FIVE WEEKS TO SYDNEY
The Era of the Passenger Liner

FIVE WEEKS TO SYDNEY

The Era of the Passenger Liner

Any proceeds from the publication of this book
will go to the **Shipwrecked Fishermen and
Mariners' Royal Benevolent Society**, 1 North
Pallant, Chichester, West Sussex, PO19 1TL

Dedication

To they that go down to the sea in ships...
(Psalm 108 v.23)

Foreword

I well remember our visits to England by ship in 1948 and 1953.

I was third selector to Don Bradman and Lindsay Hassett in 1948 and Vice Captain to Hassett in 1953.

At a cricket people gathering in Hobart a few years ago I was asked, "Mr Morris, how do you keep fit on those ships taking five weeks to get to London?"

I said, "Well, I got up and had breakfast at 9 o'clock. After that I read until noon when the bar opened. Had lunch at 1 o'clock then later had a hot salt bath and put on the black tie for the first cocktail party for the evening, had dinner, went to the bar that closed at midnight and…, next day, I got up at 9 a.m. …"

The chap interrupted me and said, "I've got the message, thank you Mr Morris."

Great memories. Pretty girls, good ships and good people to run them. What more could a humble cricketer want after most of being in the services not that long before.

Arthur Morris
Erina, NSW

A R Morris MBE:
- Created World Record in 1940-41 by scoring a century in each innings in his initial first class match.
- Scored 12,489 runs in first class cricket. Average of 55.
- Played 46 Tests.
- Australian Captain two Tests, Vice-Captain 25 Tests.
- Scored eight centuries against England. Second to Bradman in the number of individual centuries in the first 100 years of Ashes Cricket for an Australian batman.

A Note on the Poems
Poems in this volume by AP Herbert were supplied to the author by the poet himself, and to our knowledge have not been used elsewhere:

The Purser	xiii
Australia	34
Treasure Hunt	82
Chamber of Commerce	120
Distant Stranger in the Night	178
Verse Competition	190
Seagull	218

At the end of the volume, the poem *If* on p.261 is a reworking of Kipling's favourite verse by an unknown author, probably a pre-war Assistant Purser.

The verses on p.271 about the Captain, Surgeon and Purser are of unknown origin.

A Note on the Cartoon Illustrations
Neil Smith is a Cartoonist, Illustrator and Graphic Designer. The cartoons in this book were his first foray into drawing as a boy. He has continued drawing cartoons and his work can now be seen at www.neilsmithillustration.co.uk

Contents

Foreword ix

Contents xi

The Purser xiii

Introduction

1	*Orontes* Post-War Re-Fit	1
2	Junior Assistant Purser 1948	9
3	Australia 1948	21
4	The Sports Committee	35
5	Singers – Cricketers – Models	47
6	Cruising – Spithead 1953	57
7	*Otranto*	71
8	Migrants to Australia	83
9	"Keep the Mums Happy"	93
10	*Orsova* – Across the Pacific	111
11	*Orontes* – South Africa and Stowaways	121
12	The Last of *Otranto*	131
13	Refugees from Indonesia	143
14	*Oriana* – Planning – Building – Commissioning	155
15	*Oriana* – Maiden Voyage 1960	167
16	*Oriana* – Round the World	179
17	*Orion* to Tahiti and Christmas on *Otranto*	191
18	Difficult Passengers	207
19	*Oronsay* to Alaska	219
20	A Wedding at Sea	237
21	Women at Sea	251

Postscript   261

Ships   265
Ships' Ranks   273

End Notes   275

The Purser

Yes, that is the Purser with lots of gold lace
And nothing whatever to do;
Not an Officer really, but quite a nice face,
And matters immensely to you.
For he is the one that is really to blame
For whatever annoys you at sea,
But the joy of his life is to remedy same
And he will, for a moderate fee.

So go to the Purser and slip him a tip
His temper is terser with every trip,
But bang on his door,
For that's what he's for,
And say what you think of the horrible ship.
And if there is nothing to make you profane,
Invent an excuse, if it's only the rain;
The man isn't happy unless you complain,
So go to the Purser.

The moment the steamer is clear of the wharf,
Proceed to the Office and say
"My cabin would be a small size for a dwarf,
You cannot expect me to pay;
I would not confine a white rabbit of mine
To a prison so meagre in plan;
I am told that they snore in the cabin next door,
And something is wrong with the fan."

Go to the Purser and be impolite;
Call at the office from morning to night
Tackle the chap
While he's having his nap
The Purser is wrong and the passenger's right;
Make it quite clear that you are not a mole,
And cannot exist without air in a hole;
And, by the way, that the ship mustn't roll
That's the fault of the Purser.

As the voyage proceeds you may find that your needs
Take even more time to explain;
The food, as a rule, is the work of a fool,
And it's foggy again and again.
The sailors will trek overhead on the deck
Just as sleep is approaching your eyes;
Your son is too fond of that staggering blonde
And what does the Purser advise?

Go to the Purser and give him some lip
After all, you have paid for the odious trip;
And you never allowed for a positive crowd
Of Parisian vamps in this part of the ship.
A man at your table's unpleasant to see,
So either you go to another, or he;
And why is fresh milk not provided at sea?
That's the fault of the Purser.

And don't hesitate to pop in and relate
Any personal matters you can;
Describe all the rows you have had with your spouse,
And ask him to speak to the man.
If your daughters insist on staying up late,
If your husband will love you no more,
If you cannot digest, or are putting on weight,
Well, that's what the Purser is for.

Go to the Purser and sing him this song
The passenger's right and the Purser is wrong
And, alone of the crew, he has nothing to do
But listen to nice little speeches from you.
The Captain has only the ocean to fear;
The engines are fun for the Chief Engineer;
But the Purser has people to manage, poor dear
And heaven help the PURSER!!!

This poem was written by AP Herbert on board an Orient Liner. On 24th February 1969 I wrote to Sir Alan and told him that one day I hoped to write about my sea-going experiences, I asked him if I could have his permission to publish this poem.

I have his reply from 3rd March 1969:

Many thanks. Yes certainly, and good luck to the book.

Orient Steam Navigation Company Limited

Introduction

In June 1948 I made my first voyage to Sydney as an Assistant Purser in the Orient liner Orontes. The 20,000 ton ship built in 1929 had been a troop ship throughout the war. After a long refit at Southampton she was resuming her original role, now carrying 502 first class and 618 tourist class passengers, mail and cargo from England to Australia. The voyage took five weeks and five days from Tilbury to Sydney.

During the war the Orient Line lost half of its fleet of passenger ships built for the Australian trade. Until a new generation of larger, faster ships were built the pre-war liners of the Orient Line and P&O provided a much needed link between London (Tilbury) and Sydney. I hope that this book will provide a record of what conditions were like travelling to the antipodes, through the tropics, without air-conditioning, salt water baths and enduring rough weather in a ship without stabilizers.

The last of the pre-war Orient Line and P&O passenger liners was withdrawn from service in 1963, ending their days carrying new settlers sponsored by the Australian Government. First class passengers were being carried in new and more comfortable ships which culminated with Oriana and Canberra. On December 30th 1960, on her maiden voyage, Oriana completed the voyage from Southampton to Sydney in three weeks and six days.

In June 1969 an aircraft flew to the Paris airshow from Seattle, a distance of 5,160 miles, in nine hours and eight minutes. The aircraft was designated Boeing 747 and had a passenger capacity of 452. The aeroplane became known as the 'Jumbo Jet' and the roar of its four engines became the death knell of the inter-continental passenger liner. It was the end of an era.

For about ten years the liners tried to compete with the new style large aircraft. Voyages were made more interesting by visiting more ports and staying longer to enable passengers to sight-see. Speed was no longer the essence. Ships were based abroad and made holiday cruises, but these were not cruise ships. Each ship had vast cargo spaces which had contributed to line voyage earnings. These spaces were empty when pleasure cruising.

I hope Five Weeks to Sydney will remind some and inform many of what long distance travel was like – before the jumbo jet.

Nelson French
Fordingbridge, 2016

Chapter 1
Orontes Post-War Re-Fit

Iwas demobilised in 1947. I joined the Orient Line and for several months and we were re-fitting *Orontes* at the end of her war time trooping. During those re-fit days we were tied up at 41 berth in the Old Docks at Southampton, right beside where the Ocean Terminal was being built and where the giant *Queen Mary* and *Queen Elizabeth* berthed. Flying Boats took off alongside the docks – in those days the only alternative way to travel to Australia if you hadn't the time to take an Orient or P&O Liner.[1]

The weeks at Southampton were exciting, but frustrating. I and the other young men recently appointed Assistant Pursers had joined to go to sea and the furthest we ever went was from the berth to the dry dock. Other Orient Liners called in from time to time. *Otranto* still trooping was a regular visitor and twice we got a chance to see *Orion*, the only member of the Orient fleet back in peace time service.

There was one other Orient Line managed ship in Southampton at the time. The *Empire Doon* – later to be called *Empire Orwell* – a war prize formerly the *Pretoria* of the German East Africa Line. She had been handed over to the British in 1945 and spent some time swinging on a buoy off Southend pier before being brought to Southampton for conversion into what became, together with the P&O managed *Empire Fowey*, one of the most comfortable troopships ever. In 1947 she had a small caretaker crew. In charge was a Chief Officer who lived ashore and led a very gentlemanly 10.00am to 4.00pm existence, arriving on board each day just before any officials might reach Southampton on the London train. There were ship-keeping officers with little work to do, and they occupied themselves by making rocking horses – very good rocking horses.

The *Empire Doon* rocking horse factory started by one stand-by officer knocking up a horse for his child over a lonely weekend on board. On Monday morning, when others returned from weekend leave, the finished 'Dobbin' was admired by all and orders placed for repeats. One thing led to another and, before long, the bored ship-keepers of *Empire Doon* had quite a production line in operation. The factory didn't last for long. The Ministry of Transport decided to spend more than two million pounds on their

Orwell

war prize and soon the ship was swarming with shipyard workers and the standby group had no time to be toy makers.

Those who sailed in the *Empire Orwell* enjoyed the ship and peace time trooping – somewhat different from war time trooping, when converted passenger liners often carried ten times as many troops as the vessel was originally fitted for commercial passengers. By strange coincidence the first ship in which I travelled any distance was *Orontes* as a troopship – the very ship to which I was appointed on joining the Orient line as an Assistant Purser. I was a very green Second Lieutenant in the Third Carabiniers[2] taking passage to India to join my regiment, then stationed on the North West Frontier in what is now Pakistan. There were three of us newly commissioned "Cornets" as the O.C. Troops, also a cavalier, chose to call us. He decided that we should work during the voyage and we were each given a job to do.

I was Messing Officer. Little or no work was involved, but I did have the opportunity to attend meetings of the ship's catering staff and became friendly with the Purser, Chief Steward and Chef. That voyage to Bombay in *Orontes* convinced me that when I was demobilised I would become a Purser. We returned to England in a Royal Mail Line frozen meat ship called *Highland Princess*. We were

Orontes

the last British Cavalry regiment to leave India before Independence and Partition. During the voyage home the troops, who were accommodated in the holds usually used for meat, had the luxury of slightly chilled living quarters while the ship was in the Red Sea. We junior officers were sweating it out in a 24-berth cabin just below the sun deck.

It was at this time that I wrote to all the shipping companies I could think of offering myself as an Assistant Purser. I had no real qualifications and each Line seemed to want something different. I realise now that after six years of war the employers were not too sure themselves what they wanted for their post-war operations. The most encouraging reply came from the Orient Line. Perhaps somebody remembered me as Messing Officer for one brief voyage in *Orontes* – I doubt it, but I was offered an interview. This was my first and, for 27 years, my only interview for a job. I'm surprised I got it. For a start, I went to the wrong part of the Orient Line office, straight to the Stores Manager's private office. I think he must have been surprised and dumbfounded when I was shown in – it was all his secretary's fault anyway – and I said, "Good morning, sir. I have an appointment with the Managers. May I leave my coat here?"

Dressed in Service Dress and wearing a fawn British Warm without badges of rank (a privilege enjoyed by a few British Cavalry Regiments), I might have been anybody.

"Of course," said Mr Ingles and I think he was about to offer me a cup of coffee when the secretary came back in and said, "I think Mr French is a candidate for the Assistant Purser Selection Board, sir."

"Oh! – is – he?" replied my future boss. "Then take him to the others."

All very well, but my coat was still in his office when I met the other candidates sitting on a hard bench in a draughty corridor. Two of those waiting to be called to the interview room became close friends, Peter Lloyd and Mike Potter; neither stayed at sea as long as I did, but I remember that afterwards we each revealed that we thought the other two had got the job and he had failed. I can't

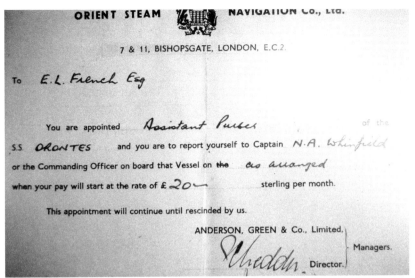

Appointment Letter

remember much about the interview. The whole encounter only lasted ten minutes and I was told, "Thank you, we will write to you."

I still had to retrieve my coat, but that wasn't as frightening as I expected as the Stores Manager was still interviewing. However, I did encounter Mr Evans, the usher, who asked me what travelling expenses I had incurred. I told him I had travelled from Wool in Dorset and would return later in the day and what the fare was. R.G. Evans had an ABC railway guide which he consulted and told me, "That is the first class fare."

"Of course," I said. Mr Evans said nothing, but looked at me over the top of his gold rimmed glasses. After a while he said, "Oh well," and gave me a chit to present to the Paymaster.

Despite my inadvertent gestures of superiority I got the job and, a few weeks later, together with Peter Lloyd and Michael Potter, I joined *Orontes* in Southampton.

Being involved in a re-fit is an ideal way in which to start a sea-going career. At the time it seemed frustrating, but on reflection we were let in gently at the shallow end, unlike some of those who followed us as the years went by (until perhaps the time when a

Purser Training Officer was appointed and the normal entry for the ships' Hotel Officers entailed a six months induction course). The only snag about entering immediately after the war and, sailing in a re-commissioned ship, was that so many of us were making our first voyage at the same time. However, at least we had six months in which to get to know one another and our ship.

The shipbuilders responsible for the re-fit were *John I Thornycroft* and they had a drawing office on board, situated most of the time in what was later to become the Tourist Class children's playroom.[3] There seemed to be miles of plans in this room, most of which were printed on pure linen. As Assistant Pursers we were always keen to acquire any unwanted plans, which were promptly boiled, dried out and cut up for handkerchiefs. Good thinking at a time when clothes rationing was still in force and coupons required for handkerchiefs!

Our Captain was N.A. Whinfield who had spent most of the war as an Assistant Marine Superintendent. Converting a troopship into a passenger liner was a job he enjoyed. As the Owner's representative he didn't miss very much and took every opportunity to check on progress, particularly in the passenger accommodation. During the day the Captain and Purser were almost entirely engaged in conferences and official inspections. It was not until the evening, when the workforce had left and all the shore officials had returned to London and their homes that, as far as we junior Pursers were concerned, the fun started.

The Captain and Purser would dine ashore most evenings – usually the Golden Hind at Hythe – and return on board full of Beaujolais and benevolence around eleven o'clock. Their first call was at the Purser's cabin, not far from the gangway. As he unlocked his cabin door the Purser, J. Gordon Thorp, would shout "Who's the duty boy?" – meaning who was the Duty Assistant Purser, and woe betide him if he had gone to bed.

"Me, sir," one of us would reply, ready for the summons.

"Come on then, let's get started."

Off we went – a little procession, the Captain, Purser and one of us. For the next two or three hours (and, towards the end of the re-fit, sometimes four hours) we would list defects, suggestions and second opinions. The Duty Assistant Purser's equipment was a clip board, a lot of paper and a supply of pencils. Captain Whinfield had observations to make on everything he saw and he wanted his observations typed out and available for *Thornycroft's* Ship's Manager by eight in the morning. Our typing ability amounted to one finger and our speed – dead slow. The sort of things we produced after our nocturnal walkabout was:

S.S. ORONTES SOUTHAMPTON APRIL 16th 1948
CAPTAIN'S INSPECTION

'E' Deck. Cabin 232 – Raise towel hooks 2".

N.B. All towel hooks throughout ship to be at least 30" from deck.

Cabin 264 – Toothbrush holder is missing.

Cabin 272 – How do you open the wardrobe if the port hole is open? Make the door open the other way.

Cabin 304 – Signs of blackout paint still apparent on port glass – examine all port glasses throughout ship.

And so it went on, page after page. Sometimes there were as many as ten pages to type onto stencils and we also had to run off copies. All this had to be done during the night, but it was an excellent training. Few Purser officers have had the opportunity to walk around the bottom of a dry dock taking notes for a Superintendent's repair conference. During our six months of standby there wasn't a part of the ship that we did not visit at one time or another. I went to parts of the ship that I never visited again at any time during the years to come, but at least I always knew what my Captain and Chief Engineer were talking about when technical discussions took place.

Preparing *Orontes* for her first post-war voyage was more than enjoyable – it was fun. Everyone involved was enthusiastic. Few could remember the Company before the war; what they did remember was clouded by six years of either serving in the Forces or trooping. No-one believed things would be just as they had been in the summer of 1939. No cruises were planned for the foreseeable future.

The first task of *Orontes* and her sisters was to get the Australian passenger trade back on a regular footing. Already there were migrants queuing up to get a passage to a new life.[4] The re-fitted troopships were fitted out with new settlers in mind. On 'H' Deck in *Orontes* just on the - water line – there were cabins with removable bulkheads which could be taken down and, together with the beds and other fittings, stowed away for the homeward voyage from Australia. The space was then used for cargo.

A lot of the teething troubles of post-war travel were being encountered by *Orion* and our Purser left us for a trip to Australia in that ship. In fact, he was away when I joined my ship at Southampton. My first encounter with J.G. Thorp was when he walked into the Purser's Office of *Orontes* with an armful of papers and said,

"What's your name?"

"Er, French, sir."

"Well, Froggy French – look at that lot and feel seasick!!" That lot was a full set of *Orion*'s menus.

"We're going to do better than that, my lad."

"Oh yes, sir," said I – and I think we did; but these were times when Pursers, Chief Stewards and Chefs could use their initiative, provided they didn't overspend. Ships were encouraged to develop personalities and to earn themselves a reputation. The Captain's name was published in the sailing advertisements in the papers. Intending passengers often wrote to their local shore office and asked who the Purser would be, before they chose their sailing.

In May 1948 we left Southampton for our home port of Tilbury and a month later sailed for Australia. I stayed in *Orontes* for four years and there is no doubt that she developed a personality. I like to think that I had a small part in creating her reputation for efficiency and happiness.

Chapter 2
Junior Assistant Purser 1948

On a glorious June afternoon the *Orontes* set sail from Tilbury for its first post-war voyage. Or so they tell me. We Assistant Pursers hadn't seen the light of day for nearly a week and this situation was to continue for weeks to come. What we lacked in experience we made up for in enthusiasm. Our Purser had spent the war trooping and had plenty of pre-war experience. The Deputy Purser had been in the Orient Line since just before the war and continued to serve in the Company's ships throughout hostilities. He was a hard taskmaster who showed little interest in the social side of pursering. We were kept in the office until midnight and beyond for night after night and I often wondered why we had been told to buy expensive mess uniforms which we hardly ever wore. Although we each hosted our own table in the First Class Saloon we rarely saw our passengers except at breakfast, an antisocial meal, and for a quick lunch. Eventually things got better as we started to understand what had to be done.

During that first voyage we were required to list every travellers cheque cashed, showing the cheque number, bank and value. This practice was soon stopped, but while it lasted it was time consuming and irksome. *Orontes* carried a lot of cargo and we had to prepare detailed lists for Customs purposes; later this job was done by shore offices, but in 1948 we Assistant Pursers had the job.

As Purser Officers we were responsible for passenger entertainment, so we did get some contact with the passengers. One Assistant Purser was designated 'Sports Assistant Purser'. For most of the four years I served in *Orontes* as an Assistant Purser I had this job, but not on the first voyage when I was designated 'Passenger Assistant Purser'.

The Passenger Assistant Purser was very 'office bound' and didn't get out much. His duties involved passenger documentation and the keeping up to date of the ship's berthing list – a sort of hotel room register. The difficulty was deciding when to pass vacant cabins on to the next port to give them time to sell the space. Way-ports knew where passengers leaving the ship at their port were berthed and could sell the accommodation which would become vacant, but they did not always know about other empty berths. There was a great temptation for the Purser to keep valuable space up his sleeve, but in doing so he can deprive the Company of valuable revenue.

Another of the Passenger Assistant Purser's duties was to organise passengers to attend various Customs, Immigration or Port Medical Authority interviews. On this first voyage I had to lean on the experience of the Purser and our Senior Assistant Purser who just, and only just, remembered voyaging to Australia in 1939, before he left to serve for six years in the Royal Artillery. Arranging these formalities was easier then than it later became, as in those days people were used to standing in queues and answering to officials. Later the travelling public, especially those who had not been touched by the regimentation of war, resented lining up for anything or anyone – and the officials and their regulations became more, rather than less, demanding with the growth of bureaucracy.

Having said that, Australia, which was then the most difficult country we had to satisfy, has since streamlined formalities to make it one of the easier countries to deal with when arriving from abroad.

The gangway of a ship in a foreign port is an international frontier and in some countries armed frontier guards stand at the gangway. In Commonwealth countries, once formalities have been completed, there was reasonably free access to and from ships from Britain. 'Entering' or submitting the required documents on behalf of the Captain was the responsibility of the Purser, and most of that work fell to me. It was a rewarding task when all went well, but frustrating if there were delays. Our route on my first voyage was from Tilbury direct to Port Said where, at that time, passengers were not allowed ashore.

The only person who left the ship was an Assistant Purser who went with the Agent's Clerk to the British Consul to have the ship's papers endorsed. I was sent and had a pleasant hour at the Consulate, but on returning to the harbour was shocked to see nothing but an open space where *Orontes* had been berthed. Looking towards the canal I saw our giant liner sliding gracefully down the harbour, passing the Suez Canal offices and about to disappear into the black night.

"Don't worry," said the Agent's Clerk, "we can catch them up in our launch."

Worried I was; but I need not have been. It took less than ten minutes to catch up with the ship whose accommodation ladder had been left lowered for me. During my absence at the Consulate a pilot had boarded and advised the Captain that if he left at once he could take the head of the queue of ships waiting to enter the Suez Canal. They considered I could rejoin at Ismailia. I didn't know that. I wish I had. A moonlight drive down the Canal road would have been fun and made me the envy of my shipmates. Years later going to Cairo and returning to the ship via Ismailia and the Canal road became a familiar routine.[5]

July is not the most comfortable month in which to travel in the Red Sea. *Orion* had air-conditioning in the Dining Room, but *Orontes* had none. Usually the only breeze came from the movement of the ship itself, and if there happened to be a natural following wind this often cancelled out the breeze made by the ship's speed. The conditions on board were hellish. Writing was difficult and we all had face towels which we placed between our hand and the paper to absorb perspiration. Our uniform tunics had high collars and inside we were all suffering from prickly heat. Stiff boiled shirts with wing collars were the dress in the evening, with white monkey jackets, white waistcoats and blue trousers. The Orient Line, and the P&O too, were more pukka than the Royal Navy, who at least had their more casual Red Sea rig comprising open-necked shirt, cummerbund and trousers. After a few years soft evening shirts were pronounced as acceptable by our Management, and several years later – when most ships were air-conditioned – open neck shirts replaced the high collar tunics.

One hot afternoon in the Red Sea an old lady came to the Purser's Office and offered us a pound note, "To buy the poor boys in the engine room some cool beer."

Purser Thorp heard this and jumped up from his desk, crossed to the counter where the lady was proffering her pound, and said, "Engine room, madam? The lads in the galley slaving over the hot stoves are more uncomfortable than those in the Engine Room."

"Oh! really?" she said , "then you had better give it to them!"

"Thank you, madam," said our Purser. He took the money, waited until she had gone and then addressed us. "Look after your department, gentlemen. The Chief Engineer can buy his men beer if they need it – which they don't."

Later the same generous lady was heard to remark to the Captain, Norman Whinfield, "How much longer do we have to endure the Red Sea, Captain?"

To which the wise Captain replied, "Just tonight, madam. I am advancing the ship's clocks a whole hour so that we will be out of it sooner!"

"Really?" she answered, "you sailors are so thoughtful."

Aden was the first port at which the passengers were able to go ashore, twelve days after leaving Tilbury. The stay was just long enough to refuel the ship. Being close to the Middle East oil wells, Aden was able to offer fuel oil at a low price and we bunkered to capacity. This operation gave the passengers and those crew members off duty a chance to spend about three hours ashore.

To the passengers, and many of the crew, the shops in Aden were like an Aladdin's Cave. Most goods were still rationed in England and pre-war luxuries were only available for export. Many of these items were on sale in the shops at Aden, as were perfumes and cosmetics not yet being imported to Britain.

The women had a field day. The children were bewildered by toys, the like of which they had never seen before, including toys mostly made in Japan or Hong Kong, many of which were operated by batteries. For days after Aden the ship's alleyways and decks became roadways for police cars with sirens, fire engines with bells and all sorts of mechanical dolls banging drums or blowing trumpets. Life was hell until someone, perhaps the Staff Commander, hit on the idea of instructing the ship's shop manager to stop selling batteries. For a couple of days the cars and dolls operated slower and slower – and slower – until at last they all expired and peace was restored.

The staff commander hit on the idea of instructing the ships shop manager to stop selling batteries

For the men there were shirts, cameras, binoculars, portable radios and a host of other items. I'm sure many migrants on their way to Australia overspent in the shops at the Crescent and Crater at Aden.

In 1948 Aden was British. The Royal Air Force was the predominant Service, except perhaps when a large warship made a call. As the Assistant Purser responsible for the preparation of the ship's papers for entering the port, I had to meet the officials from the shore. After the pilot (who boarded outside the harbour), the first person to come aboard was the Port Doctor who would examine the Health Report which I had prepared, as instructed by the Ship's Surgeon. When satisfied that we were healthy, the Port Doctor told me to inform the Bridge that the Quarantine Flag could be lowered and that the Agent and other officials could come on board. He then went off with our doctor for a cold beer – regardless of the time of day or night.

The port officials we met during those first post-war voyages were often, like ourselves, new to their job. Friendships were made which last even today. As the years went by, these friendships became invaluable and a mutual trust was established from which our Owners and passengers benefited immeasurably. Medical Officers, Customs and Immigration Officials took our word that all was well and accepted our declarations without question, clearing the gangways with the minimum of inquiry and thus getting the passengers quickly ashore and the cargo working speedily. As the British left places like Aden and Colombo due to Independence, the Colonial Service Officers were replaced by local officials, many of whom also became friends. However, there was not the same trust between us – regrettably I fear, because they did not always trust one another.

The Doctor who boarded at Aden was always accompanied by a coolie carrying a large *Thermos* canister.[6] I always assumed that the canister contained smallpox vaccine packed in ice, until early one morning, at about 4.00am, we arrived in Aden with just one passenger to land. The passenger was a woman who did not have a valid smallpox vaccination certificate and the Port Medical Officer suggested the Ship's Surgeon vaccinate her and issue a new certificate. "But you've got some vaccine there," I said, pointing to the *Thermos* which his coolie held.

"Ach no!" he replied. "There's no vaccine in that – just a cold Carlsberg!"

At Colombo we encountered some real 'pukka sahibs'. The Agents there were tea shippers and, unlike Aden, there was a large European population in Colombo. The *Galle Face Hotel* ranked with *Raffles* in Singapore and the *Peninsular* in Hong Kong. The Senior Agent called on the Captain soon after *Orontes* arrived, paid his respects and asked the Captain and his Purser ashore for lunch. Then he was off ashore again in his immaculate launch with boat's crew performing naval drill with the boat hook. That was the last anyone (except the Captain and the Purser) saw of the Agent until just before the ship sailed, when he would return and wish us all, "Good trip, chaps – see you homeward-bound," and be off ashore again.

Many passengers went on shore excursions from the ship at Colombo. We sold tickets from the Purser's Office on the run from Aden, and the cars and buses were waiting on the jetty when the harbour launches landed the excursionists. Some people were taken to a hotel at Mount Lavinia for lunch, others to a fishing village at Negombo. The really determined tourists could take a car to Kandy to visit the Temple of the Tooth and return to the ship exhausted after a long hot day.

Sometimes an Assistant Purser was instructed to accompany a shore excursion and report on the arrangements. This kept tour operators up to scratch and provided a welcome break for one of us. It is seldom that anything can be arranged that will please everyone involved. The complaints about the Colombo shore excursions were usually about the lunch provided. Half would complain that the lunch was curry and rice and, "We don't eat that kind of food." So, we arranged to change the menu. Then we would hear, "Travel all this way to eat meat and two veg – why don't they serve a genuine Ceylon curry?!"

By this stage of the voyage complaints were becoming more frequent at the Purser's Office. There were few experienced travellers on a June sailing from England, and those who were travelling were mostly making their first long voyage. For the first week the ship and its staff were considered marvellous. Passengers were called in the morning with a cup of tea and breakfast, there was no washing up, their beds made and cabins cleaned – everything was wonderful. During week two people began to take the service they got for granted – and in week three it was not being done properly!

The day ashore at Colombo came at about the right time. The passage from Aden in July was hot and sticky. The south-west monsoon blew hard and gave rough seas which forced the passengers from the outside decks to the inside of the ship which would then become crowded. Tempers became a little frayed and the odd fight broke out amongst the migrant passengers travelling in the Tourist Class, and also in crew quarters.[7]

Soon after leaving Colombo we crossed the Equator and entered the southern hemisphere. I am pleased that I was thrown in the swimming pool – resplendent in my uniform – at a ceremony provided for the entertainment of the children. If I hadn't been properly initiated into the Court of King Neptune on my first Equator crossing, I would have felt cheated.

In comparison with the well-rehearsed ceremonies we performed in later years, which were very much a spectacle with little audience participation, the jollifications around the *Orontes* swimming pool were tame. We enjoyed ourselves and the event didn't get out of hand as it might easily have done if Staff Commander Galpin had not given us a pretty tough talking to before we started. He came along to see that we really did not throw all the pretty girls on the passenger list into the pool. The Captain was persuaded to attend and was awarded the 'Order of the Ever Blowing Wind' – a delightful cherub made by the Engineers and placed round his neck by Neptune's Queen, a Bosun's Mate. The subtlety of the award was not lost on the audience. Although the citation read by the 'Clerk of the Courts' referred to the unpleasant winds we had encountered during the passage from Aden, most people read into it the pomposity of our Captain – a fine seaman who really relished commanding a first class passenger ship and

Domain of   Neptunus Rex
Ruler of the   Raging Main

To all Sailors wherever ye may be, know ye that on this 5th day of September, 1949, Ye Goode Shippe "Orontes" appeared within the limits of Our Royal Domain, and

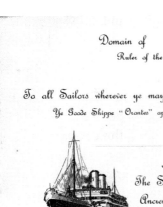

was duly admitted into
The Solemn Mysteries of the
Ancient Order of the Deep.

Be it further understood   That by virtue of the power invested in me, I do hereby command all my Subjects to show due honour and respect to him or her whenever he or she may enter Our Realm.   Disobey this Order under penalty of Our Royal Displeasure.

R.D., R.N.R.

Davy Jones   *Neptunus Rex*   CAPTAIN—
HIS MAJESTY'S SCRIBE   RULER OF THE RAGING MAIN   S.S. "ORONTES"

Orient Line

at the Equator

entertaining distinguished passengers. The Chief Officer got 'The Order of the Mop' for allegedly never clean decks. The Purser '...the never boiling kettle', and the Children's Hostess, '...the ever brimming Po!'

The run from Colombo to Fremantle in Western Australia took eight days and this was a time when passengers became fractious. During the passage we pulled out all the stops to keep them entertained and to a large extent it worked. However, the new settlers were becoming apprehensive

as Australia drew near and the experienced travellers became bored with day after day of open sea. There was seldom another ship to look at, just flying fish and beautiful sunsets.

An opportunity to steam close to the Cocos Islands, halfway between Colombo and Fremantle, was a tonic for all on board. The Cocos or Keeling Islands consist of a group of about 20 islands, for the most part of coral formation, covered with coconut trees. The *Eastern Telegraph Company*'s Station was located on Direction Island in the Southern Group. It was manned by a small group of Europeans who were visited twice a year by a supply ship. Before the war, passing Orient and P&O ships would slow down and drop a barrel of fresh food and magazines which the station staff would pick up with one of their sailing boats. At the same time the ship would pick up a sealed biscuit tin of mail for posting in Australia. For a few years after the war this custom continued, until the islands became a staging post for aircraft flying from Australia to South Africa.

The day before we reached these islands Captain Whinfield announced to all on board that he had contacted the Telegraph Station on the radio and had agreed to drop a gift barrel as we sailed past. The barrel was placed in the foyer outside the First Class Dining Room and passengers were invited to leave books and magazines for stowage inside. This was in addition to the stores which included a turkey, some fillet steak and, to be put in at the last minute, some ice cream.

The next day our first sight of land was North Keeling Island, where the remains of the German cruiser Emden, forced ashore after a battle with HMAS Sydney in 1914, were still visible on the beach.[8] The Officer-of-the-Watch gave us a full account of the battle, which gladdened the hearts of the Australians aboard, and probably bored the migrants. However, at least this was a day on which things were happening and not yet another monotonous day of sea and sky.

It was at about noon when we came up to Direction Island. The *Telegraph Company*'s boat was already in position about a mile off the shore, waiting for us. We approached cautiously and our speed was dead slow. They came up under our stern from which we were streaming a line and to which they attached their tin of mail. Then, from a ship's side door we rolled out the barrel – a real barrel. Later, on similar occasions done purely for the benefit of passengers, and in other parts of the world, plastic canisters were used; but on this, my first voyage, it was a proper wooden barrel that went over the side. It was weighted so that it floated with a flag on a mast uppermost. As it floated down the ship's side towards the stern, our passengers let out a cheer – the ship's whistle sounded and we slowly gathered speed, watching all the time the men from Cocos and their small boat which had got alongside their gift and were now sailing back to the shore towing behind them a few fresh dinners and up-to-date news.

The next day we encountered the south east trade winds and the ship began to cool down. Tempers were less frayed and an air of anticipation developed as arrival in Australia became immi-

COCOS OCCASION

ORIENT LINE

nent. The evening before we arrived at Fremantle, a Gala Dinner was served to the passengers, while we Assistant Pursers worked on in an office until 2.00am. Printed at the top of the menu were some lines from Conrad's Mirror of the Sea:

> Landfall and departure mark the rhythmical swing of a seaman's life and a ship's career. From land to land is the most concise definition of a ship's earthly fate.

For the next 25 years 'from land to land' was to be my fate.

Chapter 3
Australia 1948

The formalities required of a ship arriving in Australia have altered considerably since 1948. Preparing for Fremantle started as soon as we left the Cocos Islands. The climax came at 6.00 in the morning off Rottnest Island when our ship anchored in Gage Roads outside Fremantle Harbour.

During the last few days of the voyage from Colombo the passengers did not have time to become bored. There was Australian money to be obtained from the Purser's Office; Customs forms to fill up; Immigration declarations to complete; and, on the final day at sea, a medical inspection by the Ship's Surgeon to attend. The medical inspection entailed every person on board, crew and passengers alike, parading before the doctor and showing him their forearms and forehead. Any indication of smallpox would be apparent at these places on the body. Having seen everybody, the ship transmitted a telegram to the Australian Health Authorities confirming that the inspection had been held; then they replied saying we could enter Australian waters, although not enter port until they too had inspected everyone on board.

When we anchored in Gage Roads, about 40 officials came on board in the uniform peculiar to Australian Boarding Inspectors: sports coat, flannels and a peaked cap with a badge, 'HM Australian Customs and Immigration'. The cap was the only form of uniform. There were no badges of rank, you could tell the boss as the one who did most of the shouting. The group boarded from a large launch and entered the ship through a side door into the First Class foyer where all those on watch had been mustered so that they could be seen at once by the Doctor. The remainder of the crew were assembled on the boat deck and the passengers in the lounges.

We, as Purser Officers, had prepared a fool proof check-off system, and until every person on board had been checked off, the ship remained at anchor about a mile from the harbour entrance. The passengers at 6.00am were a motley bunch. They fell into three distinct groups – those who appeared in their dressing gowns; those who were all dressed and ready to go ashore; and those still in evening dress who thought it had not been worth going to bed. There was a fourth group, those who couldn't be bothered to get up and had to be called from their bed – that was easy if they were to be found in their own bed!

By 8.00am we had been given permission to proceed and were in our berth beside the tin sheds on the quay at Fremantle. Later, a modern passenger terminal had been built and by then proceedings were very different – the officials had uniforms and the word of the Ship's Doctor was sufficient to confirm the health of those on board.

Western Australia is a friendly place. It is said that in Perth, the capital, they say to visitors, "What's yours?" In Adelaide they ask, "Which church do you go to?" In Melbourne, "What school?" Sydney, "How much money do you have?" – and up in Queensland, at Brisbane, once again it's, "What's yours?" This attitude is about right, each state has its own atmosphere. I seldom got beyond the ports but I could detect from the passengers we carried that there was a different attitude to life from each of the various states.

Later on, when I was Purser of my own ship, I went to Darwin a couple of times and there, isolated from the rest of Australia, lying within the tropics, was a community which didn't conform to any other state pattern. They didn't ask "What's yours?" – you just took what they gave you!

Travelling round the Australian coast in an overseas liner was a popular holiday for Australians. There were small coastal steamers which provided this service and regulations ensured that these ships did not suffer by people choosing to sail in an overseas ship. However, there were many loopholes in the regulations and on each voyage we would have several coastal passengers. A very friendly group joined us in July 1948. By the time we left Fremantle, the pressure of work in the office was reducing and in the evenings we

in perth   they say to visitors 'what's yours'?

began to get out a bit more and have an opportunity to meet the passengers socially. I soon found myself involved with some of the Australians who had embarked at Fremantle. One family in particular, the Longworths from Sydney, took me under their wing and I shall always be grateful to them for giving me an introduction to Australia.

The distance by sea from Fremantle to Adelaide is 1,355 nautical miles and the journey entails rounding Cape Leeuwin and crossing

23

Great Australian Bight

the Great Australian Bight where some of the stormiest seas in the world can be encountered. July is midwinter in these parts, but in 1948 we had a reasonable passage. The giant Wandering Albatrosses which hovered over the ship were fascinating – their wing span often more than 10ft – and these great birds followed us all the way across the Bight.

Our second Australian port was Adelaide, where we berthed at Outer Harbour. There was just a wharf, some cargo sheds and a milk bar at Outer Harbour. Port Adelaide is about five miles away and the journey to Adelaide, South Australia's capital, takes about half-an-hour. When a large passenger liner was alongside at Outer Harbour a train service operated to Adelaide, which was steam-hauled and just like something from the wild west. The engine had a cowcatcher, the carriages had wooden seats with an open-air platform at each end, and the guard travelled in a caboose. I hope that delightful train has been preserved.

I didn't see much of Adelaide on this first visit as a quick dash to the milk bar with the girls from the Purser's Office was all we had time for. We had two women Assistant Pursers in *Orontes*, Joan Barker and Honor Newall, who were Junior Assistant Pursers, just like the rest of us. They had the same rank, responsibilities and privileges as we did, including a table in the Dining Room with five passengers to look after. Not all shipping companies gave their female secretarial staff officer status, but the Orient line did, and I think quite rightly. These girls had access to a great deal of confidential information, and failure to be accurate when typing lists for port officials could have delayed the ship and caused considerable expense. Their attitude to complaining passengers made them invaluable.

Joan Barker had made a voyage to Australia in *Orion* and, by the time she was in the Company, had become the senior of the Junior Assistant Pursers. She never 'pulled rank' and is still one of the friendliest people I know. Honor was one of those women who made a typewriter sound like a machine gun and was always accurate – in an office where inaccuracy could mean disaster she was a tremendous asset. She only made one voyage, so perhaps working afloat didn't suit her. If not, she never complained at the time and, like us, she had to work all the hours God and our Deputy Purser sent.

We left Adelaide in the early evening and after a day at sea arrived at Station Pier, Melbourne. We were to stay here for three days while a lot of our cargo was discharged. For the first time since leaving Tilbury the watch-keepers 'broke watches'. There were Duty Officers, of course, but the Bridge was manned by a Quartermaster with a telephone, rather than the full complement of two Officers, two Quartermasters and a messenger. The Captain and Purser lunched with the Branch Manager and even we, the lowest of the low as Assistant Pursers, had a chance to go ashore.

I was invited by my new-found friends, the Longworths, to a cocktail party at *Menzies Hotel*. This was my first experience of an Australian party. Guests were invited at 4.00pm and the women all wore hats and gloves, many with long gloves to the elbow and beyond. The men were tough-looking wool-buyers and property owners who looked out of place in a hotel lounge. After formal introductions all the men moved to one end of the room and took scotch or beer; the women moved to the other end and completely ignored their menfolk. I discovered this was the normal pattern at mixed parties in Australia. The party went on until 7.00pm, when I was taken to dinner and ate my first dozen Australian oysters. I will accept any invitation to Australia for the oysters alone – since that day in 1948 I have been addicted!

Beer appeared to be the national drink of Australia, *Swan* in the West, *Coopers* in South Australia, *Victoria Bitter* in Victoria, *Cascade* in Tasmania, *Tooths* in Sydney, and *Castlemaine* in Queensland. Each state strongly defending the supremacy of its product.

Post-war Australia had its fair share of strikes and labour disputes and I expect that it still does. A brewery strike was a state disaster to the male population. The *Carlton Brewery*, which made *Victoria Bitter*, was on strike when I called at Melbourne later in *Orion*, but our ship's Provodore had anticipated our call before the strike began and had stored in a warehouse some two thousand cases of *VB*. The local pubs were almost dry, so imagine the reaction when trucks appeared alongside our ship with cases of beer. The stevedore in charge of the gang – a man nearly seven feet tall with muscles like Hercules – stood with his hands on his hips, bush hat on the back of his head and said, "Where do you think that bloody lot's going?"

"On board the ship," replied our rather dapper little Chief Barman who appeared on the wharf to check his consignment.

"You don't think you're going to take that beer on board an overseas ship when we haven't seen a decent beer here for a month?"

By now quite a crowd of stevedores and others had gathered round. The exchange continued between Goliath in his bush hat, singlet and khaki shorts – a typical waterfront worker's rig – and the dapper little David, our barman, in his smart uniform.

The barman replied, with a blatant lie, "That beer is for the crew, not for luxury cruise passengers."

"Then buy some in Sydney – there's no strike there."

"What!" squeaked the barman, "do you expect me to sell Sydney beer to the crew?"

The gang leader took off his hat, scratched his head, smiled an endearing smile of defeat and said, "You're right, mate," to the barman, and instructed his gang, "OK, you bastards, put it aboard. I reckon they'll need it."

We left Melbourne on the evening of the third day after our arrival. The cargo for Victoria had been discharged and many of the passengers from England had now left. A few coastal passengers embarked for Sydney, but the ship felt empty after more than a month during which every berth was filled.

A full day at sea and then on to Sydney. There are not many times during a World Cruise that I would insist that a traveller rise from bed early for a sight, but entering Sydney Harbour is one. The pilot cutter had a sailing ship figurehead and the pilot was actually rowed from the cutter to the ship. After picking up the pilot, the ship then turned towards The Heads and sailed between two high promontories into what must be the world's finest natural harbour.

Tucked away behind North Head on the starboard side is Manly, whilst on the port side a succession of bays begin to unfurl: Watson's Bay where Customs and Immigration board, and Rose Bay, home of the Flying Boats – the only alternative mode of travel from England in 1948. Past Point Piper and Double Bay where

Orontes entering Sydney Harbour

expensive houses line the water's edge. Darling Point, Garden Island where we dipped our Ensign to the Royal Australian Navy and then, on *Orontes'* early post-war voyages, past Bennalong Point with its tram depot (now the site of the marvellous Sydney Opera House). The harbour bridge would now be dead ahead and from the fore part of the ship it looked as if our foremast would crash into the roadway above us, but it was an optical illusion and we passed beneath with at least twelve feet to spare. After steaming under the bridge we were assisted by tugs to make a sharp turn toward our berth, Number 13 Pyrmont, where we secured and remained for a whole week – during which our Deputy Purser gave each of us a whole day off and most evenings as well.

Sydney's social life was far more relaxed than London's. There was a lot more entertaining done in people's own homes. We did visit the odd night club such as *Sammy Lee's* where the beer was served in champagne buckets with real champagne corks floating in the ice, *The Hayden* where it was so dark that you could hardly see your dance partner and never the food you ate, and *Romano's* and *Princes*, which were more 'upmarket' – we were usually taken there by our girlfriends' parents, who would often leave early but always after first providing for the bill to be paid. I suppose those girls now have daughters who are the age we were then – I wonder if they trust them to young ship's officers until the early hours?

I have one very vivid memory of Sydney which is of an encounter I had, still in *Orontes*, a year or so after my first visit. It was with the New South Wales police, who seemed to think that I had murdered one of our former passengers, Mrs Hill of the Astor Flats, Macquarie Street. Mrs Hill was an elderly lady who had travelled with us some time before the incident and I must have made an impression on her. On the day when she was murdered, she had left her luxury flat early in the morning to meet her sister, a passenger in *Orontes* arriving at berth 13 Pyrmont. As Mrs Hill was leaving her flat her neighbour came out of the flat opposite and remarked, "You're up early this morning, Mrs Hill."

"Yes, I'm going to meet my sister who is arriving on the *Orontes*. I travelled in the same ship last year – it's a lovely ship and the officers are so friendly. I do hope young Mr French is still in the Purser's Office, he was so kind to me."

A little later that casual remark led to my interrogation by three Sydney policemen, which I hope never to have to endure again. Mrs Hill picked up a taxi in Macquarie Street and came to Pyrmont where we had just berthed. She had a Visitor's pass and came on board, although somehow or other she missed her sister (who wasn't expecting her anyway). Missing someone on an overseas liner's arrival in Sydney isn't very difficult. For about two hours pandemonium reigns with passengers trying to get ashore, luggage being carried here and there by Stewards, people saying goodbye, people saying hello, children getting lost – all the usual excited crowd events. The chaos is enhanced by newsboys wandering around the ship amongst the hoards of welcoming visitors shouting, "Pipers – morning pipers" –Australian for morning papers. There would also often be a chap in shorts, sand shoes and no socks vending, "Icy cold milk – icy cold milk" (God knows how he got a pass).

However, even though Mrs Hill did not find her sister (whom we later discovered was in the Customs shed), she did call in at the Purser's Office and ask for me. It was right in the middle of the arrival 'flap' and the foyer outside the Office was a mass of humanity and a babble of conversation interspersed with shrieks of, "How are yer?", "Good to see yer", "Mum, Mum, over here," and other human welcoming cries, making concentrated thought impossible. Inside the Office, Orient Line staff, baggage clerks and port officials were getting under our feet. This all sounds unbearable, but in fact it is a time of great exhilaration – 'We have arrived!'

I was probably talking to one of the Company's shore officials when Pat Fletcher, a Woman Assistant Purser, said to me, "There's a woman at the counter asking for you – I don't know who she is but she's covered in diamonds – at this time of day!"

I looked across to the counter and saw an elderly lady in black wearing what seemed to me to be rather a lot of jewellery for the time of day. I recognised her as a former passenger, but had no recollection of her name. I went across and said, "Hello, how are you? Nice to see you again."

She replied, "I can't stop, I'm looking for my sister, but I did want to say hello. I hope you have had a good trip." We spoke in this vein for no longer than two minutes and then she said, "You're busy now and I must be off," and that was that. Pat Fletcher said, "Who's your girlfriend?"

"Can't remember," I replied, "she travelled a couple of voyages ago, I think."

Two or three hours later, when things were much quieter, three husky great Australians came to the Office counter. They looked so much like policemen they might just as well have been in uniform.

"Ger' day," one of the policemen said to the girl at the counters, still Pat Fletcher, I expect. "You got a feller here called French?"

I overheard this and stepped across and introduced myself. Their spokesman said, "Want to have a chat, Mr French – got some place where we can be alone?"

"My cabin?" I suggested.

"OK – Let's go," and off we went down one deck to the Purser Officers' accommodation. As soon as we were inside I offered them a beer. I thought they wanted to talk about some police matter affecting the ship, such as the behaviour of a crew member in Sydney on a previous voyage, or they wanted details of a particular passenger. It was made very clear to me this was to be no social meeting.

"No beer!" snapped the spokesman and then without any preamble he barked, "Where were you at 10.00 this morning?"

"Right here, of course," I replied, "we have only just arrived, I could hardly be anywhere else."

"Do you know Mrs Hill of the Astor Flats, Macquarie Street?" one of the others asked.

"No," I said "I don't think so – should I?"

It was the turn of the third man to speak and he said "Why did you leave the ship at about 9.45 this morning?"

"But I didn't. I've already told you that we have only just arrived – none of us will get a chance to go ashore until this evening at the earliest."

My cabin was small and two of the three men sat on the settee whilst the third occupied the only chair. I stood in a corner made by a bulkhead and my high bunk. The man sitting in the chair stood up and moved towards me.

"Tell us about you and Mrs Hill, son. How long have you known her?"

Once again I denied knowing a Mrs Hill, although I did say that I met so many people in my job that I might have met their Mrs Hill, but I couldn't remember anyone with that name.

"Well, son, I'm telling you that she knows you," and with that he jabbed me just under my lowest rib – which was most painful.

This sort of question and answer conversation went on for another ten or fifteen minutes, during which I received several more painful jabs just below my ribs. It might have gone on a lot longer if it had not been for an interruption when Pat Fletcher, the Woman Assistant Purser, knocked on the door and, on entering, announced that the Shore Office Messenger was about to leave and needed some papers for which I was responsible. I took advantage of Pat's arrival to say, "Patsy, do I know a Mrs Hill from this place?"

"Don't think so," she replied. Then after a pause, "Wait a minute, that woman who asked for you today, her name is Hill. Voyage before last, 'C' deck, Starboard Side, single cabin."

"God, yes, that's right!" I exclaimed, "Lonely old soul, didn't miss much – I used to chat her up a bit now and then." I turned to the policemen and explained, "Yes, I do know a Mrs Hill. Whether she is the one you are talking about, I don't know, but we did have a passenger with that name and she was here this morning looking for her sister. I spoke to her, but at the time had no idea who she was."

"OK, mate," snorted my erstwhile assailant. "Don't leave this boat until we get back."

And with that all three walked out leaving Pat staring mouth half-open after them.

"What was that all about?" she asked.

"I'm not sure," I said. "They're are Sydney police and they seem to think I have been ashore this morning and done something or other which is connected with our Mrs Hill."

"But you've been here all morning. How could you go ashore today of all days. That woman was wearing real diamonds – her fob watch must have been worth a bomb – at 10.00 in the morning too." Patsy mused on, shaking her head from side to side. "They're a weird lot all right – thank God I'm British." Pat's father was a Rear-Admiral, a fact which she made sure we did not forget.

"Have a look at this," I said taking off my jacket and pulling up my shirt. There is not a lot of modesty amongst Assistant Pursers living in close proximity to one another. "This is where the bastard kept hitting me." There was nothing to see.

"Well, I'll be damned," I said, "there isn't a mark," and there never was, despite the pain I had felt and continued to feel for a couple of days.

I went back to the office where I told the Purser, Gordon Thorp, what had happened. He just laughed. offered me a pre-lunch gin and said, "We'll come and see you in prison!"

About 4.00 that afternoon two of the policemen returned. Coming up to the Purser's Office counter, they called across to me. "You can give us that beer now, French. Sorry about this morning, but you're clear. We'll even pay for the beer if you've got a bar open. I expect you want to know what it was all about."

We hadn't got a bar open so we returned to my cabin for a few 'Coldies' – *Resches Pilsner*, I think it was. It was explained to me that Mrs Hill had been found dead in her flat by her neighbour just after 11.00 that morning. She had been struck with an instrument which was probably a poker. The neighbour, who had gone into the flat because she noticed the door open, discovered her lying on the floor and immediately called the police. When questioned, the neighbour mentioned her earlier conversation with Mrs Hill and her remarks about *Orontes* and my name. This sent the police hurrying down to Pyrmont to find me. Their reasoning was that I knew Mrs Hill to be a wealthy woman who lived on her own, that I had seen the lady aboard *Orontes* looking for her sister and so I quickly got myself to the Astor Flats and started to rifle the place. Mrs Hill, having missed her sister, went home and found me in the act of burgling her flat. Realising I had been discovered, I hit her with a poker and rushed back to the ship as quickly as I could.

It was understandable reasoning which accounted for the treatment I received from the chaps who were now happily drinking in my cabin. They told me that my conversation with Pat Fletcher had convinced them that I was not the murderer, because my obvious realisation that I did after all know Mrs Hill could not, they said, have been rehearsed. At that moment they knew that they had the wrong man. Thank God for Pat Fletcher – I wonder where she is now.

The 'boys' drank all my beer, apologised for the rib pummelling and remarked, "You needn't worry, there won't be a bruise," and cleared off.

Later the same day a man in a stolen taxi shot a policeman, was arrested and after questioning was charged with the murder of Mrs Hill, c/o The Astor Flats, Macquarie Street, Sydney. Throughout that stay in Sydney I had dinner table conversation which made me a sought-after guest. Then we were homeward-bound.

Australia

Here is the greatest island on the Earth,
Here is a continent of British birth,
A sunny country with a sunny mind,
A cruel country peopled by the kind,
Where wealth is everywhere, but hard to find –
Australia!

A scene of stirring, like a wood in spring,
Hope in the soil and courage on the wing:
Here Eden waits for Adam to retrieve,
The fruits, the flowers, that delighted Eve,
If Adam, will but labour and believe –
Australia!

Blue hills, green gardens, and the golden plain
The birds, the herds, the gum tree and the grain:
But then, the drought that makes men hate the sun,
The fire that flies as fast as horse can run –
Nature at war with all that Man has won –
　　　　　　　　　　　　　　Australia!

In such a land, the little things must wait:
The talk is terse, and tough – the thought is straight:
Yet they find time to feel, and fight, and pray
For one small island half a world away,
A tiny island which is 'Home', they say –
　　　　　　　　　　　　　　Australia!

Here is no p[lace for sluggard or slave:
The mouth is merry and the breast is brave.
Honour today the Fathers of the State
Who found a wilderness and made it great,
Believed in Providence but fought with Fate –
　　　　　　　　　　　　　　Australia!

Chapter 4
The Sports Committee

The atmosphere on board during the homeward voyages was always different, and many factors contributed to the more relaxed feeling. Naturally the crew's morale was higher, and after the outward voyage and a break in Sydney things seemed to go more smoothly. There was more of a team spirit, and the passengers were different, especially in the Tourist Class – instead of apprehensive migrants they were fun-seeking young Australians off on their 'trip' to Europe. Even time was on our side homeward-bound, as most nights the clock went 'back' half-an-hour instead of 'forwards' as it did outward-bound, and so there was extra time in bed.

Departure from Sydney was a gala affair, with hundreds of visitors all over the ship and farewell parties in nearly every cabin. Moving round inside the ship was difficult, and trying to get from the Purser's Office to the Captain's cabin with an arm full of papers to sign was an ordeal. Every few yards a visitor would stop me and ask the way to a particular cabin or suite, or perhaps just to say, "Say, skip, this boat a roller?" or, "Say, mate, what's the tucker like on this boat?" Getting them all ashore was a miracle and although the announcement, "All visitors ashore – all visitors ashore" started an hour before we were due to leave, sometimes someone got left on board and had to travel to Melbourne. No real problem from Sydney, but from Fremantle, a week later, it would be a different matter. From there the next port was Colombo, more than 3,000 miles away.

From the wharf farewelling friends threw streamers to those lining the ship's side rails. There was an atmosphere of gaiety that we never experienced at Tilbury where Customs regulations did not allow visitors to board foreign-going ships – and anyway, Tilbury is

25 uninteresting miles from London, whereas the harbour in Sydney is the centre of the town.

The ship's leisurely progress round the Australian coast gave the homeward voyage a much better start than the embarkation of more than 1,000 passengers in the United Kingdom, all at one port, followed by an eight-day run to Port Said, where they were still confined to the ship. Just as on the outward-bound leg, the ship stayed in Melbourne for three days homeward-bound. Then Adelaide again, and finally, when it left Australia from Fremantle, people had already settled down and people had got to know one another.

At each Australian port there was the same sort of send-off, although Sydney usually provided the most riotous because more passengers embarked there. In addition to those from New South Wales, there were those from Queensland and New Zealand. Fremantle was a hectic departure, due to the need to finally clear with the Customs and Immigration. If a visitor got left on board at Fremantle, they had a long sea voyage to look forward to before they could leave the ship, and then another long voyage back home again. It happened from time to time.

My most vivid memory of a visitor failing to go ashore at Fremantle on a homeward voyage is of a man who unwillingly travelled to Colombo on my first voyage as Purser – some years after that first *Orontes* voyage when I was a mere Junior Assistant Purser. I was Purser of *Otranto*, we had dropped the Pilot, and Rottnest Island was disappearing astern. The ship was picking up the gentle swell of the Indian Ocean, and I was tidying my desk and wondering if I would bother to go to dinner or have a snack in my cabin, when the Chief Steward came in and said, "I think one of my lads has found a stowaway, sir. He's bringing him along."

"Well, that fixes it, Mr a'Court," I answered. "I'm not going to dinner. What's the story?"

"Evans, sir. 'G' Deck aft. He was checking his empty cabins when he finds this chap asleep on a bunk in 215. He woke him up to explain that the cabin was supposed to be empty and perhaps he could direct him to his proper cabin. It seems the chap doesn't communicate very well – in fact, he's drunk. So I've told Evans to bring him up here as soon as he can."

"Thanks," I said, "a stowaway is just what we don't need. The 'old man' won't turn back now. The Pilot went nearly half-an-hour ago. I don't feel much like interviewing a drunk. I suppose we had better tell the Bridge that we may have a stowaway."

I rang the Officer of the Watch and asked if I could borrow a Master-at-Arms while I spoke to our suspect, and waited for Evans and his 'find'.

We carried two Masters-at-Arms in *Otranto* and they had a busy time keeping law and order amongst our regrettably inferior crew. Unlike *Orontes*, *Otranto* only carried migrants outward-bound and those who travelled in her homeward-bound were on limited budgets. These circumstances did not attract experienced Stewards – there were plenty of fights in crew quarters and the two Masters-at-Arms or Ship's policemen had a formidable task. One was a former London policemen and the other a retired Royal Navy Petty Officer.

The Master-at-Arms (an ex-London policeman) and Evans, together with our suspected stowaway, all arrived outside my office at the same time. This was my first encounter as Purser with a suspected stowaway, although I remembered being present when Purser Thorp had conducted similar interviews. I followed the same line that I had heard him use. When the man was brought into my office I stood up and said, "Good evening, sir. I am the Purser. Do you mind letting me have a look at your passage ticket? A Steward found you in a cabin that we thought had not been booked. Perhaps I can clear up the misunderstanding?"

The man was having difficulty in remaining upright although there was only slight movement on the ship. He looked at me rather sheepishly and said, "I haven't got a ticket. I want to get off."

"I'm afraid you can't get off for at least six days," I replied. "If you haven't got a ticket, have you got any money to buy one?"

"Nope," was the answer. He said no more so I spoke again.

"Then I'm afraid you must be considered to be a stowaway and you will be treated as such. First I need a few particulars, so you had better sit down – before you fall down."

I told Steward Evans he could go and I introduced the Chief Steward who I wanted as a witness, and the Master-at-Arms who would become responsible for him after my questioning. The questions were routine and during the interview I had the man turn out his pockets, assisted by the Master-at-Arms who made sure everything came out. The exchange of questions and answer had its amusing moments when he responded to "Who is your next-of-kin?" with, "It was my wife this morning, but I doubt if it will be now," and when I asked, "What do you do for a living?" he replied, "I sell office furniture," at which he looked round my office and said, "Good office furniture!"

My interrogation, supported by documents that he had with him revealed that he was from Cottesloe near Fremantle. He had 17 shillings and 10d in Australian money, and had come on board at the suggestion of a friend to join a farewell party. He didn't know the people who were actually sailing but remembered a crowded cabin and plenty of drink. After a while he decided to have a look round the ship. He found the pre-sailing atmosphere most convivial and picked up a couple of drinks at other cabin parties. The door of Cabin 215 on 'G' deck was open and as he looked inside the freshly made-up bed looked too tempting to a man by now staggering a little, so he decided to lie down for a moment or two. He fell asleep and was later found by Evans, the cabin Steward.

I prepared the necessary telegrams for our office in Perth and for the Australian Immigration and Customs authorities. By sailing in the ship without completing Immigration and Customs formalities our stowaway had broken Commonwealth regulations. As such he was liable to heavy fines and, technically, so was the Orient Line for allowing him (even though unintentionally) to sail in their ship without Custom's clearance. I explained all this to a now very subdued man, and suggested that perhaps we could spend his 17-10d on a telegram to his wife in which he would ask her to pay the minimum fare to Colombo at our Fremantle or Perth office, thus preventing him being treated as a Stowaway and handed over in Colombo for prosecution. Later perhaps she could send some money to the ship for expenses and his return fare. He agreed to do this.

We drafted out the following message to his wife:

> ABOARD LINER *OTRANTO* BOUND COLOMBO WILL EXPLAIN LATER STOP PLEASE PAY ORIENT LINE NINETY POUNDS FOR FARE OTHERWISE WILL BE PROSECUTED AS STOWAWAY STOP PAY ADDITIONAL TWO HUNDRED POUNDS FOR MY CREDIT ABOARD LOVE VINCE.

Having got all that sorted out I sent 'Vince' off with the Master-at-Arms for a meal and went to tell the Captain all about our unsolicited passenger. The Captain knew I was conducting an interview with a suspected stowaway because I had already informed the Bridge when I asked for the Master-at-Arms. We agreed that I had done all that was needed, and the telegrams were transmitted. All we had to do now was wait for confirmation that his wife had paid her husband's fare and he would become a bona fide passenger, even though we would still have to sort out his Immigration status in Ceylon because he did not have a passport.

About nine o'clock that evening we received a telegram from Cottesloe:

PROSECUTE MY HUSBAND

I sent for 'Vincent' and told him the news. He said he wasn't surprised and told me that he had been playing up a bit lately, under the influence of a friend who had enticed him aboard and then not bothered to check that he had got ashore safely.

We let him stay in Cabin 215, although he was not allowed the use of any of the passenger amenities. A Master-at-Arms escorted him to meals in the Crew Mess and accompanied him for a period of exercise on deck. Then 24 hours before we reached Colombo we received a signal from our office in Perth telling us that his wife had agreed to pay for his keep aboard *Otranto* and for his return to Australia by the next ship, which fortunately was the day after our call. His wife had expressed a wish that her husband be kept in custody in Ceylon.

For his last night on board we let Vincent dine in the Restaurant and I bought him a drink at the bar. He was a nice chap, a little weak-willed but very much in love with his wife. He said he thought he deserved the treatment she had given him. He did spend a night in a Colombo jail, although our Agent told me he would not be put with the local looters and drunks. Immigration insisted that either the Orient Line put up a guarantee of around £1,000 or he was to be kept in custody. The Captain, Agent and I decided that the kindest thing we could do was to let Vincent sweat it out for a night. We hoped he would describe his experiences when he got back to Fremantle and perhaps discourage others who might get left on board Orient or P&O Liners.

When *Otranto* called at Fremantle outward-bound on our next voyage, Vince and his wife Barbara came to see us. Barbara was a charming girl who was just right for Vince, and told me that he had 'improved' since his trip to Ceylon! He even brought me some office furniture catalogues!

Otranto's dining room

When we were junior Assistant Pursers I think we were good officers. The voyages we made were as much an adventure for us as they were for our passengers. We were too inexperienced to be 'blasé' and sufficiently intelligent to admit it when we didn't know the answer to a question. Our 'homeward-bound' passengers (for us that is) were full of fun and the entertainments we put on for them went with a swing.

At first we did not have entertainment officers – these only came a few years later. The entertainments were theoretically run by the passengers with the help of the Sports Assistant Purser, but in fact they were run by the Assistant Purser with the help of a Passenger Sports Committee. During the early part of each voyage a General Meeting of Passengers was called by the Captain, 'to elect a Chairman and Committee to assist in the running of sports and entertainments during the voyage'. The Chairman had been selected before the meeting in order to speed up the election process, and was usually a friend of the Captain. Of course, volunteers were asked for at the General Meeting but I cannot remember anyone actually offering to do the job without a lot of persuasion beforehand.

Sometimes there were businessmen, often it was a Service Officer taking passage. I remember doctors, a judge from Victoria, an Australian QC, even several knights. Often the Chairman was no more than a figurehead, but sometimes we had a real 'live-wire' when I did not always get my own way. There was a Royal Navy Engineer Commander who was elected Chairman of the Sports Committee in *Orontes* who was a wonderful fellow. He really kept me on my toes and I used his bright ideas for years afterwards. The Committee was chosen from young people and there was no difficulty in getting sufficient to help with the entry forms for the deck games and generally assist me with the evening activities. I attended the Committee meetings and usually submitted a suggested programme of entertainment which, with minor alteration, was nearly always accepted. I let them run their own deck tournaments while I was working in the office in the daytime.

Orontes was the first ship to have a full-size tennis court on deck. The rackets were solid wood, but otherwise it was an ordinary game of tennis played on a wooden deck. There were other games such as bull board, bucket quoits, quoit tennis and, the most popular, deck quoits. Deck quoits or 'slithers' appealed to all age groups.

Old-fashioned deck games

Quoit tennis was by far the most energetic and the finals were as exciting as the end of Wimbledon fortnight. One enterprising Sports Committee organised a Quoit Tennis Finals Ball at the end of the competitions and had the winner of the men's singles starting the dancing with the winner of the ladies.

Once the Committee had been elected and the Captain gone, we had our first meeting and I would suggest that they appoint Miss So-and-So as Secretary who would then work closely with me. If the Captain's selection of a Chairman was a put-up job, then my selection of a Secretary was a premeditated plundering of the best-looking girl on board. *Orontes* Staff Commander, John Dudley Birch, considered this to be part of the Sports Assistant Purser's perks, and used to pull my leg whilst leaning over the wing of the Bridge watching a new set of passengers embark, saying, "There, Froggy – there's a potential Secretary for you" … while the Chief Officer would mutter, "They all look like Russian Princesses after a week at sea."

We carried a ship's orchestra, 'The Struggling Four!', but they were not very good. What good musician would leave the world of entertainment for three months to be lost on a voyage to the other end of the world? However, they were real live people, and as such far more valuable than a box full of gramophone records. The musicians were not available every night, as sometimes they might be playing in the Tourist Class and once a week they played for the crew, where the piano was lubricated with beer. On the nights when we didn't have the band we arranged various types of alternative entertainment.

A popular evening was the Book Dinner in which all age groups could take part. Passengers were asked to wear a novelty or motif signifying the title of a well-known book. Each contestant was given a number and during the evening people walked around recording their interpretation of the motifs. An example would be a drawing of an Egg and an Eye – 'The Egg and I'. Some were very clever. A caveman and a man in evening dress – 'Hymns Ancient and Modern'. Then there was the comic who collected a number but had no motif at all – 'Gone with the Wind'. It was usually a good evening and I would suggest to the Committee that we had a Book Dinner early in the voyage because it enabled people to walk up to complete strangers and start a conversation. This was

Ship's orchestra

acceptable at the time, although I dread to think how the Entertainment Officers we carried later would have gone down in 1948. I felt embarrassed some years later when I watched an Entertainment Officer on the first night of a cruise tell an audience to turn round and introduce themselves to the person in the row behind – but it worked and the passengers loved it! I'm sure when I was a junior officer half the passengers would have left the ship at the next port if we had conducted the entertainment like a holiday camp.

At least once a week there was a film show for the passengers. The projectors were worked by a ship's electrician assisted by an Assistant Purser. Some of the films were 16mm which were shown in the main lounge, others were 35mm and were shown from a steel projection room on the after end of the boat deck projected onto a screen mounted on the main mast. For these the audience sat out on deck under the night sky. During the open-air film shows the officer of the watch kept a look out on the radar for rain squalls and whenever possible steered round them.

Assisting with the showing of 16mm films was easy – all we had to do was rewind the spools. However, the 35mm films were different, as each was delivered in cans and the film had to be transferred to spools. It took most of an afternoon to do this and we often got into a complete mess. I remember 'spooling up' a film with my friend Peter Lloyd one afternoon and getting into a terrible muddle, with film all over the boat deck. The story was about the theft of a racehorse and the hunt to find it. The way we prepared it for showing had the finding of the horse before the actual theft!

Often passengers would offer to help with the entertainment. Some were very good, others an embarrassment. There were a couple who offered to give a demonstration of jujitsu but the husband was quite a big man and his wife an attractive 'petite' woman. We covered the hard deck of the dancing space with a tarpaulin during the interval of a gala dance. The couple appeared in the customary Japanese-style clothing and for a few minutes the man gave us a lecture on the art of jujitsu, emphasising the importance of falling properly. He went on for such a long time about falling properly that I began to wonder if we had done the right thing by allowing him to give the demonstration, and I could see that the passengers were getting bored and I feared that a slow handclap would start. However, at last he stopped talking about falling without getting hurt and then announced that, "My wife, who weighs a mere 110 pounds, will throw me, who weighs 170 pounds. Let's imagine I am about to attack her as she walks down a street – see how she throws me to the ground and see how I fall unhurt and ready to rise again."

A hush fell in the dance space. People sat or stood tense, waiting to see this big man thrown by the small woman, and of course to see how he fell; after all, he had been talking about it for long enough. The couple went to opposite ends of the dance floor and started to walk towards one another. As he came up to his wife, he made a lunge at her and, quick as lightening, he seemed to sail into the air and landed with a thump on the hard deck – and promptly broke his collar bone!

A less violent contribution to passenger entertainment was offered by a Colonel and Mrs Gratrix who said they were each champion chess players and would be willing to talk about some well-known international champions, as well as how some games had been won or lost. It was felt by the Chairman of the Sports Committee and the Sports Assistant Purser that there would only be limited interest in this sort of lecture, so a small writing room was reserved during an afternoon for the Colonel and his Lady. When the Chairman went to introduce the speakers he was alarmed to find the room crowded beyond its capacity – there were people standing on the writing desks to try to get a better view of the centre of the room from where the couple were to talk and demonstrate.

It was soon discovered that the Sports Assistant Purser – not me – had posted the following notice:

Talk and Demonstration by Colonel and Mrs Gratrix 2.30pm Wednesday 17th November in the Writing Room. Colonel and Mrs Gratrix, who have been associated with International Tournaments, will talk about and demonstrate some famous mating positions.

He had omitted to mention 'Chess' anywhere in his notice!

Chapter 5
Singers – Cricketers – Models

I remained as Assistant Purser until 1952. Most of the time I was involved in passenger entertainment, although the role of the Sports Assistant Purser changed after the first few post-war voyages. The Orient Line, first in so many aspects of passenger ship operation, quickly realised the importance of entertainment. Even before the Australian Government appointed Migrant Welfare Officers to sail with new settlers on our outward voyages, the Orient Line was carrying Liaison Officers who gave talks about Australia and generally advised migrants on what to expect. These men greatly assisted with deck sports and, homeward-bound, practically ran the Tourist Class entertainment.

Soon First Class Liaison Officers were appointed and passenger sports committees were dispensed with. There was still a Sports Assistant Purser, but he became more of a link between the Liaison Officer and the Purser's Office. Everything was becoming more professional. The informal gathering of a group of pretty girls with an Assistant Purser to tear up housie-housie tickets or to devise a scavenger hunt, was replaced by a formal requisition on the Purser's Office from the Liaison Officer. It wasn't long before Head Office in London dictated what entertainment there would be on each voyage.[9]

The world had not yet experienced the impact of the Jumbo jet, and most people still travelled by sea. *Orontes* once had a complete opera company as passengers to Australia. They had the whole of the starboard side of 'C' deck and at around 8.00 in the morning, when they were getting up, the noise was frightful. "Me-me-ME-ME-MEEEAH" and "La-La-LA-La-LAAA-AH" came from cabins and bathrooms. The Maestro was a dear man with snowy white hair, and at table in the Dining Room his dress was always impeccable – until one very hot evening in the Red Sea, whilst he wore his dinner suit, stiff shirt, wing collar and black tie, he was without shoes or socks.

"The heat – it is too much for the feet," he explained. "I feel my feet a lot," he said. "Sometimes I conduct in the slippers – no one can see and I am so happy. Tonight I go to the cabin when we have eaten – no one can see the feet when I sit here."

Plenty of sportsmen travelled, including the English and Australian cricket teams on their way to and from test matches. In April 1948, the P&O *Strathaird* carried the first post-war Australian cricket team to England. Under the captaincy of Don Bradman they played a series of County and Test matches and didn't lose a single one.[10] The victorious team returned home in *Orontes*.

I first met Bradman in the gentlemen's lavatory on the after end of 'C' deck in the First Class of *Orontes*. As I was standing there, shortly after we sailed from Tilbury, the chap next to me said, "Going to be a good trip?"

"It ought to be," I answered, "you know we have the Australian cricketers aboard?"

"Yes, I did know," replied my companion.

And that was that. He went one way, I went the other. Less than ten minutes later I bumped into my Purser, Gordon Thorp, who was talking to the man I had just been conversing with in the lavatory. Thorp in his usual brusque manner stopped me and said "Met Don?"

"Don who?" I thought, but I knew that I had to humour my somewhat eccentric Purser, so I said, "No, sir, I don't think I have."

"Don – Froggie French – taught him all he knows – which isn't much."

'Don', of course, was Donald Bradman – the man I had told that the Australian cricketers were on board. He was very understanding. Fortunately he knew my Purser from previous voyages. He was kind enough to say, "Yes, Thorpie. Froggie and I have already met."

I must admit that I felt a little ashamed at not knowing the famous cricketer the first time I met him, but cricket had never been my game. I couldn't see the ball, and it usually saw me first and was uncomfortably hard.

On their way back home the team were relaxed and there were plenty of parties. Neil Harvey, the 'schoolboy' of the team, had a birthday – it must have been his twentieth – and the others bought him glasses of liquor of different colours. Hassett, who would succeed Bradman as Captain, was a quiet Australian with a delightful sense of humour. Keith Miller enjoyed a party. Some were a little difficult, such as Sid Barnes expected preferential treatment, but most of the team were always full of fun, enjoyed the approbation of their fellow passengers, but didn't take advantage of their prowess. Bradman kept apart from his team most of the time, but he did lead them in the Fancy Dress when the whole team stripped the sheets from their beds and appeared as 'genuine Bedouin Arabs'. At dinner they arranged for the Head Waiter to remove their tables and all ate cross-legged sitting on the floor. This was always the routine for the Fancy Dress Ball whenever a test team travelled.

The Fancy Dress Ball was one of the major evenings of any voyage. Some costumes kept turning up again and again, such as Port Said traders, Ghosts or Departed Spirits (which was a ghost with an empty gin bottle) and a man dressed as a baby was usually particularly revolting, with an insecure nappy and a dummy in his mouth. Sometimes we saw something original and although the prize was supposed to be determined by ballot we used to 'fiddle' the result to exclude the 'babies' and boost up something that we had not seen before.

Lord Nuffield[11] frequently travelled to Australia in one of our ships and on one occasion he appeared at the Fancy Dress evening wearing mechanic's overalls and a cloth cap. I asked him what he represented so that I could put him on the voting list for the ballot.

"What do you mean – what do I represent?"

"Your costume, sir – do you have a title for the evening?"

"What evening?" he asked.

I realised he was pulling my leg, but I had to persist so I continued. "The Fancy Dress parade, sir – how do you want to be announced?"

49

He gave me an impish look, removed the dummy cigarette holder from his mouth and said, "I'm not in Fancy Dress – this is what I wear when I'm mending other people's cars!"

From time-to-time a leading Melbourne store brought real French mannequins to Australia on which to show off the latest fashions. *Orion* had four of these attractive models who embarked at Tilbury. For the first week of the voyage they managed to play off one Junior Officer against another and had a thoroughly enjoyable time being entertained by everybody. The few young male passengers didn't get a look in – the uniforms were too attractive for the girls to resist. By the time the ship reached Naples the mannequins were well known to all on board. They were popular, vivacious girls who didn't seem to want to become attached to any one man in particular. Their evening clothes were stunning and when they walked into the Dining Room for dinner all heads turned and admired them.

During *Orion*'s call at Naples the girls were met by a group of United States sailors who entertained them ashore. It seems they had lunch at a beach restaurant, a swim and then visited a giant aircraft carrier. *Orion* was due to sail for Port Said at 6.00pm and, as usual, dead on six the gangway was lowered, the ropes cast off and the ship moved away from the quay. At four minutes past six – the ship a good 20 feet from the shore – the four French girls and their American escorts came rushing along the quayside shouting and waving. From the ship they could be seen talking to the Orient Line Agent, who had been the last official to go ashore. He shouted to the Captain and Pilot who were leaning over the wing of the Bridge. "We'll send them off in a launch, if you agree."

Using a megaphone, the Captain called back "All right, I'll stop outside the breakwater."

Some 500 passengers and crew lining the ship's side rails, who were watching the sailing, heard this exchange and thus a wave of excitement spread along the decks.

As soon as the ship was safely through the harbour entrance she stopped, waiting for a fast naval launch which could be seen approaching from the water steps of the Stazione Marittima.

Port Said

Aboard the launch the four French girls could be clearly seen, their long hair blowing in the sea breeze and looking, as always, like a picture from the cover of *Vogue* magazine.

The launch headed for a ship's side door some twelve feet above the water line. The United States Navy gave a perfect display of small boat handling as they came alongside, and immediately a rope ladder was dropped from the ship to the launch. *Orion*'s bosun was at the top of the ladder and he lowered a rope to the US sailor who held the bottom.

The Bosun called, "Send 'em up, one at a time, and tie this round 'em in case they slip."

"Okay, sailor," called the navy man, "here's number one, nice to have had her aboard."

He quickly tied a bowline around the waist of a tall Parisienne called Collette and helped her onto the first rung of the ladder. Collette reached up and after four or five hesitant steps was able to take the hand of one of our seamen stretched down to welcome her. A loud cheer went up from the passengers and crew watching the operation.

Number two mannequin came aboard safely, although she seemed very embarrassed by the whole thing. The third girl must have had some experience with small boats. She paused halfway up the ladder, removed one hand and waved to the hundreds leaning over the rails and then blew a kiss to the US boat's crew.

The last to leave the launch was a petite blonde, less outgoing than the others, but very popular with all on board *Orion*. It was obvious that she was nervous and the sailor who tied the safety rope around her was having to reassure her that all would be well if she did exactly as her friends had done. After climbing very hesitantly halfway up the ladder she stretched out to take the hand of *Orion*'s seaman, but she wasn't as tall as the others and they didn't connect – at the same time her feet slipped and the poor girl twisted sideways and the breeze caught her skirt which finished up over her head. The quartet were travelling to Australia to model top wear – this one must have displayed her French underwear to the largest audience on record!

During my last voyages as an Assistant Purser, I was acting as Deputy Purser, which meant that I was second-in-command of the Pursers' Department. On one of these voyages we carried the Governor-General of Australia and his family from Melbourne to England – his Excellency, the Right Honourable William McKell, Mrs McKell, their son and their daughter. Accompanying them was the Governor-General's Military Secretary, Lt Colonel William Orr. Bill Orr and I were to become firm friends. The Purser was called Sindall, known affectionately throughout the fleet as 'Sinbad'. He showed little or no interest in running his department, but provided the figurehead for the hotel side of the ship. I never let him down, but I suspect that if I did, he would have soon put things straight and then, once again, left me to 'get on with it'. Sinbad behaved impeccably with the Governor-General and I often found them together putting the world to rights, while Bill Orr and I were worrying about the arrangements for the Vice-Regal party at the next port of call.

It was a voyage during which things didn't always go too well. At Fremantle the harbour tugs all went on strike. The ship delayed sailing until slack water and then Captain Burnnand swung *Orontes* right round, without the aid of tugs in a not very wide harbour, and set off for Colombo. During the sea passage to Ceylon we got to know the McKell family very well. The Governor-General and the Captain became firm friends – they were both very much 'men's men', gruff and 'straight-to-the-point'. The McKell children were a bit of a problem, especially their son, who was a typical Australian teenager who wanted to disassociate himself from his parents. This is a difficult thing to do in a ship, and if your father is the King's representative in Australia it is impossible.

The day before Aden the ship broke down. The starboard engine had to be stopped and we entered and left Aden on just one engine. No tugs in Fremantle, and only one engine at Aden… we began to wonder if we had some sort of Vice-Regal voodoo cast on the ship. Four hours after leaving port the Engineers had us back on full power and we reached Suez in time to enter the Canal as scheduled.

A week later *Orontes* steamed into Gibraltar and received a Vice-Regal gun salute from the Garrison. We thought it a great pity that Orient Liners no longer carried a saluting cannon. When we sailed we had yet another Crown representative with us, the Governor of Gibraltar. The night after we left the Mediterranean Mr McKell gave a dinner party. Purser 'Sinbad' Sindall had a severe chill and I was required to represent the Pursers' Department. Although the party was supposed to be informal, Bill Orr told me that Vice-Regal protocol should be observed. So at lunchtime the Military Secretary briefed those of us who were being invited to represent the ship – all of us except Captain Burnnand who was detained elsewhere. We were told that at 7.00pm sharp we should present ourselves at the McKell suite on 'D' deck. We would be offered sherry, and only sherry. Nobody was to smoke during the pre-dinner reception. We would be offered cigarettes, not cigars, after the loyal toast at the end of the dinner.

At 6.45 the Staff Commander and I met in the Chief Engineer's cabin for a stiff gin because, apart from being a little nervous in case we let the side down, we needed something to prepare us for the sherry none of us were accustomed to drinking. Suitably fortified, we presented ourselves at the *Orontes* Special Suite on the starboard side of 'D' deck at exactly 7.00pm. A Steward was circulating with a tray of sherry, the Chief Engineer grimaced and took a glass, the Staff Commander and I took ours more graciously – I hope. The Governor of Gibraltar came over and chatted to us and all the time Bill Orr was dancing attendance on his Master and Mrs McKell.

Then in came McKell junior and the first thing he said was, "Bought these in Gibraltar," and producing a packet of Lucky Strike cigarettes asked, "Anybody want one?" By now he had already got one in his own mouth and was proffering the packet to the Chief Engineer who immediately took one. Bill Orr caught my eye and almost imperceptibly shrugged his shoulders. So much for our lecture on protocol! However, it was our own Captain who really brought the party down to earth. Stanley Burnnand arrived late – he had warned the McKell's that he might be held up on the Bridge, so when he came into the now crowded room he was the last guest to arrive, so the Governor-General personally offered him a sherry from the Steward's tray.

"What's that?" says 'our Stan' with his fog horn voice.

"Sherry, Captain," says His Majesty's Governor-General of the Commonwealth of Australia.

"Sherry!" grates the fog horn, and to the Steward he says, "Bring me a gin, man."

The evening was a great success. Protocol was observed in that, on board his own ship on the high seas, the Captain is 'Master-under-God'. The request for a gin broke the tension which some of us were feeling and without meaning to, Stanley Burnnand had established the atmosphere which was to prevail all evening.

Soon after the McKell family disembarked, the Governor-General had a private audience with King George VI at which the King knighted him. Sir William and Lady McKell travelled back to Australia in *Oronsay*, then the latest ship in the Orient Fleet. I like to think that despite *Oronsay*'s modern comforts they retained a soft spot for the dear old *Orontes*.

I met Sir William again when I stayed with Bill and Jean Orr in Canberra. The Military Secretary had a house in the grounds of Government House and when I stayed there they still had a parrot in a cage by the kitchen door. The parrot had been at 'Yarralumla', the home of the Governor-General, since the time when the Duke of Gloucester was the King's representative. It had picked up the remarks most often heard in the kitchen, the chief of which must have been "Never do for His Grace", because that is what the parrot said all day long.

For a long time the Governor of Victoria was Sir Dallas Brooks who travelled in *Orcades* when I was responsible to the Purser for the Tourist Class section of the ship. Sir Dallas, of course, travelled First Class, but I was allowed from time to time to venture up into the 'West End' and have a taste of the high-living that was denied to my Tourist Class charges. I had very little contact with this particular Vice-Regal party until their last few hours on board.

As usual, we picked up the pilot off Port Philip Heads in the early hours of the morning. As dawn broke, a Royal Australian Navy Destroyer came close alongside us acting as an escort to *Orcades* with the State Governor aboard. At about this time the Chief Officer on watch glanced towards *Orcades'* solitary mast and to his wrath observed atop the mast a chamber pot! His roar of disapproval might almost have been heard aboard the destroyer, which fortunately hadn't yet noticed the decoration.

"Bloody Assistant Pursers," he roared – which was a bit unfair because he had no proof that the offending article had been placed there by Assistant Pursers. I think (and secretly hope) it was Cadet and Assistant Pursers who climbed the mast with the pot, but to date no one has admitted the 'crime'. As soon as a seaman was observed being sent up the mast, the Australian Navy realised what was going on and a group on the destroyer's Bridge could be seen pointing and laughing – which annoyed the Chief Officer even more.

The weather in Melbourne can be unpredictable, and as we approached Station Pier quite a strong off-shore wind began to blow. A sudden gust caught *Orcades* as she was edging in towards the Outer West berth and the tugs had difficulty holding the stern. Eventually the ship was got alongside, but facing down Port Philip Bay and not 'head in' as planned. This in itself would not normally present a major problem, except that when everything had been prepared for the ship to be starboard side to the wharf, gangways and baggage discharge suddenly have to be changed to the port side. On this occasion there was an added complication. The reception arrangements on the pier for the Governor had been made at the point where the First Class Foyer gangway came alongside. By the time we were tied up the wrong way round the red carpet, band, guard of honour, Lord Mayor and everyone else were opposite a seldom used ship's side door into the Tourist Class restaurant, close to the galley.

A hasty consultation with the Shore officials and Ship's Officers resulted in a decision that it would be easier for the ship to change the point of exit, than for the shore to move their red carpet, band and guard of honour. This meant that with 20 minutes' notice I had to prepare a corner of the Tourist Class restaurant while the Deck Department opened a seldom-used door. Everything was ready with about two minutes to spare. There was a patch of linoleum in the corner of *Orcades* Tourist Class restaurant that was cleaner than the rest for the remainder of the ship's life – it had been bleached.

Sir Dallas Brooks disembarked, passing between a few hundred Tourist Class passengers munching eggs and bacon, onto a wharf where the band struck up the National Anthem, the guard of honour presented arms and a flight of RAAF fighters passed overhead – dead on time.

Chapter 6
Cruising – Spithead 1953

In January 1953 I was promoted to the rank of Deputy Purser. I had been the second in command of the Pursers' Department for several voyages and at the time I was in *Orcades*, the first of the post-war Orient Liners. My first sight of *Orcades* was from the ship's side door of *Orontes*, off Gravesend waiting for the Port Doctor at the end of a homeward voyage. This was in December 1948 and *Orcades* was in Tilbury dock preparing to sail on her maiden voyage. She was a revolutionary ship with a unique appearance summed up by the seaman standing beside me.

"Cor, look at 'er – looks like a Liberty ship gone pregnant!!" Liberty ships were mass-produced cargo ships built during the war. In the new *Orcades* of 28,000 tons – nearly half as big again as *Orontes* – the single funnel, a tripod mast and the Bridge were a composite unit almost amidships, certainly much further aft than in previous passenger liners. Deck Officers and Pilots soon appreciated having the Bridge in this position, which made control easier when manoeuvring because they were standing almost at the centre of the axis. The future Orient Liners, *Oronsay*, *Orsova* and *Oriana* had their Bridge in the same position. *Orcades'* speed also enabled her to reduce the passage to Australia from 36 to 28 days.

The interior of the ship had many improvements on the 24,000-ton *Orion*, the newest surviving pre-war Orient Liner, although not all the modern decor was appreciated by the passengers. The First Class Dining Room had fluorescent lighting which presented a problem for the ladies. With ordinary make-up on their faces, women looked a sickly green under the lights in the Dining Room and several used to slip down from their cabin to make up amongst the waiters laying tables for dinner.

Sir Colin Anderson, a Director of the Line, gave a great deal of personal attention to the decorative detail of the ship incorporated many fine features. This included some modern paintings, one of which just outside the First Class Café looked to me like the back of a garage door. This painting, Sir Colin told me, had cost in excess of £1,000. I didn't feel so ashamed as I did when he asked later in the Main Lounge, "French, that picture there – how long has it been like that?"

"Always, as far as I know," I said.

"Well," he replied, "it's upside down!"

Just before *Oriana* was commissioned in 1960, I was wandering around the after end of the Bathing Deck one evening when I came across Sir Colin hanging a picture called 'Corroboree'.

"Good evening, sir," I said. "Can I help you?"

"Yes, please," he answered. "You can hold this when I have decided which way up it goes."

I was highly delighted to think that he wasn't always sure of these things himself. I didn't have the courage to remind him of our conversation in *Orcades* seven years previously.

The Coronation of Queen Elizabeth II took place in Westminster Abbey on 2nd June 1953. I was aboard *Orcades* at the time, cruising the Mediterranean. We were at sea all day on passage between Venice and Rhodes and our Captain was Norman Whinfield under whom I had served in *Orontes*. Most of the day was taken up with the BBC broadcast from London, but Captain Whinfield never missed an opportunity to address his ship's company and addressed us all before we started to pick up the broadcast. We were fired with loyalty as he enthused about a second Elizabethan age, and although some of us had a quiet smile about our eulogising Captain, we had to admit that his flair for showmanship impressed the passengers.

Norman Whinfield took advantage of any situation that offered itself to make a speech. At times he would offer a brief sermon at his Sunday church services, but because he was a short man, we used to build a platform with a lectern on top from which he could conduct the service and be seen by his congregation. It was Empire

Day – in those days we had an 'Empire' Day celebrated on Queen Victoria's birthday, whereas now there is Commonwealth Sunday which seems to slip by unnoticed by most people. However, on this occasion 'Winnie' decided he would give a short address. As usual, his lectern was draped with a Union Jack and, as he worked up to his theme, he took hold of the flag and said, "What is it that unites us – we have the Crown – we have this." At which point he took hold of the flag and held it up, revealing the boxes from which we had built his platform, all clearly marked 'WORTHINGTON EXPORT ALE'. I suppose today his performance would make a good TV commercial, but at the time it generated a few stifled smirks from the front row of his audience.

Orcades had her problems during Coronation year. Homeward-bound from Australia the port engine broke down between Melbourne and Adelaide, where we arrived three hours late. We crossed the Australian Bight at a reduced speed and were late arriving in Fremantle where we embarked the Australian Test Cricketers for the 1953 series in England, with Lindsey Hasset their Captain. Despite our engine troubles, we reached the United Kingdom on the correct day and disembarked our passengers at Southampton before carrying on empty to Tilbury. We spent the summer cruising in the Mediterranean, but throughout the programme the port engine continued to give trouble. Whilst berthed in Venice the Engineers decided to do some tests on the engine which entailed flushing a green dye through the system. There was an embarrassing consequence from the use of this dye, as after passing through the system, it was automatically discharged over the ship's side and for several hours the Grand Canal was a beautiful green colour!

Often, when a ship was in port, one of the Deck Officers would arrange for a motor lifeboat to be lowered and sent away, and we used to take advantage of this exercise to go for picnics and swimming parties. In Venice, Fred Woolley, then the Junior Second Officer (and eventually Commodore of the P&O fleet in command of *Canberra*), got permission to take a boat for a run round the canals. There were about 15 or 20 people aboard, including several

Engineers, a Radio Officer, Nursing Sister and Hostesses. Fred took us up some pretty smelly side streets and under some low bridges, but we managed to navigate without too much trouble.

After a while the girls announced that they wanted to disembark and go shopping. This idea was taken up by the majority of those aboard and at some convenient steps most people left us. Only Fred, an Engineer and I remained to take the boat back to *Orcades*. Now the fun began – the low bridges we had chugged under on our outward trip were now too low for us without our passengers to increase the boat's draught. However, the problem was soon solved, as a group of urchins saw our plight and jumped aboard for a jolly joy-ride… although we had difficulty in persuading them to get off after we had regained the Grand Canal.

The day after the Queen's Coronation we arrived off Rhodes. The Greek island was a regular cruising port and we got to know the local officials quite well. A very attractive Greek girl came on board from the local Post Office to sell stamps. Our Senior Assistant Purser was Stan Rawdon and it was his job to see that people like the stamp seller, currency exchange operators and others were looked after. The Rhodes stamp seller received his special attention.

"Is this table all right for you? Have you got enough light? Would you like a cool drink? Do you smoke?" Stan took care of everything and seldom left her alone for more than half-an-hour at a time, when he would quite casually pass by her table to say, "Everything all right? Can I get someone to bring you a cup of coffee?" It was on the Coronation Cruise that Stan said to the lovely Greek, "Would you care to come aboard for dinner this evening?"

"Yes, thank you, that will be very nice," she answered with a winning smile.

"Fine, I will be at our gangway at seven o'clock and I look forward to seeing you then."

All afternoon Stan bored the staff with descriptions of the lovely girl he had booked for dinner. He was right about her beauty – she really was most attractive, and I felt very privileged when he asked me to join them for a drink beforehand. However, at 7.00pm the laugh was on poor Stan. She arrived, looking stunning – with mother, father, sister and small brother in tow!

* * *

After the Coronation Cruise we returned to Southampton, disembarked our passengers and then had 24 hours in which to prepare *Orcades* for the Spithead Naval Review where we were to be an Admiralty Guest Ship and be part of the procession following the Queen's ship, *HMS Surprise*, on its progress through the assembled fleet.[12]

Servants, whether they are the general manager or commis waiter of a hotel or restaurant, react to the attitude of the customer. There are hotel guests and ship's passengers who will never get the best service, even though they pay the highest prices, because they are not respected by the staff. Some of the biggest snobs can be Stewards in the First Class section of a ship. A man considered by a Steward to be a 'gentleman' will receive service fit for a 'gentleman'. However, a passenger whose behaviour does not meet his Steward's standards will not get that little extra service that can always be found, whatever tip he gives at the start of a cruise. Our Government guests were Ambassadors, Governors-General and High Commissioners. There were three Admiralty guest ships *Orcades*, *Pretoria Castle* and *Strathnaver* – *Orcades* had the most distinguished guests and the entire ship's company gave splendid service.

First impressions always count for a lot. The first impression the Admiralty guests received of the Orient Line was when their special train steamed into the shed alongside the ship in the New Docks at Southampton. On the platform was a line of white-coated Stewards, and as the train came to a standstill the Stewards opened the carriage doors, went inside and took a compartment, each saying, "Please leave your luggage on the rack, I will take it to your cabin. Captain Whinfield and Captain Traill, the Admiralty Host, are waiting to greet you at the gangway."

Whilst the passengers walked towards one gangway, a chain of Stewards saw the baggage aboard on another. At the head of the First Class gangway stood our Captain and the Chief Admiralty Host who shook hands with everybody and welcomed them aboard. For the duration of the Review Charter by the Admiralty, Stan Rawdon and I were officially classed as Executive Officers and were required to carry out gangway duties – a rare, if not completely unknown, distinction for a Purser Officer in the Merchant Navy. All it really meant was that for 24 hours we took our orders from the Chief Officer instead of the Purser, but it was published in the Staff Commander's orders for the Review, and we are still proud of that distinction.

During the embarkation, our Purser 'Bill' Rope stood in the foyer a little apart from the two Captains – he was not part of the official reception party. Hardly any of the guests knew Captain Traill, the odd one who had travelled with him recognised Captain Whinfield, but a large number on seeing our Purser went to him with hand outstretched asking, "Bill, how are you?"

Nearly all the Australian and New Zealand representatives knew him, but many others like the Speaker of the House of Commons, the Prime Minister of Malta and Bishop of London also knew him at once. I

was very proud of my Purser and my profession – they didn't know the Captain, but they knew him – even the Archbishop of Canterbury said "Good morning, Rope."

As soon as the passengers were on board we sailed down Southampton Water to Spithead and through the assembled fleet to a point where we were required to anchor and wait for *HMS Surprise* to come from Portsmouth with the Queen aboard. Whenever *Orcades* was stationary she was dressed overall with flags – that is, there was a line from the bow to the masthead and to the stern from which hung down signal flags as decoration. Putting up and taking down these flags quickly presented a problem which was solved by an ingenious method, credited to our Bosun, Jack Kite. A permanent wire was rigged from bow and stern to the masthead and to each flag two big rings were sewn. The rings were then threaded onto the taut wire and the flags hauled up or dropped down very quickly. After the Review, the way we rapidly dressed and undressed ship was remarked upon by many experts.

Lunch on board *Orcades* was not very formal. At the time we were anchored at the eastern end of the lines of assembled ships, close to one of the Forts which guard the approach to Spithead and Portsmouth Harbour. I was on gangway duty at the head of the forward accommodation ladder. The ship's three restaurants were named (for this operation only) the Red (First Class), the White (a special Grill Room on the Boat Deck), and the Blue (the Tourist Class).

At 3.00pm *HMS Surprise* led by the Trinity House Vessel *Patricia*, with Sir Winston Churchill on board, and escorted by *HMS Redpole*, left Portsmouth for Spithead. As this little procession approached the Fleet a salute of 21 guns was fired, and as the three small ships followed by *Standing, Fleetwood* and *Helmsdale* entered the Review lines, the Government guest-liners led by *Orcades* fell in behind and the Coronation Review of the Fleet began. Behind us steamed *Pretoria Castle* and behind her came *Strathnaver*, followed by two small vessels with Admiralty staff aboard, *Brading* and *Southsea*.

It was a fine day, but there was quite a breeze and we were steaming very slowly. *Orcades* was the largest vessel moving during

"Stan took care of everything".

the inspection, and at one stage seemed to be bearing down on *HMS Vanguard*, the flagship of Admiral Sir George Creasy, Commander-in-Chief of the Home Fleet. Thankfully, we pulled out of that one, and almost did the same thing to the aircraft carrier *Eagle*, but from then on things went satisfactorily (although Captain Whinfield is reputed to have said some unkind things to our Trinity

House Pilot). As we moved slowly down
the line we had the large Royal Navy
capital ships on our starboard side and
on the port side were visitors from
foreign navies, headed by the United
States Heavy Cruiser *Baltimore*. The
foreigner who stole the show was the
Italian Sail Training Ship *Amerigo-
Vespucci* with her crew manning the
yard arms – they made a slight error
in cheering the Trinity House Yacht
Patricia with Churchill on board
instead of the *Surprise* wearing the
Royal Standard.

NAVAL REVIEW
BY
H.M. THE QUEEN

AT SPITHEAD
JUNE 15th, 1953

At the end of the line we had
to turn and steam back between
different ships. The port engine was still 'dicky', but
we made it without mishap and returned to our anchorage off
Portsmouth Harbour. There now began a busy and interesting time
for those of us on gangway duty. Several of our guests went off to
visit other ships and Captain Whinfield went in our launch to a
reception aboard *HMS Surprise*. Our launch was in charge of a
Deck Officer called John Bensley who was always getting himself
into some sort of strife, even though he was a very competent
seaman. He took our immaculate launch across the short distance
to *Surprise* and took it alongside with skill. John Bensley and his
crew then lay off the Royal Yacht with all the other launches which
had brought guests to the Queen's reception. About an hour after
they had left, John and the Captain returned. As soon as the Captain
had left the foyer, John, who had left a coxswain in charge of the
launch, turned to me and said, "I saw her – I saw her – I actually
saw her!" He was so thrilled that as soon as he had finished his
watch he went and called on the Children's Hostess, but fell asleep
in her cabin and missed the evening fireworks display.

While the Captain was visiting *Surprise* there was a lot of coming
and going from our gangway. General Freyberg[13] went off to the New

Orcades at the Spithead Review

Zealand cruiser *Black Prince*, and Clement Attlee[14] arrived from the Trinity House Yacht *Patricia*. A group of Russians headed by their ambassador went off for vodka in *Sverdlov*, and later another group of Iron Curtain attachés left for drinks in the Russian cruiser. They intrigued me by their repeated inquiry whether it would be all right if they returned after dark. I emphasised that, "Dinner is at half-past-eight"; they appreciated this, but repeatedly asked if they could move amongst the Fleet in darkness. I said that as far as I was concerned they could, but they seemed to have their doubts. Nevertheless, they went away in the *Sverdlov* launch and returned with the Russian Ambassador in time for dinner.

Dinner was a grand affair and our Chefs did us proud. I was able to 'host' my table in the Red Dining Room, where I had to entertain the Egyptian Ambassador and his wife, an Admiral and his wife, and someone who held a senior post in Ulster. Mrs 'Egypt' was a bit heavy-going, but Mrs 'Admiral' was so talkative that I had little difficulty in keeping conversation going. At one stage (I think it was between the Boiled Salmon and the Roast Ribs of Scotch Beef as we changed from Batard Montrachet '47 to Chassagne Montrachet '45) the Admiral, resplendent in his uniform with gold braid halfway up his arms, was trying to speak to me, when his wife tapped my arm and said, "Don't bother about him, he's only an ignorant sailor."

One of our Women Assistant Pursers had a somewhat traumatic experience during her dinner. The guests at her table were South American diplomats and the group around the table resembled a meeting of Chicago gangsters. Molly Drury firmly believed they each carried a gun and this belief turned to conviction when one of them, after listening to another discussing his country, leaned towards her and whispered, "He is a liar and we will kill him." At which Molly quickly grabbed a handy bottle, filled his glass, and said, rather like an English nanny, "Not now please; have some champagne and tell me about the ships you saw today."

The day ended with a splendid fireworks display whilst I watched from *Orcades'* darkened deck. After a while a man came and stood beside me and enthused at the sight, becoming boyishly excited as each cluster of stars burst from the sky. When it was over he turned to me and said, "Wasn't that wonderful?" Just then the lights came on, and I realised my companion had been the Archbishop of Canterbury – the man who, a few days before, had actually crowned the Queen.[15]

The next morning we were back in our berth at Southampton and the distinguished guests disembarked. Our Captain broadcast to the crew after the passengers had gone and thanked everybody for the way we had performed our duties. The greatest praise came from Sir Colin Anderson, Director of the Orient Line, who had been on board throughout. That afternoon as he walked into the Orient Line Office in Bishopsgate, London, a secretary asked, "Did it go well, sir?"

"Faultless," replied Sir Colin.

Chapter 7
Otranto

O n Friday 1st January 1954 *Oronsay* left Sydney at 4.00pm to
commence a trans-Pacific voyage which proved to be the
beginning of a new service by the Orient Line, followed
later by the P&O. The Canadian-Australasian line's *Aorangi*, built in
1924, had reached the end of her days and, grasping the initiative,
the Orient Line stepped in to maintain the Commonwealth link.
Soon the ports of Auckland, Suva, Honolulu, Vancouver and San
Francisco became as familiar as Colombo, Aden and Port Said.

Oronsay's first voyage from Australia to North America was a
success, although for the Pursers' Department there was little time
for relaxation. The office staff was supplemented with typists from
the Sydney office assisting with the mountain of documents for the

Otranto in the 1950s

United States Immigration Department. Canadian requirements were also as complex as the US demands.

I watched *Oronsay* sail from *Orcades* and then one-and-a-half hours later we sailed for Melbourne and home through the Suez Canal. A year later *Orsova* crossed the Pacific from Sydney and carried on home through the Panama Canal and *Orcades* went round the world in the other direction. We had became a worldwide passenger fleet.

1954 was to be an important year for me. During the last few days of the previous year, whilst on a Christmas cruise, I had became engaged to the Nursing Sister of *Orcades*. We were steaming past Norfolk Island when I proposed, en route from Auckland to Noumea. Soon after our arrival in Tilbury I was sent for by the Stores Manager, RG Evans, now in the London Office. I was a bit apprehensive as I knew there had been some complaints from the Tourist Class where I had been in charge during the last voyage, and although I had a clear conscience, I was a little worried about this sudden command from our boss. Joan, at the time my fiancée, came with me and chatted to the Lady Superintendent, Miss Metherell, while I was closeted with 'RG' and his assistant, David Peters.

The interview started off rather frighteningly with, "Good afternoon, French. Have you signed on *Orcades* again?"

"Yes sir, as soon as we opened the new Articles."

"Well, you will have to sign off again. You are going to *Otranto*."

Otranto was the oldest and least popular ship in the fleet and my heart went straight to my shoes... until he continued, "as Purser", and then, as an afterthought, he added, "acting".

I was 27 years old, engaged, had been at sea a mere six years. Here I was sailing as Purser of a 20,000-ton liner. As soon as we got out of the office and into Bishopsgate, Joan asked me if we still had a job. I couldn't resist treating her the way Mr Evans had treated me so I said, "I've got to go to Tilbury and sign off *Orcades*." Her face fell and she said, "Oh dear," but when I continued, "and then we have to pack and go across to *Otranto* where I am to be Acting Purser for one voyage", I was given a whopping great kiss right in the middle of a busy city pavement!

The 'Acting' didn't last long. I remained in *Otranto*, with one short break until June 1957 when we took her to the breaker's yard. I still have the ship's bell. It was not until my ship was broken up that I got a chance to make a Pacific voyage like the one we witnessed *Oronsay* set off on 1st January 1954.

My first ship as Purser was built in Barrow-in-Furness by *Vickers Limited* in 1926. By the time I joined her she was 28 years old and a One Class ship employed principally to carry migrants to Australia. *Ormonde* had gone to the ship-breakers two years before, so *Otranto* was the 'old lady' of the fleet. I had made one voyage in her when I was an Assistant Purser and at the time was rather glad that it was only one voyage. However, I eventually grew to love the old lady, despite her shortcomings.

There was no running water in any of the passenger cabins, and there would not have been running water in the Purser's cabin if it had not been for the initiative of the Purser standing by during her post-war re-fit. Seymore Hart noticed that the pipes to the wash basin in the Surgery ran through his cabin, so had a 'branch line' drawn off from the Doctor's supply. The cabin itself was vast, again due to Purser Hart's quick thinking when somehow or other he managed to get the next door cabin incorporated into his own!

Orama entering Sydney in 1931

Seymore Hart had been in a German prison camp from 1940 until the end of the war – he had been Purser of *Orama* when she was sunk during the evacuation of Norway. Prison camp experience gave him the instinct to grasp quickly any opportunity of increasing his comfort.

There was a tank above the wash basin in the passenger cabins. Each morning and evening the Stewards filled these tanks with fresh water using garden hoses attached to taps in the deck pantries. Twice a day for an hour each time, the main alleyways in the accommodation were strewn with water hoses as the men went from room to room, tanking up. Hot water was brought to passengers in a small can, just like a miniature watering can, in the morning with tea and in the evening when requested. All the baths were salt water and, on a board across the bath, there was a tub filled by the bath Steward with fresh water. A salt water bath was very good for treating prickly heat, from which most people suffered in the tropics.

The Officers fared better than the passengers in that there was an Officer's Mess, although the Captain, Staff Commander, Chief Engineer, Purser and Surgeon each had their table in the former First Class restaurant where we usually took dinner with the passengers. There was none of the glamour of *Orcades* about *Otranto*. We still wore mess kit in order to set an example to passengers, some of whom turned up for dinner in chain breaker singlets until they saw us, and then most made the effort to at least wear a clean shirt.

Our passengers were a very mixed bunch. Some very charming people setting off to a new life, professional people who became an asset to Australia, as well as some real 'dead beats' who would never succeed wherever they went. These latter types had usually tried everything but had never bothered to learn a trade and unfortunately were not prepared to try. They thought Australia would offer an easy life but found they had made a big mistake as soon as they got there. Most of the professional men and craftsmen taking their families were doing it for the sake of their children and were to be greatly admired.

Otranto

Homeward-bound *Otranto* carried young Australian holiday makers, most planning to work their way around Europe. They were all full of fun and we had many happy homeward trips. There was the odd disgruntled returning migrant, and we seemed to get all the deportees from the Commonwealth who sometimes managed to take the edge off our enjoyment.

The crew of *Otranto* left a bit to be desired and maintaining discipline was a hard job. My Leading Hands were a tough and loyal bunch and somehow or another we managed to get to Australia and back. The passengers didn't help on the outward voyage when they treated their Stewards as their 'chums', encouraging them to give inferior service, disregarding our normal standards. For several days before we sailed, inexperienced waiters were instructed on how to serve at table. By the time the passengers embarked they had a reasonable idea of what was required of them. Then, up the gangway came a thousand migrants. The conscientious Steward, serving dinner for the first time, pulls out a lady's chair, presents a menu to her and her husband, who promptly says, "My name's Jack, this is Dot – the wife – what's your name, son? – just bring us what's good – there's a good lad." The poor young Steward, wanting to do what he has been taught to do, doesn't get a chance.

Some of the young Stewards did not even want to try to get it right for the passengers. Many were only at sea because being a Merchant Seaman made a man exempt from being called up for National Service with the Armed Forces. These 'artful dodgers' of service with the colours were determined to do as little as they could for their wages, which also included full board and lodging. They were a constant source of trouble and seldom made more than one voyage in a ship, constantly changing to another shipping company where their behaviour was as yet unknown.

There was another type of Steward we encountered in *Otranto* – the 'old lag' who knew enough to keep out of trouble and to do as little work as possible. This type had his passengers organised from the moment they met. If he was a bedroom Steward he would introduce himself and then explain that the Captain or another Senior Officer held an inspection each morning at sea.

"They'll be along here at about 11.00am and they won't want any of you lot hanging around. If it's the Purser he'll look under the bed – so no dust there please. Beds 'as got to be properly made and baggage tidy. I'll be round about half-ten to see things is proper. If it's the Old Man 'imself he'll feel along the top of the wardrobe, and Staffy likes the porthole brass polished. I'll get you a bit o' Brasso if I hear he's coming!"

I have even heard of old lag Stewards actually paying migrants to do his work for him. Of course, the crew were better off financially than the people they were paid to serve. I remember remarking to an old rogue of a Steward during our inspection that the deck was filthy in a certain cabin. "Quite right, sir," he said, "I'll tell them about it!"

This sort of relationship between families and their cabin Steward did not really do a great deal of harm. Most migrant mothers became bored with the voyage, so keeping the cabin clean and making beds was a familiar routine they were glad to keep up at sea.

I did have to draw the line regarding a waiter about whom I received an official complaint. It seems that this chap would do nothing until everyone had arrived at the table. He then stood at the

stewards actually paying migrants to do his work for him.

end of the table, called his passengers to order by using a spoon as a gavel and said, "All read the menu? Right, hands up for porridge – now hands up for Corn Flakes. Porridge gets it, you all have porridge. Now hands up for kippers – bacon and egg? Right, today it's porridge and kippers all round."

The children, at least 200 of them, had their meals separately and always got everything they wanted, even if it was chips and ice cream on the same plate! It was amazing how the roughest and toughest

Stewards bent over backwards to do things for the kids. Likewise, when an emergency occurred, such as a burst pipe flooding part of the ship, these 'bad hats' rallied round and worked like slaves.

Punishing crewmen for misdemeanours in the Merchant Navy was an elaborate process and could technically only be done by the Captain as Master of the Vessel. Unlike an employee ashore, every crew member signed a legal document in the presence of a Board of Trade Official agreeing to conform to certain regulations. This Agreement was between the man and the Master, who in return certified that he would provide wages and food at a scale recorded in the Articles of Agreement. There was a list of 'Offences' for which the Master could inflict a fine of ten shillings, and if a man was absent from his place of duty he could be made to forfeit his wages for the length of time he was missing.

There were three essentials in imposing a fine or wage forfeiture on a member of the crew. One – the man had to be told what he had done and exactly what deductions were being made from his wages. Two – the man had to have the opportunity to comment on the action being taken by the Master. Three – the offence, punishment and comments of the defaulter had to be recorded in the ship's Official Log Book. Hence, the whole procedure was known as a 'logging'.

There were various ways in which the legal requirements could be met. One company just put a slip of paper on the defaulter's bunk telling him what he was charged with and the fine that was imposed. The recipient was then invited to record his comments on the back and return the slip to the Captain via the Chief Steward. If the slip was not returned the log entry read, "In reply the charged had nothing to say."

Other shipping companies had different ways of administering justice, but none was as impressive as Orient Line's Captain's defaulters. The 'Court' was held in the Chart Room, which in itself gave the event grandeur as this was a part of the ship inaccessible to the majority of those on board. The Captain stood (or sometimes sat) behind a lectern or table draped with a Union Jack – a reminder that British justice was being dispensed. To the left of the Captain stood the Staff Commander and to the Captain's right the Purser, who in the Orient Line was the keeper of the 'Official' (as opposed to the 'Sailing') Log Book. The defaulter stood on a mat about six feet in front of the Captain, and behind the defaulter stood a Master-at-Arms. Also present were any witnesses who might be asked to speak and always the Chief Officer, who together with the Captain, would sign the Log entry.

Defaulters were formally charged by the head of their department, Chief Officer, Chief Engineer or Purser, after the 'crime' had been investigated. Charge sheets were prepared by an Assistant Purser who noted on the sheet the maximum fine and forfeiture that could be imposed. When the 'court' was assembled, the Captain would say to the Master-at-Arms "Bring in the defaulter."

So in comes, for example, a waiter from the after Dining Room. "Stand on the mat and face the Captain," says the Master-at-Arms.

"Are you Article Number 321 William Young, Waiter?" the Captain asks, and having received a "Yes, sir", he continues, "Read the charge, Staff Commander."

The Staff Commander reads. "321 William Young, Waiter, is charged with being absent without leave from 0730 until 0930 and from Noon until 1400 on Monday 12th July while the ship was in Sydney."

"Is the charge correct?" asks the Captain.

"Yes, sir," says Young.

At this stage some Captains might ask the Head Waiter, Chief Steward or Purser for a character reference; others might deliver a homily on the sin of letting the ship down; some might ask, "What happened?" and then some fantastic stories could emerge and at which it is difficult to keep a straight face. The most experienced Captains carried on from the defaulter admitting the charge to:

"Fined according to the scale – Purser, read the Log Entry."

The Purser reads, "321 Young, W, Waiter, is charged with being absent without leave from 0730 to 0930 and from Noon until 1400 on 12 July 1954. He is fined the sum of ten shillings for absence and is to forfeit half of one day's pay."

The Captain to the defaulter, "Anything to say?"

"No, sir."

The Purser continues, "The above entry was read over to Young who admitted the charge and had nothing further to say."

With that the Captain nods to the Master-at-Arms who takes Young back to crew quarters and the 'Court' breaks up – usually for a gin in the Captain's cabin.

In the old *Otranto*, after each port there were usually a dozen or more defaulters. On one occasion leaving Naples there were 40, which was after a weeding out by the Heads of Department. The important thing was that the process was carried through and no one thought he could get away with it. The difficulty for those of us who had to maintain discipline was that ten shillings didn't mean that much to a seaman at the time. It was some years before the scale of fines moved up in relation to the increase in rates of pay.

There were some amusing moments at defaulters and some of the Captains were able to inject a little comic relief into the proceedings. Captain Norman Smith was confronted with an apparition from the Dining Room in the shape of a scruffy-looking waiter, long in need of a haircut, who had been kept standing for some minutes outside the Chart Room in a high wind.

"I've seen you before," said Norman Smith.

"No sir, not me sir, I've never been logged before, sir."

"I see you every morning on my marmalade pot – get your hair cut!"

Once there was an Oiler stood before Captain Charles Pinkney. He used to get through his logging sessions at breakneck speed – no homily or discussions just, "Read the entry – next case." This Oiler had managed to get himself in a lot of strife and the Second Engineer persuaded the Chief Engineer to charge him with practically everything in the book. He finished up with nine fineable offences and I read out, "… is fined the sum of ten shillings for drunkenness, ten shillings for making an unnecessary noise, ten shillings for absence from his watch, ten shillings for being in passenger accommodation when not on duty, ten shillings for using abusive language to the Second Engineer, ten shillings for fighting with his cabin mate, ten shillings for damaging ship's property, ten shillings for returning on board after the expiration of crew leave, ten shillings for disobedience of a lawful command in that he refused to go to his quarters when ordered to do so."

"Anything to say?" asked his Captain.

"Yes," replied the Oiler. "What does it add up to?"

"Four pounds and ten shillings," I answered.

"Right," replied the still a bit drunk Oiler. "You lot can go to hell! – that will make it a round fiver!" "Five pounds ten!" snapped Captain Pinkney. "Second offence – you've already been insubordinate to the Second Engineer."

"Sorry," muttered the Oiler.

"Too late – take him away. Master-at-Arms – next case!"

It wasn't rough justice. The men understood Captains like Smith and Pinkney and they respected them. There was no messing about, everyone knew what the book said, and as long as the charges were correct, the men accepted their punishment.

Treasure Hunt

It can no longer be ignored
That there is gold concealed on board
Gold is a curse (and so they say
The wise man throws his gold away)
Gold is a curse, so they are kind
Who make it very hard to find;
We hope that we've been kind enough
To keep you from the horrid stuff,
And if you stumble on the chest,
Well, don't blame us, we've done our best.

At [time] o'clock, or just before,
Be present on the dancing floor,
First choose your partner; but to-night
Let not more charm attract the sight.
    Forget, young Sir,
    That graceful Her
Whom in the Polka you prefer;
'Tis not her ankles, but her wit,
'Tis not her dimples, but her grit,
    Will help you through
    The artful clue –
If she be agile, it is true,
Agility will do no harm –
But on the whole beware of charm;
For plodding Wisdom here may find
While nimble Beauty
Lags behind.
    Let your sweet She
    A wall-flower be
For once in her experience;
    Far better choose
    To read the clues
Some Matron of Uncommon Sense,
But, young or old, and wise or not
To hunt the Treasure you have got,
Maybe the Matron will not play –
Then you must do the best you may;
And if no Matron hears the call
Bring charming … after all.

                APH

Chapter 8
Migrants to Australia

Most of the time during my first voyage I thought it was going to be my last. Regrettably I did not have the very necessary confidence shown to me by my Captain. He was, of course, much older than me and had been at sea for many more years than I had. I think perhaps that he resented my having reached my position as Purser after only a few years at sea, whilst he had taken a lifetime to get his first command. He was supported by a Staff Commander who echoed the Captain's attitude. However, my Assistant Pursers were totally loyal to me as were the Chief Steward, Chef and our Leading Hands. There were times when the Captain and Staff Commander would humiliate me in front of others. On one occasion the Captain decided he would include the Purser's Office, including the contents of the safes, in his daily inspection of the ship, an event unheard of by anyone else on board.

My Captain was a gourmet, or at least he thought he was, and he used to send for the Chef and plan dinner parties to be held in his cabin. The Chef would take notes and would always say as he was dismissed, "I will tell the Purser, sir – I'm sure he won't mind me preparing this for you." Dear, dear Chef – he knew what I was going through, but remarks like that only made matters worse. The standards were terrible and needed constant supervision by the Leading Hands. One Sunday night 200 plates, eleven vegetable dishes and the Chef's desk were thrown overboard. I had many sleepless nights worrying about my relations with the Captain and what seemed to be going wrong in my Department. I was firmly convinced that by the end of the voyage, I would at best revert to Deputy Purser and that I might be sacked altogether. In actual fact,

plates, eleven vegetable dishes and the Chef's desk were thrown over board

my appointment was confirmed and the Captain left to take leave, and although he remained in the Company for several more years we never sailed together again.

After that first unhappy voyage I never looked back. For my second voyage my own departmental team remained practically the same. The Captain was Charles Pinkney, a giant of a man who was full of character, and there were many stories about him as a junior officer before the war. During the war he had served as a Royal Navy Reserve Officer with distinction. Charles Pinkney loved to make an impression, and he did it in delightfully harmless ways. He had been known to travel in a Sydney tram wearing top hat, tails and opera cloak and he was such a big man that the toughest Australian would think twice about ridiculing him.

When we were off the Cocos Islands he appeared on the Bridge wearing a large uniform topee. The Officer-of-the-Watch, John Spiers, was taken aback and couldn't conceal his amusement. Pinkney bellowed "Second Officer – are you ridiculing me?"

"Well, sur," replied John in his delightful Worcestershire accent, "you do look a bit like Trader Horn."

One evening I was talking to two young ladies at my table during dinner, Pam Hardy of the South Australian wine family and Gill Peren, whose father was a New Zealand academic. A mutual friend came up in conversation, and I remarked that I had a picture of the friend in my cabin and I could show it to Pam and Gill. As we had to walk past the door of my room on the way to the lounge for coffee, I invited them in to see the picture. We were standing in the middle of my cabin with the door wide open and every light switched on, looking at a photograph album, when Captain Charles Pinkney came in saying, "Ah, ha – I find my Purser closeted with two young ladies!"

"We're looking at a photograph, sir," I replied, "and then we're going to have some coffee." I meant that we were on our way to the lounge for coffee.

"Oh good," says Pinkney. "I'll join you," and promptly sat down. I had no choice but to ring for coffee. The time was about 9. 15pm.

The girls left at 2.00am, and the Captain left at 6.30am, when it was broad daylight. For at least four hours he entertained us with songs from the Bing Boys: "Dapper Dan was a Pullman man on the trains that run through Dixie – all you had to do was ring – he would bring you anything", and very many more such songs.[16] We were entranced and after the girls left we just chatted and time flew.

The next morning, when we met for a meeting in his cabin, he took me aside and said seriously, "Pay. I don't think you should entertain young ladies in your cabin after dinner and you have a big responsibility in this ship – I don't think you should keep the late hours you apparently do!"

Charles Pinkney was a remarkable man. He said and did strange things. He was a great trencherman, although perhaps that is an unkind assessment of a man who needed food to fuel his large frame.

The Captain's Steward is always referred to on board as 'The Tiger'. Many Tigers take advantage of their privileged position, knowing that few people, Chefs and Senior Stewards in particular, will argue with him if he says he is asking for something on behalf of his Master. When Pinkney was in command of *Otranto* he had a particularly 'fly' Steward whom the Chief Steward, Mr Charles a'Court, and I often suspected him of ordering tins of biscuits or fruit juice and other stores which never got near the Bridge.

One day in Sydney the Captain phoned my office and asked me to arrange for the office car to be at the gangway at 1230 as he was lunching with the Orient Line General Manager. At about 12 noon I observed the Tiger in the galley collecting from a large Indian curry with all the trimmings of poppadoms, Bombay duck, chutney and condiments, but I just watched, didn't say anything and thought, 'At last I've got you'. I saw the Steward leave the galley and decided it would not be right for the Purser to actually follow, so I went back to my office and then up to the Bridge to tell the old man his car was coming, and that at last I could prove his servant was using his name to get things for his own use. Entering the Captain's day room I was astonished to see Charles Pinkney, dressed for the shore, sitting at his table with a large linen napkin tucked under his chin, devouring a heap of curry and rice. "Hey," I said, "you're supposed to be lunching with the General Manager – I've ordered the car."

"I know that," said the great man, "but they don't give you much at that Club he takes you to."

I had been to 'that Club' – the Union Club in Bligh Street – and had never got away with less than a dozen oysters and a large steak!

Although I had a different Captain for my second voyage as Purser, the original Staff Commander remained, but without the support of Pinkney's predecessor he found he could not harass me as before. Eventually this difficult Staff Commander got his own command and on his first voyage as Captain I was the Purser, by then quite experienced. His whole attitude to me became very different. It is rare for people at sea not to get on with one another – the ship is so important that personal dislikes have to move into the background, and having done that they nearly always melt away completely.

My promotion to Purser and appointment to *Otranto* was sheer good luck and in no way due to my being brilliant. There was no one else to take the ship and I was the senior of the Deputy Pursers, all of whom were pretty junior by pre-war standards. However, it did mean that I stayed in the junior ship for quite a long time and as a result of this I kept getting newly promoted Captains. I had known them all as Chief Officers and Staff Commanders, and some even as Second Officers.

It was interesting to see how some of them changed when they got command. There is no doubt that the Captain must be the loneliest man in the ship – the ultimate responsibility for the life of everyone on board is his. Men who were poor Staff Commanders sometimes became natural Captains. Others, whom everybody expected to make a superb Captain, were not so good. A very few only made one voyage and were then found a convenient shore job. Those few had the professional skill, but lacked the moral strength to assume the responsibility. Very few pretended they 'knew it all', and if they did they soon realised they did not. The Purser was in a special position because, together with the Surgeon, we were all professionals at occupations beyond seafaring. Many Captains, both those experienced as well as those in command for the first time, have confided in me when they were reluctant to talk with men of their own calling. At such times I felt very privileged.

Charles Pinkney was making his first voyage in command of a passenger liner when he came to *Otranto*. As with all newly appointed Captains, he was unfamiliar with the routine for sending arrival advice telegrams to ports as the ship approached. I remember going to him soon after leaving Tilbury with the

Gibraltar arrival signal for him to sign; then a few days later the Naples message; then Port Said… and so on, for the rest of the voyage. He studied each telegram carefully and filed his copy. During the next voyage he used to tell me the day before each message had to be sent: "Gibraltar arrival signal tomorrow, Pay. Don't forget to tell them how much mail we have and the numbers landing." This went on all the way to Australia. Never once did he fail to tell me in detail what to put in an arrival telegram, although on the previous voyage it had been I who had told him what needed to be transmitted.

Late one night, after midnight, I was sitting in my cabin thinking about going to bed when over the loudspeaker system I heard the Officer-of-the-Watch broadcast: "Will Mrs Coates, passenger to Adelaide, please go to the Purser's Office on 'D' deck, now."

'Strange,' I thought, 'there is no one in the office now. Why is the Officer-of-the-Watch making the announcement.?' I went from my cabin to the foyer outside the Office where I met Captain Pinkney and the Staff Commander coming down the staircase from the deck above. They had a passenger with them whom I did not recognise.

"Pay," said the Captain. "This is Mr Coates – he has been to the Bridge to say that his wife is missing."

"Oh dear!" was my spontaneous reply, thinking she might have gone over the side. The man must have read my thoughts because he said, "She's around the ship somewhere, Purser – probably drunk." Just then she appeared, fortunately alone, as I'd had fears of her turning up on the arm of a man. Her husband rushed towards her with a, "Where the hell have you been?" and I thought he was going to hit her.

Pinkney intervened with, "Ah! She who was lost is found." And to the enraged husband, "Rejoice! Embrace her, come now and kiss your beloved."

The couple were so astonished at the Captain's reaction to the wife's appearance that they had no alternative but to embrace in front of the three of us. What he said to her when they were out of our hearing I dread to think about, but 'Pinks' in his unconventional way had prevented a scene which would have otherwise embarrassed all of us.

We had little official entertaining to do in *Otranto* – on the outward voyage there was almost none at all, but homeward-bound social contact with the passengers looked up a bit. There was nothing like the lists of specially commended passengers that had been sent by the shore offices to Captains and Pursers in the First Class ships. Nevertheless, from time-to-time there was a VIP or two aboard *Otranto*. A regular passenger was a naval officer's widow called Mrs Gregory, an old lady with a daughter in Scotland and another in Western Australia. She travelled with us once, and sometimes twice, a year and every morning, after breakfast, she called on me at my office. She considered daily contact with the Purser important. She never dealt with anyone on board except the Purser and Captain, and she kept us on our toes. She was quite open with us about her frequent voyages from England to Australia.

"I have one girl in Scotland and one in Australia. I spend a few months with one and then she gets fed up with me and her husband pays for me to stay with the other one. After a while the same thing also happens there so, you see, I get a lovely sea voyage every year."

Each time she travelled, Mrs Gregory gave a small cocktail party. The arrangements were always the same, but we had to go through the planning ritual every time. After she had been on board a few days, during our regular morning interview, she would say, "Mr French. I think I would like to give a little party for some of the Officers."

"Certainly Mrs Gregory, when would you like to do this?" We then discussed whom she would ask. She knew whom she wanted, I knew whom she wanted, but we had to go through the motions every time. I suggested she spoke with the Chef about canapés.

"What a good idea – tomorrow perhaps?"

Usually there were only about half-a-dozen of us at the party, but the arrangements took several days and gave her an interest and an opportunity to relive the days when her husband entertained as a Senior Naval Officer and she was the hostess. Our invitations stated that, 'Mrs Gregory requests the pleasure of the Company of…' except the Captain's invitation which requested 'the honour of the Company of…'.

After the party, during the morning call, I would be presented with a letter of appreciation for the canapés addressed to the Chef. This was always written in French, even though the Chef came from Grays in Essex and didn't understand a word of French beyond names of dishes – and even then he didn't know many of them!

Several days before we reached Naples on a homeward voyage, Mrs Gregory asked me if I would buy her a basket of grapes in Naples so that she could take it home to her daughter. I promised to do this, but every morning she reminded me so much so that I was beginning to get a bit fed up with being told, "You won't forget my grapes, will you?" or, "I've written to my daughter and told her about the grapes you are going to get in Naples."

The day after Port Said we made a short call at the Greek port of Kalamata and by sheer coincidence the Agent brought me a beautiful basket of grapes. The next morning I was ready for my regular caller. In she came, sat down, looked me straight between the eyes and said, "Naples tomorrow, Purser – don't forget the grapes."

I was waiting for this. I reached down behind my desk and produced the Greek Agent's gift. "I'm a jump ahead, Mrs Gregory" I said, "there you are – lovely fresh grapes from Kalamata."

"Oh", she said. "What a nice basket. This will do for the Italian grapes you buy tomorrow – I'll eat these now."

When she died, one of her daughters wrote to one of the old lady's favourite Captains, Ricky Harris, who had last seen Mrs Gregory on Waterloo Station, when she had said, "So nice to meet you, Captain. I can't find a porter – will you get me a taxi?" She must have been a formidable Senior Officer's wife in Plymouth or Malta when her husband was serving.

Otranto often called at a Greek port on either the outward or homeward-bound journey. Sometimes we picked up more than 100 Greek migrants for Australia, many of whom were young brides just married by proxy to a man who had gone to Australia several months previously. When the man found a job and a home he would marry his fiancée, appointing a proxy to stand in for him at the ceremony in Greece. The bride would then travel to Australia and enter the country as his wife. Homeward-bound we carried Greeks returning for a visit and several Australians would leave the ship at whichever port we called at, Piraeus or Kalamata, to start their European tour.

In mid-November 1954 *Otranto* steamed into Kalamata bay just as the sun was setting. We anchored and prepared to embark a handful of passengers and a car which we could see being towed out from the shore by small tug. The car was on a large pontoon attended by three Greeks whose job it would be to fix the cradle we lowered from the ship's deck under the car wheels ready for hoisting aboard. There was a moderate swell in the bay and our Captain was anxious to get the car and the passengers aboard. A tender brought the passengers and took those landing away, but by now it was quite dark and still the pontoon with the car was not secured alongside. The wind was getting up and the swell increasing. At last the small tug managed to get its tow alongside and two of the three attending the car endeavoured to secure the ship's line to the heaving platform. The third Greek stevedore was being very sick over the edge of the pontoon. All the while the Captain and I were leaning over the wing of the Bridge watching this performance.

"They can do it if they hurry," said the Captain, "but this wind will increase." Just then there was a loud crack as the tug's tow rope broke and the pontoon, car and stevedores began to drift off into the night. While one man continued to be sick over the side of the pontoon, the other two jumped into the car, switched on the headlights and started blowing the horn. A little later it started to rain, so no doubt they set the windscreen wipers going! I hope they let the third man join them when he had finished being seasick. The last we saw of them was two bright lights drifting shoreward, pursued by a tiny tug sounding off pathetic toots in reply to an aristocratic electric horn's demands for assistance.

"No point in staying here," said the Captain. "Officer-of-the-Watch, hands to anchor stations, tell the Bosun to secure that derrick. We're off. If we wait much longer we'll drag the anchor."

"But Captain," the Chief Officer remarked, "the Pilot's still here, sir, and there's no boat to take him off."

"Too bad," replied the Captain. "He'll have to come to Naples." The Greek Pilot overhead this remark. "But I cannot come to Naples; I am the Harbour Master and the only pilot. And tomorrow another ship comes. Who will pilot the ship?"

"Don't need a pilot for this place anyway," said our Captain. "I'll give you half-an-hour to signal for a boat to take you off. Then I'm going to Naples."

Frantic signals with the ship's whistle and a lamp did not bring a boat from the shore. The small tug chasing after its lost tow made no attempt to turn back for the stranded pilot who was now pacing up and down the chart room announcing, "I am the Mayor, I cannot go to Naples. I am the Station Master. Tonight the train goes to Athens." At this point the Junior Officer of the Watch asked the Pilot if he could have his name to enter into the sailing log. "My name is Christopoulos. Too difficult eh? Put down Christ – Mr Christ, it's easier."

"That's it," said the Captain. "With a name like that he can walk ashore."

Around midnight the wind had dropped and we passed a Greek fishing boat to which the Pilot transferred. I don't know where the fishermen were bound, but I'm sure it became Kalamata as soon as 'Mr Christ' had a word with them.

Chapter 9
"Keep the Mums Happy"

When *Otranto* was all migrant, as it was on most outward voyages, Australia House in London used to appoint three chaplains for the voyage, usually Australian clergy returning home after a visit to Europe. There was always one Church of England minister, a Roman Catholic and another, usually a Methodist, who looked after what was broadly described as 'other denominations'. I enjoyed having this trio at my table for meals. Their conversation was usually lively and it gave me a chance to keep in touch with their activities in an informal way. They were well chosen by the Australian Immigration Department and I never had an official migrant chaplain sailing with me who did not pull his weight. I am sure there are hundreds of new settlers in Australia who were baptised aboard the ship that carried them from Europe.

One Bishop whom we carried as an Anglican chaplain held a Confirmation Service, having given classes throughout the voyage. He insisted on sending a telegram to the Bishop of London, as Bishop of the High Seas, seeking permission before he held his Confirmation Service. The Roman Catholic priest was always good for a jolly conversation at meal times. On one occasion, the 'other denominations' chaplain, who was usually grumbling about something or other, gave me a real ear-bashing at breakfast about noise during the previous night. "There was somebody outside my cabin," he said, "stacking deck-chairs. He was throwing them about and calling to his workmates. Altogether a most unnecessary disturbance. Then the wind got up and my window began to rattle." He was on 'C' deck, the promenade deck, where deck-chairs were put out in the daytime and then later removed at night so that the deck could be washed down at dawn. "What with the sailors and the sea and the wind," he continued, "I didn't get a wink of sleep."

I replied, "I'm sorry you had a bad night, Padre. I'll have a word with the Chief Officer about his sailors, they must be told to be quieter. I can't do much about the sea and wind – that's more your department." As quick as a flash the Roman Catholic priest spoke up with his delightful Irish brogue, "And if he wanted to do anything about that he'd have to ask me."

Although he had ordained clergy on board, the Sunday morning service was conducted by either the Captain or his deputy. In the rare event of a death, the appropriate minister would conduct a burial at sea, but we did not have many on migrant voyages when our passengers were young and healthy. However, we did have the occasional baby born and then the appropriate chaplain, if we had one, would conduct a baptism – using the upturned ship's bell as a font. During one voyage, a Greek woman was discovered to be going into labour and the medical staff had to make hasty preparations. The Greek interpreter, who was appointed from amongst the passengers by our Athens agent, was adequate but not considered suitable to be present at the birth. So, together with the nursing sisters, he made a series of cards to be held up in front of the mother. The cards read, in Greek, "Push", "Relax" and other such instructions that the Sister thought might be needed. All went well, except that when the baby was born and was being washed, the medical staff realised they did not have cards for "boy" and "girl". So the Assistant Surgeon looked at the mother, pointed between his own legs, and waggled a finger – she got the message.

Each Sunday at sea the master or, if he could not leave the bridge, one of his senior officers was required by both Orient Line and P&O managers to conduct an inter-denominational church service for the passengers and, if they wish to attend, the crew.

The attitudes of captains to this duty varied considerably. For some this half-hour on Sunday morning was the highlight of their week; to others it was a chore to be avoided and delegated at the slightest excuse. Most masters of passenger ships, however, accepted, and still accept, that it is their duty to lead the community in prayer when at sea on Sunday.

During my time at sea Divine Service on Sunday morning was an event to which I was pleased to give my personal attention. Orient Line Captains, most of whom were officers in the RNR, tended to treat their Purser as a Captain's secretary and looked to their "Paymaster" as a personal aide when it came to handling situations beyond seamanship. As Captain's secretary the Purser worked closely with the master on such matters as correspondence with shore offices, liaison with agents when in port, arrival signals, guess list for cocktail parties…and arranging Divine Service.

Many people may think that arranging a simple service on the lines of Anglican matins is not a very difficult task. Not so. Some Captains found it difficult to decide exactly how these 30 minutes on a Sunday morning should be occupied and when it came to Remembrance Sunday or Anzac Day – they were impossible! I must admit though, that most of the masters with whom I sailed were perfectly reasonable, but not all.

Perhaps the most difficult sea-appointed "high priest" I had to deal with was a Captain who used to start preparations for his Sunday service on Tuesday, when I was required to submit suggested hymns and give a reason for my choice. I enjoyed doing this. The *Order of Service,* which would eventually be printed with a copy for every person attending, had to be as balanced as the menu for a good dinner but I prepared many of my submissions with tongue in cheek. In the Red Sea I suggested *As Pants the Hart for Coming Streams.* Approaching Fremantle *As Near the Wished-for Port we Draw* and on the last Sunday of a long voyage, *Now Thank We All Our God.* The "cruising hymn" was *New Eve Morning is the Love.*

At the Tuesday meeting we decided who would read the lesson and we would choose what the lesson was to be. In the Red Sea the congregation was told how the sea had divided to allow the Israelites to pass, and then closed to drown the Egyptians. The lesson reader, who might be any officer the Captain decided to detail, was sometimes allowed to choose his own Bible passage. Pursers often chose the part of the Sermon on the Mount which affirms that "No man can serve two masters" and having read it they would pause and look at the Captain and Staff Commander.

The hymns and perhaps a psalm having been decided the *Order of Service* went to the printer who was instructed to produce a proof for use at choir practise. Not every Captain attended choir practise and very often the Purser found himself a reluctant choirmaster. Ideally, the choir was provided by crew members; volunteers and conscripted boy ratings. I found that the way to get the boys singing was to start the practise with *Roll out the Barrel* or some such song. After a good "lung blower" the boys were more willing to have a crack at *Lead us, Heavenly Father, Lead us Oh'er the World's Tempestuous Sea.*

✝

Order of Service

Hymn No. 175
"Conquering Kings Their Titles Take"

Prayers

Venite (Page No. 45)

Lesson

The Battle Song

Creed and Collects

Hymn No. 217
"Thy Kingdom Come, O God"

Prayers

Hymn No. 172
"Praise To The Holiest In The Height"

Prayers
"O Trinity Of Love and Power"

National Anthem

During the singing of the last hymn a collection will be taken in aid of Marine Charities

Sometimes the Captain would insist that passengers be invited to join the crew at choir practise but I found the presence of passengers on these occasions to be inhibiting, and I know that many of the crew felt the same way. We were a bunch of shipmates running through the hymns to be sung on Sunday to support the Old Man at his church service. The type of passenger who wanted to sing in the choir was usually a dedicated churchgoer who disapproved of our "Sunday morning sing-along" attitude.

One of the stumbling blocks at church service was often the pianist. Where there was not a permanent member of the crew who played the piano the pianist from the orchestra had to be used. Most ship's orchestra pianists were versatile but some had a repertoire restricted to dance music and the odd palm court piece. An instruction to accompany hymns and play a voluntary while waiting for the Captain and his lesson reader to appear was often met with "what's a voluntary?" I can remember walking out of a service with the Bible tucked under my arm to the strains of *Blue Tango.*

The first job after a successful choir practise was to tell the printer that he could go ahead and print the *Order of Service*. After the Purser had corrected the final proof it was assumed that the finished article would be perfect but not all printers could be relied upon to get it right every time. A ship's printer spends most of his time producing menus, which probably explains why one of them produced 100 *Order of Service* sheets which advertised the first hymn as *Jesu, Lover of my Sole*. He then compounded his crime by putting "Grilled Soul" on the lunch menu.

If things were going to go wrong they would go wrong on the first Sunday of a voyage when a new ship's company had not shaken down. For a few minutes before church a recording of bells was played throughout the ship but the recording always seemed to get lost between voyages. A responsible person usually stowed it away in a safe place, went on leave, and failed to tell his relief where he had put it. One Saturday evening I said to the staff in the Purser's Office, "I hope there won't be last minute panic tomorrow to find the church bells record".

The office bell boy answered, "Oh, no sir. I know where it is." That was a good thing because it was his job to play the record.

I happened to be in the radio office just before the bells were due to be broadcast and decided to look in at the gramophone-room from which the boy would play the record. On the turntable was a recording of Bing Crosby singing *The Bells of Saint Mary*.

"What's that?" I cried.

"Church bells, sir."

With the aid of the chief radio officer we found the recording of various changes rung at St Paul's Cathedral which was the customary Orient Line call to Sunday morning devotions.

Sometimes things went wrong during the service and then we had an interesting post-mortem afterwards in the Captain's cabin. The service always ended with the Grace followed by the National Anthem. One Sunday our Captain read the Grace and then immediately left the lectern and began to walk out of the room. The lesson reader and other officers had started to follow when the pianist struck up the National Anthem. The Captain stopped in his tracks; the lesson reader walked into him and a nursing sister walked into the lesson reader, and so on down the line. It was superb unrehearsed slapstick comedy. At the end of *God Save the Queen* we started moving again and I whispered to the chief steward, "We can't be blamed for that one!"

"Don't you be so sure," whispered the chief steward.

When we arrived in the Captain's cabin, where it was customary to have a glass of sherry after church, "thirsting after righteousness", the Captain barked: "Pay! That was all your fault."

"How could it be my fault?" I responded. "You forgot the National Anthem, not me."

"Ah," said the Captain. "Look at this *Order of Service*. After 'The Grace' there is a full stop."

"So what?" I said.

"A full stop means end, finish. If there hadn't been a full stop there I would have known that there was more to come. That 'lash up' was all your fault. Now have a drink."

The chief steward nudged me: "I told you so!"

When the Captain had to on or near the bridge he would delegate the morning service to one of the senior officers, usually a deck officer but not always. One Sunday morning I was taking a service and had persuaded the Chief Engineer to read the lesson. He chose I Corinthians Chapter 13, which is easy to read and usually generates a good collection for marine charities from the congregation. However, right at the start the chief got tongue-tied and read: "Though I speak with the tongues of men and of angels and have not chastity, sorry, charity ..." I am sure that if he had not corrected himself no one would have noticed.

Very often there were clergymen travelling as passengers and they were sometimes invited to preach at the Captain's service. The clergy didn't always accept the invitation and none considered that they and not the Captain should conduct the service. I have travelled with archbishops and bishops who always insisted that the Captain or one of his officers is the correct person to lead the shipboard community in prayer.

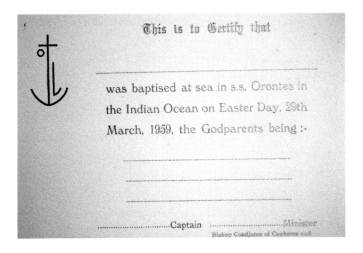

This is to Certify that

....

was baptised at sea in s.s. Orontes in
the Indian Ocean on Easter Day, 29th
March, 1959, the Godparents being :-

....

....

....

...........................Captain ....Minister
Bishop Coadjutor of Canberra and

The chaplains from Australia House were usually a cheery bunch and demonstrated a true ecumenical spirit long before the start of the present drawing together of the churches. They worked hard and many settlers were baptised aboard the ship which carried them to a new life in Australia or New Zealand. We used an inverted ship's bell as a font and *Certificates of Baptism* were prepared by the printer which gave the ship's name and position at the time of the service. People of all ages were baptised, many parents along with their children.

The baptism of a child born on board was a great event with the baker contributing a christening cake and the Purser providing suitable liquid refreshment for all present to "wet the baby's head" after the ceremony.

Burials at sea were not uncommon but a birth was an unusual event. Women who knew that they might be going to have their child soon did not choose to travel and, anyway, the Company would not have accepted them as passengers. However, there were premature births and, especially in the case of foreign migrants, mothers-to-be who deliberately failed to disclose their condition.

Over the years I accumulated a number of *Forms of Service for the Burial of the Dead at Sea* which Captains used for Roman Catholics, a Jew and a child. One of the most impressive services I attended was the burial of an Asian seaman conducted by the *serang* (Indian seaman in charge of Indian sailors) in the presence of the Captain and other Christian officers.

A request to scatter ashes, usually of a former seaman, was not uncommon and we developed a routine for this operation, after one or two embarrassing miscalculations. At first we attempted to literally scatter the ashes on the water but more than once they blew back on those solemnly gathered at the ship's side. Eventually we committed the whole casket, first ensuring that it was going to sink.

This was after a notable scattering when the Captain decided that a former Chief Steward's ashes would be dispatched from the wing of the bridge. After church on the first Sunday of a voyage to Australia, somewhere off the Portuguese coast, a group of officers stood round the Captain while he read a prayer and then, in what appeared to be an ideal light breeze in the right direction, removed the lid of the small casket and allowed the contents to be taken by the wind. A small cloud drifted away and downwards and then curled back into the ship at "B deck" where the lunchtime buffet was being laid out.

"Typical chief steward," muttered the Purser. "Checking on the buffet to the last".

It is well known that the master of a British registered ship is not licensed to perform the marriage ceremony but there is nothing to prevent an ordained priest, licensed to marry people, performing the ceremony at sea if he is satisfied that all the usual formalities have been observed.

* * *

The Purser and Surgeon always have to work closely together. Both are responsible for service to the people on board, and neither has anything to do with the sailing of the ship. I encountered several Surgeons in *Otranto*, most of whom were making their first voyage in the Orient Line, with some taking their first voyage to sea before moving on to one of the more senior ships. Leonard Goodman had been a medical officer in the Colonial Service before

Deck buffet and ship's Chefs

joining the Orient Line. He was a good doctor and an experienced administrator. Public Health was one of his interests. He was in his element whenever we conducted an inspection of the galley where his favourite theme was questioning the Chef about the frequency with which his staff washed their hands. There was a wash basin just by the kitchen entrance from crew quarters, and as soon as we started a galley inspection, Leonard Goodman would go straight to this basin to check that everything was present: soap, scrubbing brush, and clean towels.

One day he noticed the taps were very greasy because a man with greasy hands had just used the basin. This observation prompted the Surgeon to write to the Medical Superintendent in London, suggesting that the hand-operated taps be replaced by foot pedal taps. During our turnaround in London I was consulted about this and agreed. As a result, the taps were removed and new ones installed, which operated from pedals underneath the basin. I warned the Chef that during the first galley inspection of the voyage the Surgeon would certainly make a point of showing his latest contribution to hygiene to the Captain. The Chef had a twinkle in his eye when he said, "Leave it to me, sir; I'll see the Old Man and the Surgeon are suitably impressed."

An hour before the galley inspection started, the Chef got hold of one of his scullions and told him that when the inspection party were grouped round the wash basin he was to barge through and say, "Excuse me, I've been to the lavatory. I must wash my hands." He was then to wash his hands, in front of everybody. The scullion came from Southern Italy, and was one of several we signed on in Naples from time-to-time. All went exactly according to plan… or almost. On entering the galley, the Surgeon said to the Captain, "May I show you the arrangements I have made so that the staff don't have to handle greasy taps at the wash hand basin?"

"Of course, Doctor," said the Master. "Let's go there first."

The 'brass' were grouped round the solitary wash basin – Captain, Chief Officer, Purser, Surgeon and Chef admiring, they are not sure what, but the Surgeon was waffling on about hygiene when along came the Italian scullion. Pushing everyone aside, he commenced his speech, almost as instructed by the Chef. "Excusa me, excusa me, good morning, Captain, good morning, Purser. I just make the peepee – now I washa the hands. I always washa the hands when I go peepee. Every time, like the Chef say to me, every time." He takes the soap with one hand and moved with the other to press the tap – which is no longer there. A blank expression appears on his face as he looks at the Chef, and says, "A Chef, where is the tap?"

Sometimes, when the ship was all migrant, we were virtually under charter to the Australian Government. Passengers did not book their cabins and were allotted a berth by Australia House. Very often husbands and wives were split up. The husbands would be berthed in an all-male part of the ship and the wives in another along with any young children.[17] One day the Assistant Purser at the office counter told me that a passenger wished to see me on a personal matter. I invited her into my office and asked her what help I could give. She was a gorgeous raven-haired woman with a darkish skin and piercing eyes, very gypsy like.

"It's me 'usband." she said. "Is 'e allowed in my cabin?"

"Well," I said, "technically he shouldn't be in your cabin without your invitation, but we don't get severe over things like that where husband and wife are concerned."

"He comes in, sits on the bed and cleans his shoes. That's all 'e does all day long – polishes his shoes."

I said, "I'm sorry about that, but what can I do to help you? I can hardly forbid him to visit his own wife. Don't you like him visiting you?"

"No, I don't. I can't stand the man. Always getting in the way."

I tried to be sympathetic and said, "Surely you love him, you're on your way to a new life in Australia?" While she had been talking I stole a quick glance at my passenger list and noticed that they had three children. The youngest was only three months old. I continued, "I see you have a new baby. You must be very proud of her."

"They are fine, it's me 'usband who gets in the way and I want you to tell 'im to stop bothering me."

There were times when we had more than 400 children on board. There were advantages in having a lot of children. I had a theory that on voyages where there were families on board, the person to look out for was Mum – keep the mothers happy and the fathers become automatically happy. If Mum was miserable in the close confines of the ship, then life for all on board was hell. Following the logic, the quickest way to win a mother's approval is to make a fuss of her children, and if at sea she can get them out of her hair for even a few hours each day, she will be your friend for the voyage.

I cannot take the credit for inventing a daily school at sea, as this had been done in *Ormonde* when she was a migrant carrier, but I do claim to have introduced a school to *Otranto* and later *Orion* and *Orcades*, when they became migrant ships. The idea was that, at least for the morning, all the children on board would attend classes – what, if anything, they learned was not important, rather the object was to get them all corralled for a few hours while mothers got on with their washing or just relaxed.

When every passenger was travelling under the sponsorship of the Australian Government, the organisation was easy, whereas full fare paying passengers cannot be regimented and told what to do. We could only offer a school facility, and for migrants attending school, it could be (and was) compulsory. The first move had to be made as soon as we sailed from Tilbury, the same evening if possible. With my two Children's Hostesses, three chaplains from Australia House, our Liaison Officer and, if he was available so soon after sailing, the Staff Commander, we would invite all those passengers with teaching or child care experience to a pre-dinner sherry party. We knew who the teachers and others were, because Australia House had provided us with a list showing, amongst other things, the profession of each of our passengers. We then explained exactly what we wanted to do and no one ever objected to having to work during their voyage. After all, it was only a couple of hours a day and most teachers found that taking a class alleviated the monotony of the long sea passages.

At our sherry party meeting, we appointed a headmaster or mistress and I introduced the Assistant Purser, usually a woman, who was going to be the Head's link with me. The relationship between the Woman Assistant Purser and the Head was very much like the old link between the Sport's Assistant Purser and the Chairman of the Sports Committee. My girl let the Head think he was running the show, while she was tactfully giving him all the ideas.

Having our teachers organised, the next move was to inform the parents of the arrangements. Once again it was important to act quickly, because we had to get the families into a routine from the start of the voyage. If we had left the opening of our school for a week we would never have got the children into the habit of spending the morning under supervision.

The next morning, during the first day at sea, we called a meeting of all parents and this, of course, meant almost everybody on board except the children themselves. I introduced myself and explained what we were going to do, as well as other information about what would happen during the voyage and to explain shipboard routines. I introduced the three chaplains and some of the ship's staff.

School started at 9.30am on the second morning at sea, when all those under the age of twelve were summoned to the after end of 'E' deck by the school call – a call which been chosen by some genius in *Ormonde* a few years before, 'the Syncopated Clock' played on loud speakers throughout the passenger section of the ship. Each morning the children went marching off to their class area to the rhythm of "tick, tock, tick, tock went the syncopated clock". It was just the right summons for our type of school, as a bell would have been too formal.

There were children who tried to play truant, but it is difficult to hide in a ship when every adult knows where you should be between 9.30am and noon. Even if the parents didn't co-operate, there was a crew of 400 who knew where children ought to be each morning and they sent any child they found around the deck straight off to the school area. Anyway, it was soon realised by the would-be truant that our school was somewhat different from the type they had been used to.

At about 11.00am ice cream was served, but only to those at school. Each day one of the 15 or so classes was taken to the Bridge and shown around by the Officer-of-the-Watch and, sometimes, by the Captain himself. There were mornings when children found that they were taken off to a film show of cartoons. Deck Officers gave a talk on navigation to older boys, and the baker taught girls how to ice a cake.

Children over 12 years of age paid a full adult fare, so we didn't make then attend our school. However, after a few days I received a request from a group of teenagers to be included in the classes. It was clear to me that to do this we would have to create one, or maybe two, new groups, which would mean more teachers that we did not have. The Woman Assistant Purser I had appointed to work out the school details with the headmaster offered to take the teenagers herself. She was very good and persuaded a lot of other officers to talk to her class.

each day one of the classes was taken to the bridge and shown around

There was one amusing consequence of the teenagers' class, which started with one young man putting up his hand at the back of Ann, the Assistant Purser's, class and asking, "Miss, will you dance with me tonight?"

"Only if you dress properly and brush your hair," said Ann. He did, and so did the rest of the boys in her class.

By tradition the Purser was Treasurer of the Crew Club. The full title of the Club was 'The Otranto Social Athletic and Benevolent Club'. It was social in that its committee arranged social events during the voyage (usually indoor games such as chess, draughts and darts, as the crew had insufficient deck space for outdoor games); it was athletic in that football and cricket matches were arranged at ports of call. The benevolent side of the Club allotted funds to assist members who might have to fly home to be with a sick wife or other sick relative, or to a man left behind in hospital abroad. Each member of the crew paid a subscription each voyage to belong to the Club and the Management gave a sum to be used at the Captain's discretion. The discretionary authority of the Captain was important because committees would often review their assets and decide to have a free beer-night in the crew bar.

The Purser's job of Treasurer was no sinecure. I can remember many long meetings in which I had to persuade an over-enthusiastic committee that having money in hand did not mean that it had to be spent on the first idea they had. The idea of carrying credit on to the next voyage was at first considered madness, but after a few voyages I was able to convince them that having a bit in reserve might be a good thing.

The Club funds were supplemented by a percentage taken from the weekly crew football sweep. In *Otranto* this was run by the Donkeyman, who was one of the two leading hands in the engine room. His job is to look after all the smaller pieces of machinery, such as fan motors, washing machines and several pieces of galley equipment. These responsibilities made it necessary for the Donkeyman to visit most parts of the daily, and he was therefore the ideal man to run the football sweep. For a stake of two shillings, a punter drew two pieces of wood from a canvas bag. Each piece of wood was about one inch by a quarter of an inch and had the name of a football team written on it. The teams drawn were recorded by the Donkeyman. When the results came through to the radio office, the aggregate score of the two teams was determined and the person with the highest score took the pool, less the percentage for Club funds.

During a turnaround in Sydney the Club Chairman, Secretary and Donkeyman came to me and said someone had stolen the football money. It had been in the Donkeyman's locker and he had left his cabin door open. We suspected a stevedore, but we had no proof.

"How much?" I asked.

The Donkeyman said that he estimated at least £200, as the crew had had a cash advance just before Sydney and several had staked more than the usual two shillings. "Well," I said, "we can't do much until we know whose money it is. And we won't know that until the results come in. If he's a decent sort of bloke he will settle for getting his two bob back. If he wants to be awkward, we may have to pay him from Club funds." The Club officials left me and for a couple of days I thought no more about the theft. We did tell the local police, but they were not very interested, saying they thought we were a bit stupid leaving £200 lying around in our crew accommodation – and of course they were correct.

On Sunday evening I was sitting quietly in my cabin when the Crew Club delegation arrived. There was a smile on the Chairman's face, and I had a feeling that we were going to be all right over the payout.

"Who has won?" I asked.

"You 'ave, sir!" came the reply. The result must have been fiddled – never before, or since, have I won anything in a crew sweep.

The Donkeyman, who ran the sweep, was a loveable rogue and had a love-hate relationship with the Engine Room Storekeeper, the other petty officer in the engine room department. One Christmas morning I was in the ship's main bar when the Storekeeper came up to the door and asked for a beer. Whilst he was standing there, up came the Donkeyman and, seeing his mate, he says, "Happy Christmas, Bert."

The Storekeeper put down his glass and said, "Why. Ain't your birthday. It's Jesus'."

The Donkeyman took up the challenge with, "You wouldn't even know who Jesus is." Now the Storekeeper was ready for the sort of argument he loved to have with his friend. "I've got ten shillings here that says you don't even know the Lord's Prayer!" To which the Donkeyman replied, "Oh yes I do. Here's ten shillings to cover yours." I was asked to hold the stakes while the Donkeyman took a long swig of beer. He put down his glass and started, "The Lord's my shepherd, I'll not want." The Storekeeper immediately called out, "Give him the money Purser! I never believed he knew it."

Chapter 10
Orsova – Across the Pacific

In November 1955 I was given a respite from my voyaging to and from Australia in the old *Otranto* when I was appointed Supernumerary Purser of *Orsova*, the flagship of the fleet, under the command of my old Captain, now Commodore Whinfield, with Thorp as Purser. The position of Supernumerary Purser is not to be envied. He has all the privileges of the Head of Department, but none of the responsibilities, and for a person who is used to authority and responsibility this is can be a frustrating role. I was therefore delighted when, literally hours before sailing, I was told that I would have to carry out the duties of Deputy Purser even though I retained the rank and privileges of Purser. This gave me something to do and a definite responsibility to Thorp, who would otherwise have had the embarrassment of carrying another Purser around with him, whom he would have had to politely tolerate.

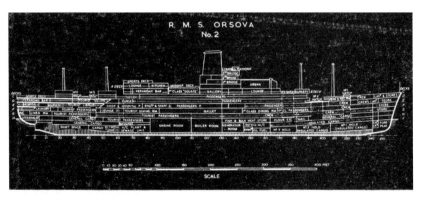

ORSOVA No. 2. Built 1953. Approx. tonnage 28,000 gross. Length 722' 10" o.a., 668' b.p. Moulded breadth 90' 6" depth to "C" deck 67' 3" draught 30' 7". Twin screws, solid 4-bladed manganese bronze 19' diameter. Parson's turbines, 34,000 s.h.p. with propeller 130 r.p.m., and 42,500 at 140 r.p.m. Boilers. 3 superheat Foster Wheeler, pressure 525 lbs. per sq. in. Approx. passenger accommodation 670 first class, 818 tourist, with 533 crew

I had been sent to *Orsova* because, after a routine voyage to Sydney and a cruise to Tasmania and New Zealand, we were to cross the Pacific to Vancouver and San Francisco. I enjoyed being a Deputy Purser again, especially with the rank, salary and privileges of a Purser, and Thorp was the perfect senior partner of our management duo. During the routine voyage to Australia I made several visits to the Grill Room of *Orsova*. Sometimes I was the host, but usually I was the guest of passengers who were so different from (although not necessarily better than) my *Otranto* migrants. At last I was able to return to port officials the hospitality I had received ashore. At Naples I enjoyed wining and dining *Thomas Cook*'s Manager, Luigi Maestri, who had always entertained me in delightful restaurants around the harbour of Santa Lucia.

Smoked salmon and grouse were gastronomic treats for the Port Said agents, which only a visiting first class ship was able to provide. The European staff at Aden used to come on board with a shopping list, and there was a regular arrangement for any Agency around the world to purchase ship's stores for the staff in exile. Even in Australia Branch Managers would seek out a box of kippers. On one occasion I offered the wife of the head of the P&O organisation in Hong Kong a pound of English sausages – she became my friend for ever after. English sausages and kippers were in demand from friends resident ashore from Yokohama to Juneau in Alaska, and I am sure we took too much for granted in our floating luxury hotel.

In all those ports where Customs officers did not seal the shop up, it was descended upon by shore officials and even then many senior Customs men turned a blind eye to the purchase of things which were unobtainable ashore. In fact, the wife of the Senior Customs Officer sometimes headed a group of women seeking perfumes, scarves, twin sets, jewellery and other items. There was a wife in Colombo who made a hair appointment in the Ladies' Hairdressing Salon every time the ship called and afterwards took the hairdresser ashore for lunch. After our merger with P&O, the hairdressing concession was given to the London firm *Steiner*. As a result, the wife of the P&O agent at a port like Aden could visit

Government House with a West End shampoo and set, while 'Her Excellency' had to manage with the attentions of a native maid.

Throughout the outward voyage and during the short cruise to Tasmania and New Zealand, we were preparing for the Pacific Voyage to come. We carried one extra Woman Assistant Purser whose responsibility was Pacific Documentation. Later, when we actually started on the journey from Australia to North America, we embarked two secretaries from the Sydney office of the Orient Line. Together with our Woman Assistant Purser, they formed a team which handled the complex documentation needed to get us in and out of Canada and the United States. Amongst other things the Pacific Woman Assistant Purser spent the outward voyage preparing a Crew list for visaing by the US Consul in Sydney. We were a British ship with a British crew and at United States ports we were aliens. Of course, we were aliens at Naples, Port Said and at many other places our ships visited, but it was only the United States that insisted on having our fingerprints and photographs before we could even take a walk ashore.

Before we set off on the voyage to Vancouver we had a twelve-day cruise to Hobart and New Zealand. While we were in Hobart, Thorp told me an amusing story about a pre-war call at the port when the annual regatta had been taking place. The Hobart regatta was one of the social events in the Australian calendar and the Australian Navy provided a guard ship for the occasion. The State Governor gave several receptions at Government House and the Captain of a visiting Orient Liner was invited to attend. The Captain in question was a Captain in the Royal Naval Reserve and an aide-de-camp to the King, who decided to attend the reception in his RNR uniform. Whilst dressing for the occasion the Captain was attended by his Steward who was unfamiliar with dressing his master in frock coat, medals and sword.

Meanwhile the Purser was being asked by a female passenger, who had been asked to the Governor's Reception, whether she could go ashore in the Captain's launch and share his car to Government House. The Purser agreed to ask the Captain and went to the Bridge to deliver the passenger's request.

"Sir, Miss Speer from Vaucluse has been asked to the reception, and asks if you will allow her to accompany you ashore and if you will let her share your car to Government House," asked the Purser.

"Suppose I'd better," barked the Captain. "Tell her to come here in half-an-hour."

Twenty minutes later the Captain was resplendent in uniform wearing his decorations and his sword. His Steward stood and admired him, being particularly proud of the sword which he had not seen before. The Quartermaster on the Bridge, right above the Captain's cabin, sounded seven bells – 11.30am. Adjusting his aiglet, the King's ADC shouted, "Where's Miss Speer?"

"Spear, sir?" said the Steward. "Didn't know we had one of them!"

Three days after leaving Hobart we were sailing off the entrance to Milford Sound on the west coast of New Zealand – at least, that's where the Officer-of-the-Watch broadcasting from the Bridge said we were – all we could see was a wall of rain. Commodore Whinfield managed to get in contact with the hotel at the top of Milford Sound and learned that, despite the wall of rain at the entrance, inside the Sound was clear and sunny. We headed straight for the rain wall and after a very short time emerged in a fairyland of steep sides, clear water, lush vegetation and waterfalls. The trees and ferns came right down to the water's edge, thus making Milford different from the Norwegian fjords we had visited whilst cruising from England, where the sides are more barren. We spent two hours cruising in the Sound and then we steamed back through the rain curtain and turned north for Wellington, where most passengers disembarked to travel overland to Auckland and rejoin us there later. In the meantime, we had a peaceful day at sea with hardly any passengers on board. 23rd January found us back in Sydney for a break of four days before we set off for what was to be my first visit to North America.

The first two ports of call were already known to me as cruising ports – Auckland and Suva. The port officials were old friends and the immigration and Customs requirements were familiar to me. The documentation Woman Assistant Purser and the two secretaries from the Sydney office who had now joined us spent the days at sea interviewing those passengers destined for Honolulu, Vancouver and San Francisco. Most of the crew lists had been prepared and visaed before we had left Australia.

At Suva two US Immigration Officers joined the ship and during the voyage to Honolulu interviewed every soul on board, passengers and crew. They were cheery shipmates and on their last evening on board we had an enjoyable dinner in the Grill Room; nevertheless they had a job to do and regulations to observe. Having my first encounter with United States officials, I was interested in their unflinching attention to their Government regulations. British Immigration and Customs officers seem to have the right to use their discretion in certain circumstances, whereas the US men had no authority to do anything that was not covered in their instruction manual. Once I understood this, I found that my relations with them were very cordial. In many ways the US.system has advantages and it certainly ensures that we prepare our returns correctly.

Arrival in Honolulu was similar in some ways to arrival in Australia, in that before the gangways could be opened every passenger had to be seen by the Port Health Inspector. However, at Honolulu there was an incentive to get up early – in addition to a fine view of Diamond Head and Waikiki Beach, as soon as the Medical Inspection was over the passengers were entertained by a troupe of Hawaiian dancing girls who distributed leis made from fresh flowers. The girls embarked from a tug at about 7.00am, and once aboard they went to an agreed space on deck or sometimes a ballroom and began their Hula Hula act. Whenever they performed inside the ship, the smell of sweet scented island flowers was overwhelming and for that reason we tried to have them perform on deck. The girls had to be rushed off ashore again as soon as we were alongside because they nearly all worked at Woolworth's which opened at 8.00am!

At about 10.00 in the morning, when most of the passengers were ashore, we were visited by US Coastguard Officers who required the entire ship's company go through our emergency drills, including lowering all the lifeboats on the off-shore side of the ship. It was not until this operation was complete that any member of the crew was allowed ashore. Other inspections (which did not involve all the crew) were made of our galley and food store rooms, the ship's hospital, and they conducted a search of the ship to ensure that we were not carrying any fruit, plants or flowers from previous ports of call. On arrival morning at Honolulu there was no grapefruit on the breakfast menu – any fruit we had remaining on arrival had to have been sealed up in a special store room the night before.

Eventually I got ashore. Purser Thorp arranged for the Chief Steward, Chef, Baker and me to have lunch at the *Royal Hawaiian Hotel* where the beach buffet was supposed to be of the highest international standard. We were not over-impressed, which was very good for our morale, as our ships had been trying to introduce 'haut cuisine' to the Pacific Ocean and we four marine caterers considered the Grill Room of *Orsova* a good match for the Waikiki hotels. We had been provided with a 'U-drive' car, which I had to drive, but the car seemed twice as long as anything I had driven before and had power brakes. Twice the Chef nearly went through the windscreen before I got the feel of the car. We drove around the island, which was interesting, but I think I had built up a Hollywood image of Hawaii and I was a bit disillusioned with the real thing. By teatime it was raining.

We sailed for Vancouver at midnight. Tradition says that if you want to return to the Islands you must throw your lei into the water as the ship leaves the wharf, although it seemed a pity to see so many expensive flowers floating away as we sailed. As we steamed off Waikiki beach towards Diamond Head we gave a fireworks display which must have looked impressive from ashore. At around 2.00am I fell into bed. I had spent my first day on United States soil, and although I hadn't reached the mainland, I now knew a nickel from a dime.

About 4.00 in the afternoon on the fifth day after Honolulu we were slowing down off Victoria having just entered the Juan de Fuca Strait. We were now up by the 49th parallel and the weather was foul.

The morning had been spent by sticking notices up all around the inside of *Orsova* telling passengers where to go when the Canadian officials came on board. The ship was like a London Underground station with coloured notices: "Follow the Red arrows if you are a Canadian citizen returning home. The green arrow if you are a through passenger for a port beyond Vancouver. The white if you are a Visitor. The yellow if you are an Immigrant to Canada"... and if you are an immigrant you would need to take chest X-ray plates amongst a whole host of other certificates and visas.

Out of the cold uninviting mist came, first a launch with a Canadian doctor who boarded us and had a quick word with our Surgeon, then after a signal from the Medical Launch, alongside came a tug with about 30 other officials. The procession of people coming in through the ship's side door was greater than I had seen at any other port in the world. There were doctors, nurses, Immigration inspectors, Customs officers and men from the Orient Line agents. The doctors and nurses were with us to check vaccination certificates of all on board as well as the medical papers and X-ray plates of the immigrants. The journey up the Strait to Vancouver took about six hours and as the Canadians finished their work they tended to relax – after all, they had been in a pretty uncomfortable tug waiting to join us and must have left home early that day to get to Victoria to join the boat. It is not surprising that some jolly parties developed during the last hour of the approach to our berth.

Apart from an official visit to the US Consul with some ship's papers, I didn't see much of Vancouver during that first call. We stayed for a day-and-a-half. Just before we sailed, a brass band paraded on the wharf and we left to the strains of 'California, here I come'.

One day at sea and the next morning we were steaming into San Francisco Bay, under the Golden Gate Bridge and to our berth not far from Fisherman's Wharf and opposite Alcatraz Island, which was at that time a working prison. By now, we and our passengers had completed most of the US Immigration requirements and our gangways were clear as soon as we tied up.

In the evening Thorp took me ashore to the Barbary Coast, which was then a collection of sleazy strip clubs, where we also met most of our Assistant Pursers. In one club the star turn was a girl with tassels attached to her nipples who could shake her body and make the tassels swing round and round. The really clever part was when she made each tassel rotate in a different direction. After a while even she got boring so we tried to move on, but one girl Assistant Purser wouldn't budge – she was almost hypnotised by the 'tassel girl' and kept murmuring, "Incredible". I sometimes wonder if she tried to do the same thing when she got back on board.

The next day we sailed off towards Honolulu and began the long journey home. On subsequent visits to the West Coast of North America we made a Los Angeles call at either Long Beach or San Pedro. Formalities at Honolulu were simpler on the southbound call, but the port was our final departure from the United States and the authorities made a thorough check that everyone was on board before we sailed.

At Suva a Fijian Chief joined the ship for the voyage to England. He was called Ratu – which means Chief – Sukana, and was already a Knight who was travelling on behalf of the Government of Fiji. I was fascinated by his dress which was European in all respects except that instead of trousers he wore a sulu or skirt. I suspect most of his clothes had been tailored in Savile Row. After our arrival in England his photograph was in *The Illustrated London News* showing him with a top hat, morning coat and sulu. Ratu Sukana sat at Commodore Whinfield's table and the Commodore assured me that the following story about the Fijian's first meal was true.

Amongst those at the Captain's table was a particularly giggly woman who could manage little intelligent conversation and had been looking forward to a Fijian Chief joining the group, ever since Whinfield had mentioned his impending arrival a couple of days before Suva. Soon after the Ratu joined them on the evening he embarked, the lady remarked, "Is it true, Ratu, that your ancestors were cannibals?"

Just at that moment a Steward appeared at the Chief's elbow and proffered a menu. After a moment of hesitation, the smiling Fijian looked at the lady and then at the Steward and addressed them in turn, "Ancestors, Madam! Steward, bring me a passenger list."

Before he left *Orsova* I invited Ratu Sukana to a drinks party in my cabin; he wrote in my visitor's book "9.iv.56: In memory of a very fine and select party, may I give you 'good luck' in four languages of the South Western Pacific – 'Aloha oe' (Hawaii), 'Aloaoe' (Samoa), 'Ofa Atu' (Tonga) and 'Bula' (Fiji) – Sukana of Suva, Fiji."

This entry appears at the beginning of my visitors' book, which I started on my first Pacific Voyage and which I still bring out when I have justification to do so. There are many familiar names following the Fijian Chief's. I am most proud of two entries on 4th March 1967 – Alexandra and Angus Ogilvy.[18]

My taste of First Class luxury was for one voyage only and after a few weeks at home I joined *Orontes*, now a one-class ship similar to *Otranto*. My Captain was Clifford Edgecombe, who had been Staff Commander on my previous *Orsova* voyage to San Francisco, and was now experiencing his first voyage in command. It was the beginning of a long Purser-Captain association. Cliff had remarkable confidence in himself and displayed a much appreciated trust in his subordinates, which led to ships he commanded being happy, efficient units. Our paths crossed frequently and I think I helped him to run a good ship – our ship was always happy, despite the difficult situations we sometimes found ourselves having to deal with. That first voyage in *Orontes* had its problems, which started even before we left Tilbury dock.

Chamber of Commerce

In the latest ocean liner, there's an object made of china,
In a dinky little cupboard by each bed,
It's a honey-coloured beauty, of design both chaste and fruity,
With amusing lines of green and blue and red.
Before the war each locker held a white repulsive shocker,
On which the letters 'P & O' offended,
But the modern sleek utensil is devoid of any stencil,
You are left to guess for what it is intended.
Ah! The old one was unsightly and lay unsullied nightly
So it never really stood the acid test.
But now from here to Sydney, every patriotic kidney
Is persuaded to deliver of its best.
And this is good democracy – goodbye to class hypocrisy –
The era of equality survives.
And the richest and the poorest in the First, Saloon or Tourist
Gets a little splash of colour in their lives.
Though its mention is forbidden, it's a shame to keep it hidden,
For the whole affair is just a hollow mockery;
And really we should never rest until they place on 'Everest'
The jewel of the 'Himalaya' crockery.
Perhaps you may be tempted to see it filled or emptied,
It's a natural reaction, goodness knows;
But, although there be restriction on the subject 'Fact' or 'Fiction',
It's not a real conviction – merely Poe's.

A.P.Herbert
'Himalaya', en route, Melbourne – Sydney.

Chapter 11
Orontes – South Africa and Stowaways

We were due to sail from Tilbury dock in *Orontes* at 2.00pm on Tuesday 26th June 1956. The previous evening we had the usual Orient Line sailing night dinner when the Managers of the Company came down from London and dined with their officers and later walked round the ship alone. The atmosphere was friendly and the effort made by our managers to treat us as trusted servants of their Company was much appreciated. Later, when we became part of the mighty P&O, this personal relationship between sea staff and board room got lost in a vast impersonal organisation.

On sailing morning the passengers had already started to embark when we learned that part of our cargo, already loaded and secured, was suspected of being inflammable and unsafe to carry in a passenger ship. Off came the hatch covers and we started discharging cases that had been carefully stowed during the ship's stay in port. The work took all afternoon and carried on during the night so that it was 1.00pm the following day, 27th June, before we eventually sailed. Poor Cliff Edgecombe, he was already late on his first voyage in command before he had even started.

Throughout his career as Captain, and later as Commodore, Edgecombe had a charmed life. Even this first setback had a silver lining. The previous night when we should have been off Dover there had been thick fog in the Channel, but the next night when we were steaming down channel it was a clear starry night.

We had with us Peter Smith of *Smith, Imossi*, one of our Gibraltar agents, as a passenger as far as Gibraltar. Peter was a charming man whom I had met before for brief moments when we called to land and embark passengers. Often our Gibraltar call was in the early morning, usually around 6.00am. At this time of day both Peter Smith and Paul Imossi were pretty sleepy, Peter in particular. I remember sipping rum with milk and honey with the pair of them early one dark winter's morning when Peter kept murmuring, "I feel quite odd. I don't know why. I went to bed quite early last night, but I really do feel odd. My legs feel funny."

He obviously wasn't ill, but he kept going on about this strange feeling he had. Then suddenly Paul Imossi noticed, "No wonder you feel odd – you even look odd. I can see what it is – you've got your shoes on the wrong feet!"

He had.

At Naples the Captain and I lunched ashore, the first of many meals ashore together all round the world. At Navarino Bay we made a brief call to embark about fifty Greeks. The passage down the Red Sea was unbearably hot and I remember the Storekeeper being upset when I insisted the full ration of Board of Trade lime juice should be put in the Crew Mess. I was puzzled about this – I knew the Storekeeper to be an honest man and not the sort of chap who would want to hoard lime juice to sell in, perhaps, Aden or Colombo. Eventually I discovered that one of the reasons for *Orontes'* dry store room being so spick and span was due to the fact that the deck and wooden shelving had been bleached with Board of Trade lime juice. 'Stores' felt it was far too good a bleach to issue to the crew simply to dilute with water and drink.

The Staff Commander was 'Tommy' Thompson, a thrifty Tynesider. He upset the Chef when he was called to the galley shortly after we left Aden and experienced the full force of the south-west monsoon. One minute we were steaming along in a calm sea and then as soon as we left the lee of the land we started to roll with heavy waves crashing along the weatherside of the ship. The ship's side door in the galley started to let in water and the Chef telephoned the Bridge where the Staff Commander happened to be, so he went down himself to assess the situation. The leak was attended to by the Bosun and a seaman who soon tightened up the door. However, 'Tommy' Thompson took no notice of the leaking door. He occupied a full ten minutes telling the Chef that an egg he saw resting on the Chef's desk might roll off and break, and that eggs in the UK were currently two shillings and sixpence a dozen, or 2½d each. The Chef should therefore immediately secure the egg. Throughout the conversation the Staff Commander was impervious to the water lapping round his feet from the leaking door which, if not quickly closed up, might have caused thousands of pounds' worth of damage.

It wasn't until we had passed the Cocos Islands that the weather began to cool off. Throughout the period of hot sticky weather we had managed to remain more even-tempered than was usual in those non-air-conditioned and overcrowded ships. We had a remarkably good team. The Chief Engineer was a character about whom an apocryphal story has since been told, alleging that there was an occasion when he fell asleep at dinner at his table in the restaurant. The passengers were so embarrassed that they left the table. The Chief told the story against himself and I therefore always felt there might have been a grain of truth in it, especially as he finished up with, "And there I was, exhausted, I might have fallen in my soup – I might have drowned!"

My own staff made a great team. I was not granted the privilege of a Deputy Purser but I had John Manton, Senior Assistant Purser, as a number two. John was very nearly seven feet high and for some reason or other always chose tiny girlfriends. He later married a girl with whom he could never have danced cheek-to-cheek. One of the Assistant Pursers was Mike Maher, a giant of a young man, with a permanent grin on his face. Mike was friendly with, and later married, a Woman Assistant Purser, Celia Johnson, who had a truly seductive deep voice and would sing with the other Assistant Pursers "On top of old smokey", taking low notes while the boys crooned away higher up the scale. The cabin opposite mine was occupied by Philip Saywell who later took Holy Orders. He was studying by correspondence during the voyage, but that did not prevent him doing his share of entertaining the girls. I often heard the swish of taffeta around 10.30pm when junior officers had to leave the passenger decks.

The Chief Steward was a dapper little Scot called 'Jock' Harcus, a real martinet. It was said that once he had put on his white duck trousers when we were in tropical uniforms, he would not sit down, thus avoiding creasing them. 'Jock' was not an admirer of the Staff Commander, particularly as they had too much in common with their attitude to detail. 'Jock' was as mean with ship's stores as 'Tommy' was about waste. One morning, whilst browsing around the Bridge, the Staff Commander found an apple in the flag locker. "Quartermaster," called Tommy Thompson. "Is this your apple?"

"Yes, sir," replied the Quartermaster.

"Take it back to the Chief Steward and tell him you stole it from your mess room. You know the rules – all food to be consumed in the mess rooms."

"Very good, sir – now?" asked the Quartermaster.

"Yes now, and come straight back, no lingering for a quick smoke while you are away," instructed Staffy.

The Quartermaster took the apple and, much to the amusement of the second Quartermaster who was at the wheel, he left the Bridge. Arriving at the Chief Steward's office the 'thief' explained the reason for his presence and proffered the apple. This was right up the little Scotsman's street – a chance to get a dig at the Staff Commander – so Harcus picked up his telephone and rang the Bridge.

"Chief Steward here, I wish to speak wi' the Staff Commander." Pause. "Staff Commander, I have yon Quartermaster here. He's just awa' to the store-keeper with yon apple. Ye're quite right, sor, it's a poor wee apple. I've told him to ask for a bright red rosy one!" With that he hung up, grinned at the amazed QM and said, "Off ye go, lad – and mind ye show Staffy your new apple."

By the time we reached Sydney we had made up the time lost by our sailing late from Tilbury. The homeward voyage started on 8th August. A few days earlier President Nasser of Egypt had announced the nationalisation of the Suez Canal. When we sailed, the Canal was still available to international shipping. However, at lunchtime on 16th August the Third Officer heard on his radio (which he tuned into a Western Australian station) that, "The Orient Liner *Orontes* due at Fremantle tomorrow will sail for the United Kingdom via the Cape of Good Hope, thus avoiding the present troubles in the Suez Canal."[19]

124

I was having a pre-lunch gin with the Captain in his cabin when the Third Officer came and gave us the news. "Interesting and typical." said Edgecombe. "No doubt we will get an official signal soon." We stayed together waiting for the expected instruction and at about 2.00pm I was brought a radio message from the Sydney Stores Superintendent telling me to order stores at Fremantle for a ten-day sea passage to Durban, and that we would subsequently call at Cape Town, Dakar and Las Palmas on our way home to Tilbury.

Receipt of this message understandably upset the Captain somewhat. First one of his Junior Officers told him his ship was diverted, then his Purser confirmed it, and still he had been told nothing. Edgecombe immediately sent off a signal to Sydney, repeated to London:

AM RECEIVING DEPARTMENTAL
INSTRUCTIONS ABOUT AMENDED
ITINERARY WHICH I DO NOT UNDERSTAND.

That did it. Within the hour he received an official alteration of his Sailing Orders and plans were laid for our voyage to South Africa. While John Manton, my Senior Assistant Purser, was interviewing those passengers booked to Colombo, Aden and Port Said, who would now have to leave us in the morning, I attended a conference in the Captain's cabin.

I was confident that my department could cope with the new arrangements. Durban and Cape Town were major ports used to servicing large passenger liners. We would not have the proper Customs and Immigration documents, but we would provide all the information they were likely to require.

There would be no trouble over stores. I was not too sure of current prices in South Africa, but this was an emergency and I intended to buy what was necessary whatever the price. In fact, when we did get there, we found the quality of most things to be excellent and the prices reasonable. Our conference had its amusing moments, the chief one being provided by the Second Officer, who was the Captain's chief adviser on navigation. He was affectionately known as 'Harpic' because he was considered to be 'clean around the bend'. He asked, "Shall we go Great Circle, sir, or do you want to stay to the North?"

Edgecombe looked at his navigator and replied, "Great Circle! Oh yes, Great Circle and steam into Durban with a Penguin on the fo'c's'le,[20] looking like an advertisement for chocolate biscuits."

As far as I can remember that was the only contribution 'Harpic' made to the conference. The Chief Engineer and Captain discussed speeds and fuel requirements, but the major subject for discussion was fresh water. Ten days at sea would be a long haul for a passenger ship equipped with running water in most cabins, showers and a large laundry. The engines consumed some two hundred tons a day and we feared that rationing of water between Fremantle and Durban would be necessary – which in fact, it was, although with the co-operation we got from our passengers who thought the diversion to South Africa was an adventure we had no real difficulty. Later voyages round the Cape of Good Hope would cause us more anxiety.

Largely due to the efficiency of Basil Staniland, the Orient Line Branch Manager in Western Australia, we got away from Fremantle with everything we needed for a voyage home by an unaccustomed route. He even remembered a South African National Ensign for us to fly as a courtesy flag when we reached Durban. We sailed from Fremantle at 5.00pm and about an hour later, after we had dropped the Pilot, I was sitting in the Captain's cabin with Cliff Edgecombe and Tommy Thompson when an attractive girl came to the open door and said to Tommy, who was sitting just inside the room, "Excuse me, are you the Captain?"

Tommy jumped up and said, "No. If you want to see the Captain you must make an appointment with the Purser."

"Where do I find the Purser?" she asked.

"On 'D' deck, Miss, at the Purser's Office," replied the Staff Commander. We heard her move away and Tommy turned to us, out of sight from the doorway. "Pretty girl looking for you, Pay. I expect she wants to change her cabin, or maybe she has lost her baggage."

I answered, "My team are all in the Office. I'm sure they will solve her problem."

They did not – it seemed the pretty girl decided to try and find me personally and not just settle for an Assistant Purser. When I got to my cabin my Steward told me that, "A young lady has been looking for you".

I didn't think much about it and went off to have a bath and then started to change for dinner. While I was changing, a barman, 'Scotty' from 'E' deck aft, came and told me there was a young girl with four children in his bar saying that she 'must' see me. I asked him to give me five minutes to finish dressing and then to bring her along, adding, "You had better stay, Scotty, in case I need a witness to whatever it is that she is going to say."

Five minutes later he returned with a most attractive young woman who immediately announced, "I am a stowaway and I want to go to Holland and so do my brothers and sisters."

"Your brothers and sisters?" I questioned.

"Yes, they are outside – can I get them?"

"Well, yes, I suppose you had better," I replied, looking vacantly at poor Scott who was as astonished as I was at the pretty girl's announcement.

Off she went and returned immediately with two girls and two boys. I was now sitting in my chair and without any hesitation the youngest, a boy aged six climbed on my knee, poked me in the stomach and said, "Hello – we're stowaways."

And stowaways they were – and would be all the way to England – although they were stowaways with a difference.

By now the time was getting on towards 8.00pm and I felt that the first thing that needed to be done was to feed the youngsters and put them to bed.

Children's Hostess

127

Turning back to Fremantle was out of the question and I knew I didn't need to consult the Captain over this. Getting to Durban on time was going to be difficult as it was, without going back and thus adding at least six hours to our journey time.

While the Children's Hostess looked after the four children, I talked to the elder sister and learned her story. She told me that the family lived near Perth in Western Australia and that her parents came from Holland. Their mother was at present in Holland and had been taken ill, but their father was out of work and depressed. The children had spent the afternoon at Fremantle looking at the ships. When they realised that they could get on board *Orontes* with the visitors seeing friends off, they came up the gangway to have a look around. It was then that they decided that if they stayed on board they could get to Europe and eventually see their mother.

That evening while the family was put to bed in a large six-berth cabin, the Captain and I sent off several telegrams to Australia and to London. We then decided that we would accommodate our unexpected family in the ship's isolation hospital until Durban, from where we assumed they would be returned to Australia. Cliff Edgecombe summoned his senior officers and told us that, "There is to be no sloppy sentiment over these children. They are stowaways and therefore criminals. They are confined to the hospital area and the Surgeon is to see that they don't leave. Purser, you will feed them good plain food, and they will wash up the plates and cutlery themselves. Give the adult girl washing powder and she can wash their clothes and do the ironing. Remember, gentlemen – no sloppy sentiment, they're stowaways."

A couple of days later I found the Captain in the ship's shop buying jars of boiled sweets. The shop in *Orontes* was close to my cabin so I remarked, "Can I get those taken up to your cabin while you come and have a gin?"

"No thanks, Pay. I can carry these. I'll be with you for a drink in a few minutes," and with that off he went aft, not upwards towards the Bridge. After a while he appeared in my cabin and claimed his gin, although I noticed that he no longer had the jars of sweets. We consumed two quick ones and then he went off to discuss the

Remember gentleman – no sloppy sentiment

speed to Durban with the Chief Engineer. While we had been drinking I had been thinking about the present whereabouts of the boiled sweets and my thoughts led me, as soon as the Captain had left, to our young 'criminals' in the hospital. Sure enough, there on the table were two bottles of boiled sweets.

"Has the Captain been to see you lately?" I asked.

"Oh yes! sir," the little one cried. "He just brought us these sweets." So much for our Master's instruction: "No sloppy sentiment, gentlemen!"

I noticed that although it was lunchtime, the two boys were still in bed. I was told it was wash day for their clothes and big sister wouldn't let them get up until their shirts were dry and ironed. I tried to be 'official' in my dealings with the children, but it was hard not to show sympathy with their plight. The Surgeon was caught, by the Captain and me, with the 21 year old at the cinema show one evening, but both of us pretended not to notice.

A couple of days before Durban we learned that the family was to remain on board until London and not to be sent back to Australia; an instruction which pleased all of us. Somehow or other the presence of the stowaway children on board leaked out. At Las

Palmas a photographer and reporter from *Picture Post* joined us, bringing with them the children's mother. The pictures of the family reunion were excellent 'copy' for the magazine, but we who had been 'in loco parentis' for nearly a month did not entirely approve of the publicity given to our charges.

Although the stowaway children still provide the most vivid memories of that first voyage I made round the Cape of Good Hope, there were other distractions. At Dakar, where we called in for oil, we were told that yellow fever had broken out ashore and that all our passengers and crew were confined to the ship. Las Palmas was more successful as our passengers and crew did get a few hours ashore before the final run to Tilbury where we arrived on 15th September.

We had spent eleven days at sea between Fremantle and Durban and another eleven days confined to the ship between Cape Town and Las Palmas. We kept our passengers amused, despite the long monotonous sea passages, and we encouraged the crew with their own distractions by supporting a boxing tournament and other entertainments. Under a lesser man than Clifford Edgecombe we might all have been at one another's throats long before we reached South Africa.

Chapter 12
The Last of *Otranto*

The Suez Canal remained closed until April 1957. During the closed period Britain and France had invaded the Canal Zone in an attempt to exert their rights in an International Waterway of which they were the principal shareholders. Eventually the Canal became Egyptian property, as it remains today.

I made my first post-Suez war visit in *Orion* when we passed through the Canal southbound in July 1957. I was interested to know how our old friends 'Harry Lauder' and 'Mr Macgregor', local traders, had fared during the invasion. Although Egyptian nationals they, together with many others who had traded with the ships in Port Said, were really international, giving their service and apparent loyalty to whoever suited them at the time.

Otranto's games deck.

There were two Harry Lauders, Young Harry and his father. As usual, Young Harry was among the first on board when we tied up at the northern entrance to the Canal. "Hello, Harry," I said in greeting. "How did you get on in the war? I'm glad to see you don't seem to have come to any harm."

"No trouble, Mr French," he replied. "When the British came, my father and I are on the beach and we get the order for their stores!"

During the time the Canal was denied to us I made two voyages with migrants to Australia in *Otranto*. These voyages were real headaches – *Otranto* was older than *Orontes* and had not had as good a re-fit after trooping from 1939 to 1948, and we carried 1,400 passengers and had a major fresh water problem. On the first of these two voyages Captain Roberts was in command, a small, slight man who was known as 'gin and listen'. He seldom stopped talking, which made conversation difficult, and even though he was a kind and thoughtful man, at times he was a bore. Often I nearly fell asleep listening to him – one Staff Commander assured me that on one occasion I did fall asleep, but he was there listening for both of us and contributing the necessary, "Really – you don't say – incredible."

Captain Roberts was a great man for going ashore whenever possible. I had sailed with him on previous voyages when we had called at Marseilles, where he used to like his Purser to organise a picnic. This was rather fun and we often took the Chief Engineer and some of the female officers or friendly women passengers with us, and the Agents owned an old *Rolls Royce* which was put at our disposal, together with its ancient driver. On one of these excursions we were cruising along through some woods in the Aix-en-Provence area with our hamper of goodies strapped on the back I was inside the car with the Captain, Chief Engineer, a Nursing Sister and Woman Assistant Purser. The driver suddenly announced, "Captaine, Mesdames et Messieurs – now we are coming to the hotel where your Winston Church is staying sometimes."

"Oh really?" says Robbie. "We must stop and have a drink. Driver, we will visit the hotel, take us there."

"Oui, Monsieur," replied the veteran, and a minute or so later we came upon a large building which looked like a country house. Seating ourselves in the lounge we ordered drinks and, while we were waiting for them to be served Robbie gave us a run down on Churchill. A stranger, or maybe one of our more gullible passengers, would have believed that Robbie and Churchill were intimate collaborators in winning the war. However, we were used to his monologues and waited for the drinks to arrive. When they did, Robbie asked the waiter if he could look at a Luncheon Menu which was duly produced.

After some "Uhms and ahas" to himself while he studied the menu, he announced, "We will take lunch here, it will be nice to eat in the dining room Winston uses. Pay, the picnic isn't wasted, the food can go back on board." To the waiter he called, "Garçon – we will take lunch, please bring more menus." We weren't asked by Robbie if we wanted to lunch at the hotel – he just told us, "We will take lunch here."

Fortunately I was prepared for a sudden change of plan – it often happened when ashore with Captain Roberts, and I had plenty of money with me to pay for our meal. We would square up with each other when we got back on board, although I knew the Chief Engineer wasn't over-keen on contributing towards lunch for a couple of our female officers. I cannot remember what each one of us ordered, but I do remember the Chief Engineer asking for ham and eggs because he had not had any breakfast. I also suspect it was the only dish he could translate from an extensive menu.

In due course we were seated and our food began to arrive. The Chief had placed before him a plate from which two beautifully fried eggs looked up at him. The waiter moved away to be called back immediately with, "Oi garçon, où est mon bloody jambon?" – to which the waiter replied in faultless English, "Underneath the eggs, sir."

Captain Roberts commanded *Otranto* for her penultimate voyage, and for the final voyage the Master was Clifford Edgecombe. At the time we did not know that we were making the final voyage of the, by then, 32 year old ship, but this last voyage was a chapter of disasters. We sailed from Tilbury at 9.30pm on 14th February 1957; we broke down for one hour at lunchtime the next day; a week later the hot salt water system became defective (apart from baths we needed hot salt water to wash down the galley after each meal); then somehow the fresh water supply became tainted with fuel oil; finally the Chief Engineer announced that he could not, for the time being, distil sea water for his boilers. This meant that each day some 200 tons of precious domestic-use fresh water had to be diverted to the engine room.

At Cape Town repairs were effected and after Durban we set off on the long haul to Australia. We had more than 300 children on board and an epidemic of chicken pox broke out. After a few days of isolating the cases in the ship's hospital with two children in each bed, one at each end, the Surgeon realised that all of the 300 who had not contracted chicken pox were going to get it, so we accepted the inevitable and let them stay in their cabins and convalesce on deck. One of my Woman Assistant Pursers caught it and, being an adult, suffered more than the children.

The passage across the bottom of the world to Fremantle was not without incident. The lavatories were becoming blocked by children throwing whole packets of toilet paper into the pan, and sometimes the overworked plumber extracted such interesting things as Teddy bears, dolls and once a toy double-decker bus.

We reached Fremantle on 18th March where more than 400 of our migrants were told they were not going to the part of Australia they thought they were heading to. That news didn't cheer up many of our already apprehensive passengers. We had another small engine room problem whilst crossing the Australian Bight and arrived in Adelaide six hours late. When we reached Sydney there were some adverse comments about the ship in the *Sun* newspaper. This upset our remarkably loyal crew, who were never shortcoming with their own criticism of the Orient Line, *Otranto* and their Officers, but there was no way in which they were going to allow a Sydney newspaper reporter to run down their ship.

It came to my ears that they had invited this reporter to visit the ship and intended to duck him over the side in the same way that witches were ducked in the village pond in medieval days. The crew had rigged up a chair, into which they intended to strap their victim and drop him into the dock, immediately hauling him out again, for as many times as was necessary to get the reporter to agree to write another article admitting his first was an exaggeration. The scene was set, but the newspaperman must have received a warning because he didn't turn up when expected. Incidentally, we did receive a fair criticism of our ship, and the way we ran it, from an author who had arranged to travel out with us to write a script for a film about migrants. The author was Ted Willis, later Lord Willis.[21]

We were in Sydney for six days and sailed in the early evening of the sixth day. The final gangway was from a ship's side door beside the main bar, so as soon as I had reported by telephone to the Bridge that all shore officials had left, I went into the bar for a drink. While we were passing under the Harbour Bridge I remarked to the barman, "I have no evidence for this, so don't say the Purser has told you the ship is on her last voyage; but somehow or other I feel the old lady is passing under the Bridge for the last time." My premonition proved to be correct.

Thirteen days later, whilst on passage from Fremantle to Durban, we received a telegram from London telling us that the ship was to be taken out of service on our return to Tilbury. It is a pity that Australia did not get an opportunity to 'farewell' *Otranto*, as there were many who remembered her from her pre-war glory, and the ship represented a very tangible link with Europe for thousands of post-war migrants. Instead of the glorious farewell accorded to so many old ships, the old lady just quietly left Australian waters. Even after the announcement of her withdrawal she steamed through unfamiliar waters, except perhaps Durban where several residents remembered her wartime trooping visits. Had that voyage included a visit to Naples she would have received an affectionate farewell from many Italians who remembered travelling in *Otranto* to Australia as prisoners of war many years earlier.

Just before we left Tilbury in February the Orient Line Stores Manager remarked to me that our wine stock included several dozen bottles of pink champagne. He felt they had been in the ship for too long, so he instructed me to try and sell them during the voyage. Outward-bound we gave away the odd bottle as a prize at Gala dances, but pink champagne is not a popular tipple with migrant passengers. I remember Ted Willis bought a couple of bottles, but that was about all we sold.

Homeward-bound I decided that we had to make an effort to get rid of the remaining bottles, so at the Race Meeting (held on deck some days after Cape Town when we were close to the Equator) I arranged for a Pink Champagne Bar. The Chief Officer asked the carpenter to make a frame for a red and white striped awning and some trellis work through which we wove paper roses. Inside the 'tent' was a table upon which we had ice buckets, glasses and, of course, bottles of pink champagne. The bar was staffed by a barman with a striped jersey and black beret, and assisted by a Woman Assistant Purser and a Nursing Sister each wearing black fish-net tights and very short dresses with small white aprons – all very French and 'ou-la-la'!

The race commentator was instructed to advertise the 'Champagne Tent' whenever he had an opportunity and soon the pink liquid began to flow – for a while sales were quite good. The Race Meeting was held after dinner under a starry sky with the moonlight reflecting on the water.

At about 10.00pm the Captain came across to my Champagne Bar and, after congratulating the 'staff' on their appearance, helped himself to a glass. I explained how I was desperately trying to sell the remaining stock we had on board. The Chief Engineer had joined us with a couple of 'jockeys' from the last race and mischievously suggested that in order to boost sales I should offer a kiss from the Captain with every glass. "Oh! Yes," cried the girls, "buy us a glass, Chief – and Captain, we want our kiss."

This started something and another nearby group of girls exclaimed, "Captain, can we really have a kiss if we have a glass of champagne?"

"Of course," smiled Clifford Edgecombe. "For two glasses the Purser will kiss you. The Chief Engineer comes a bit more expensive – you need to buy a bottle before he will give away

A race meeting

kisses." Trade now improved, although the Captain kept the kiss dispensing business to himself and didn't share it with the Chief and me. A lot of fun was enjoyed and at one stage it was hard to see Cliff for all the pretty girls crowding around him.

The sequel came the next morning when, shortly after breakfast, the Assistant Purser on duty at the counter of the Purser's Office informed me that a gentleman and two ladies wished to discuss a delicate matter with me. I went to the foyer outside the main office and ushered them into my private office where I seated them and asked how I could help. The man, who was elderly, as were his companions, looked a little embarrassed and spoke: "Purser, these two ladies have asked me to speak for them about the behaviour of the Captain last night. I did not witness what they report, but it seems the Captain was allowing himself to be set upon and embraced by young women. The ladies with me now consider your Captain's behaviour to have been most frivolous and not in keeping with his responsible position in this ship. One of the ladies is a shareholder in your sister company, the P&O, and she informs me that she intends to write to your Chairman about what she considers to be a shameful demonstration of irresponsibility by the Master of a British passenger vessel."

. to boost sales i should offer a kiss from the captain with every glass.

Strong words, I thought. We may have trouble here. Thank God they have come to me first, so I replied, "I am sorry you feel as you do, ladies, but I can assure you the Captain was only endeavouring to enter into the spirit of the evening. Entertaining passengers of all ages is our responsibility and this particular Captain has a reputation for joining in whatever entertainment we arrange for our passengers."

"Humph!" said one of the ladies, "I haven't seen him join us for Whist yet."

"Oh, he will," I answered. "I know he has it in mind."

"We shall see," came the response, and with that she rose saying, "Come, Edith, Major. We have a letter to write." She turned and led the others out. Dame Edith Evans could not have made a better exit. I went straight to the Captain's cabin, where he was sitting at a table in his day room, eating stewed prunes. "Good morning, Pay – good night last night, did you sell all your ghastly pink champagne?" he asked.

"Yes, almost," I replied "but we have a problem," and I told him about my early morning visitors. Whatever the situation, Cliff Edgecombe was always calm. Even when there was a fire in the galley he remained unruffled. Another time his ship was in collision with a United States aircraft carrier and he averted any thought of panic on his Bridge by calmly saying without raising his voice, "Full astern both."

The day in question he slowly ate another prune and announced, "So, this afternoon we play whist. Pity, I could do with a little sleep after lunch in this weather. Have a cup of coffee. There's one snag: I don't know how to play whist – do you?"

"No, not really. I did once. I suppose I could pick it up again. But I don't have to play whist, it's you they're expecting."

"Froggie, my boy. If I have to make a sacrifice, so must you. We all run this ship, not just me. Now get hold of Les Hunt after rounds this morning and tell him to be here at noon ready to teach us how to play whist." Les Hunt was the Entertainment Officer.

By 2.30pm we were whist experts. By 4.00pm we were, in the eyes of the whist enthusiasts in *Otranto*, the most popular officers on board. By 5.00pm the spokesman of my morning visitors had called again to tell me that his ladies were still going to write to the Orient Line Chairman, but that they were going to say what a versatile man our Captain was, and how charming he was to elderly passengers who can often be ignored by ship's officers. At 6.00pm I sent Clifford Edgecombe one of the few remaining bottles of pink champagne. At five minutes past six the bottle came back with a note, 'You don't expect me to drink that terrible stuff? Come up here and have a pink gin – PS That's an order. PPS Bring Hunt.'

When we reached Tilbury most of our stores were offloaded. Amongst the items which we discharged were several hundred chamber pots, but the newer ships didn't need to carry many of these, so there was nowhere else for them to be transferred to and They were sold off at sixpence each. If an American antique dealer had heard of the sale and bought them, he would have probably made a fortune.

We were a month de-storing in Tilbury during which everything portable went ashore, but some beautiful wood remained in the public rooms and went to the shipbreakers in Scotland. Very few of us sailed the ship to Faslane on the Gare Loch, and when we arrived we were met by the local manager of the *British Iron and Steel Corporation (BISC)* who had bought the ship for breaking up and selling the scrap metal. The 'run' crew who had sailed the ship from Tilbury were soon paid off by the one Assistant Purser I had brought with me, in the presence of a local Shipping Master who came on board as soon as we were alongside.

My own responsibility was to hand over the Ship's Register to the new owners, but we knew that *Otranto* would not be accepted by the BISC until all the remaining fuel oil had been pumped out of the ship – the normal practice when a ship is handed over to the breakers. After we had seen the crew away in a coach to take them to Glasgow, there remained on board the Captain, Cliff Edgecombe, the Staff Commander, the Chief Engineer who alone was watching the oil being pumped into a barge, the Company's Marine Superintendent, Paul Sargent, and myself.

We sat in the Captain's cabin as the lights grew dimmer because the generators had been stopped soon after the Bridge had rung for the last time after 32 years – 'Finished with Engines'. The emergency batteries were operating the lights, but they had little capacity, and as it was a beautiful summer evening, we didn't need lights anyway. We sat talking, waiting for the Chief Engineer to report that all the oil was pumped out. The Staff Commander kept sticking his head round the door, grinning and going away again. Eventually the Marine Superintendent got tired of this pantomime and on his fourth visit asked, "What's your trouble, why don't you come in and join us?"

"It's all right, sir," replied the Staff Commander. "I'm waiting for you to leave so that I can have the carpet!"

"For God's sake, take it," said the Captain. "I'm fed up with you peering round the door every ten minutes." With that we all sat with raised feet while the Staff Commander rolled up a not inconsiderable area of good-quality carpet. Our Staff Commander had shown considerable initiative when he asked the Stores Manager before we left London if he could have any odd bits of carpet still on board when we reached Faslane. He had just bought a house in Bournemouth and, although I never visited it, I understand it was almost entirely furnished with ex-*Otranto* carpet.

'Staffy' was a nice chap, but most unlike the average person's image of a seaman. He was tall, thin and almost bald. He looked more like a Company Secretary or Accountant than a Master Mariner, and it always seemed that he 'missed out' when things were happening – while some people are 'accident prone', he was 'not knowing about it prone'. When the whole ship knew that the rig of the day had become white uniforms, he would come to breakfast still in blue. If, as sometimes happened in port, the times of meals were altered, it could be guaranteed that Ralph would be the only officer to turn up at the wrong time.

His classic misfortune was in *Orontes* on an occasion when, off the island of Crete, we were affected by an earthquake which shook the ship badly. At the time we thought we had hit an underwater obstacle until we noticed heavy rocks falling into the sea at the shoreline and realised the cause of the shake-up. After the event we all met in the Captain's cabin to compare notes. The Captain had been on the Bridge and immediately broadcast to the passengers telling them not to be alarmed, the Chief Engineer was having breakfast, and I was writing a letter to home. Poor 'Staffy' told us, "I was sitting on the lavatory – and my bottom got wet!"

As soon as the oil had been pumped out of *Otranto*, I handed over the Register to the *Iron and Steel Corporation*'s manager, and we left for Glasgow and the train south. The old ship had played us up a bit over the last couple of years, but it was sad to say goodbye to what to us was a living thing. The Chief Engineer swore that when the Bridge rang 'Off-engines' in the Gare Loch she really did expire – I don't doubt his opinion.

Chapter 13
Refugees from Indonesia

When I reported to the London office of the Orient Line on my return from Scotland I was expecting to be sent on leave for at least a month; however I was instructed to sign on *Orion* as Supernumerary Purser. This was a disappointment as I was looking forward to an English summer at home. As it turned out, we left Tilbury on 27th June 1957 for what I expected to be a six-month voyage to California via Australia and back, but I was back in England on 13th July having been flown home from Aden to join *Orontes*, whose Purser was unable to sail on the voyage due to depart on 23rd July.

I am glad I didn't have to endure the long *Orion* voyage as a supernumerary, but the few days I did spend with Captain Birch and Purser Banister were most enjoyable. They let me spend my last night on board in the Special Suite which happened to be unoccupied at the time. Part of the arrangement was that I would give a farewell party before dinner and the Suite seemed to them the best 'out of the way' place to have such a party. For the first few days of the voyage we had Captain Sargent and his wife on board who were travelling to Naples. At the time Paul Sargent was Marine Superintendent of the Company and he had been there when we took *Otranto* to Faslane. Captain Sargent had once been in command of *Orion* and while he was with us I was reminded of his encounter with a stowaway. The Captain, who was later to become Marine Superintendent, was very fond of swimming, and whenever possible at sea would take a dip in the First Class swimming pool at around 6.30am. He would stroll down from his cabin under the Bridge in a bath robe with a towel over his shoulder, and sometimes he would meet the morning watch washing down the decks and often encounter the Chief Officer and Bosun making their morning rounds. There was seldom anyone in the pool at that time so usually the Captain had it to himself. The morning after departure from Adelaide *Orion* was just about to enter the Australian Bight when Paul Sargent set off for his morning swim.

There was a gentle roll on the ship and the water in the pool was slopping about a bit, but not dangerously. However, the Captain was surprised to find that he had a companion this morning, already in the water, and as he took off his robe and hung it across the pool rail he called to the swimmer, "Good morning – lovely day – mind if I join you?"

"Come on in," called his new companion – "it's great."

They swam around for a few minutes and then both clambered out and sat on the pool edge dangling their legs in the water.

"Have you just joined the ship?" asked Paul Sargent.

"Yes, Adelaide. I'm headed for England – I hope," replied the other.

That 'I hope' seemed an odd remark to the Captain, but he let it pass and continued the conversation.

"Holiday or Business trip?"

"Neither. I'm on my way home – I've had enough of Australia. The wife's left me for some chap who earns twice as much as I could hope for, working up at the Woomera Rocket Range, as a security man. I wouldn't trust him with my dog, let alone a high security research base."

"Tough," said the Captain, who was now suspecting that his companion might be a Tourist Class passenger. It was not unusual for Tourist Class passengers to sneak up to the First Class pool for an early morning swim. However, whatever the Captain's thoughts, he was not prepared for the next remark.

"Say, friend. Do you have a cabin near here? You couldn't get me a bit of breakfast, could you? Like a bacon sandwich or something like that?"

"There's no need for that," answered Paul Sargent. "You can go to breakfast in a short while."

"Oh no, I can't, my friend. I'm a stowaway. I've got it all fixed except for the food. Give us a hand, mate. No-one need know."

"Where did you sleep?", asked the last person on board in whom the stowaway should have confided.

"Come, I'll show you. Just round the corner here there's a big cupboard marked 'Lifejackets'. They keep it unlocked and I don't expect they ever go in there unless the ship's going to sink."

The stowaway then led the Captain to a Lifejacket locker and showed how he had made a bed amongst the lifejackets. There was also a suitcase serving as a bedside table and a suit hanging up from a sprinkler pipe.

"Very nice," observed the Captain. "Will you be here if I come back in about half-an-hour?"

"No, don't come here, someone might see you. I'll go and have a shave in one of the big lavatories I found last night and meet you over there by the rail, then we can pretend we are just watching the water rush past, while I eat whatever you can get me."

Paul Sargent, now dry and wearing his bath robe, made his way back to the Bridge. On the way he encountered the Bosun's Mate in charge of a gang washing down decks.

"Tell the Chief Officer I would like to see him in my cabin in fifteen minutes," he told the crew member.

"Sir! – Chief Officer to Captain's cabin – fifteen minutes – aye aye, sir." Yes, Orient Line Bosuns did respond to Senior Officers like that!

When the Chief Officer reported, Captain Sargent was dressing but broke off to tell him about his strange encounter at the swimming pool. "I want you to go down with the Master-at-Arms and bring this fellow to the Bridge. He hasn't told me in front of a witness that he is a stowaway and, anyway, he thinks I am a passenger. You had better get his gear from the lifejacket locker and warn the Surgeon that we will want to lock him up in the isolation hospital. Oh! and I am going to have breakfast before I see him. Get a bacon sandwich for him while he is waiting for me – I'd hate to think that he felt that I let him down!"

Two hours after their first meeting, the early morning swimmers met again. This time the second person to arrive at the swimming pool was dressed in the uniform of an Orient Line Captain, whilst his companion stared in awe at the equipment in the Chart Room of a 24,000-ton liner and the majesty of the man in command of the vessel in which he had chosen to stowaway. The interview was not unfriendly but the outcome was inevitable. The stowaway was landed at Fremantle, but at least, he had a story to tell. There can be few stowaways in a ship with some 1,500 souls on board who have asked the Captain to, "Get us a bit of breakfast'."

On leaving *Orion* I then signed on *Orontes* under the command of Captain Pinkney for two voyages. The first was as reasonably routine as any voyage was in those days, but on the second we received information while we were steaming between Adelaide and Fremantle that we were to divert to Singapore and pick up some refugees from Java. This time the signal came addressed to the Captain (thankfully not like the embarrassing moments when Cliff Edgecombe had heard secondhand that this ship was to sail home via South Africa).[22]

Our passengers from Australia were delighted with the change of itinerary which, although extending the voyage by two days, gave them a visit to Singapore and nearly every passenger was asked to move to a more expensive cabin at no extra charge (to make room for the Dutch refugees). Sailing to England in December was not the most popular time to travel, and had it not been for the diversion to Singapore we would have sailed all the way home half-empty. The cabin changes took place on the run between Fremantle and Singapore. This period included Christmas Day, which we celebrated steaming through the Sunda Strait and passing close to the coast of Sumatra.

We reached Singapore at 8.00am on 27th December where we embarked 600 refugees for Holland. There were many children, most were Asian, and the few Dutch government officials who embarked (chiefly to look after the children who were nearly all orphans) were inexperienced and gave the impression of not being really interested.

We sailed at 5.00pm, but during the stay in port I was able to go for about half-an-hour for a drink at *Raffles Hotel*. I was determined to do this on my first visit to Singapore, just in case I never called there again. (In fact, later I did make several more calls in cruising ships when we stayed for much longer, often overnight.)

After we sailed in December 1957 we had a hectic evening getting the orphans berthed and put to bed. Our Children's Hostesses and Nursing Sisters were wonderful, as were a group of Nursing Nuns travelling from Australia – they had no connection whatever with the Dutch, but who spent the whole voyage working with the ship's staff in caring for the children. Unfortunately the official Dutch escorts didn't seem to care what happened to their charges. Once we had got ourselves organised, the voyage went quite well and the passengers from Australia accepted the Dutch refugees as fellow passengers.

I have several memories of that unusual voyage. I was most impressed with the way the Dutch kept the ship tidy. Unlike British migrants, these people took the trouble to put toffee papers and orange peel in the receptacles provided and not just drop refuse where they stood or sat. I still wonder from time-to-time what happened to a little boy called Ferdinand, aged about nine, who seemed to 'adopt' the Assistant Surgeon whose cabin was opposite mine. At one stage I think the Assistant Surgeon was seriously considering adopting Ferdinand.

When we reached Naples in mid-January, one of the United Nations organisations placed on board winter clothing for the refugees from Indonesia. Among the articles sent were several pairs of woollen gloves and Ferdinand received some. However, in all his short life he had never seen gloves of any sort and he was thrilled with his present – he put his gloves on in Naples and refused to take them off, except perhaps to wash his hands. The Children's Hostess confirmed that he went to bed wearing his beloved gloves, and I never saw him without them during the day.

We called for a couple of hours in Cowes Roads off the Isle of Wight to land some of our commercial passengers and pick up a group of press and television reporters covering the refugee story.

When we reached Rotterdam snow lay everywhere and the temperature was below freezing – not a very pleasant first impression for those arriving in a new country from the tropics. Our last sight of Ferdinand and his companions was in a convoy of coaches leaving the ship's side, shivering and looking completely lost.

There was an amusing incident associated with our bitterly cold arrival in Holland. Amongst those who joined us in Cowes Roads was an Assistant Marine Superintendent, Captain Jim Kidd, and a Management Trainee (or 'Student Prince' as we used to call them) named Francis Burne. The Assistant Marine Superintendent arranged to be called by the Bridge when the Pilot joined off the Hook of Holland, so that he could observe the approach to Rotterdam. Our expected time of arrival off the Hook was 3.00am. At about 2.45 on this dark winter's morning the Senior Second Officer who was on watch telephoned the 'C' deck night watch and instructed him to call Captain Kidd.

"Captain Kidd? 'Oose 'e?" said the elderly watchman over the telephone.

The Second Officer explained. "He joined from the Southampton tender this morning and is berthed on your deck."

"Oh, yus – I know. Young chap. Went to bed early. Call 'I'm, you say – aye aye, sir. I'll get 'im up – want 'im on the Bridge, do you? – I'll fix it." And with that the night watchman rang off, made a cup of tea, and set off for the cabin he thought Captain Kidd was in. He did not realise that two people who joined off Cowes were in cabins on his deck: Jim Kidd and Francis Burne.

Francis was woken from a deep sleep by a loud hammering on his door. He called out a sleepy "Come in" and in came the watchman with a cup of tea putting on every light in the cabin, including the bedside reading light about ten inches from Francis' sleep-laden eyes.

" 'Ook of 'Olland, sir. Bridge just telephoned."

"So what?" yawned a sleepy Student Prince.

"Come on – feet on the deck. I've 'ad trouble with young men like you before. Up you get."

"But why?" pleaded Francis. "It's 3.00 in the morning."

"I know what time it is and you're due on the Bridge now. There's yer tea," placing it just out of reach from the bed. "Do you want a bit of toast? Five minutes; and when I get back I expect to see you up and getting dressed."

Burne could see that the night watchman was determined and that he would get no more sleep that night, so he got up, had his toast and went up to the Bridge where the Captain greeted him with a cheery "Good morning, Mr Burne. Come to see us enter harbour, have you? Didn't expect to see you up as early as this, but now that you are here – welcome!"

Jim Kidd, an experienced seaman, awoke as soon as the engines slowed down. He made his own way to the Bridge where he berated the Second Officer for not calling him and promptly drank the watch-keeper's tea which had just arrived from the galley.

Francis Burne sailed with me as a Supernumerary Assistant Purser in my next ship, *Orion*. The Orient Line gave their trainee Managers experience in every part of their operation and a voyage to Australia was considered to be an important part of the training.

'ook of 'olland, sir bridge just telephoned"

Francis was a useful member of my team, and what he lacked in experience he made up for with enthusiasm. Amongst the New Settlers for Australia who boarded at Tilbury were about 30 Finns who spoke no English. Francis decided to teach them English, although he had no knowledge of Finnish or any Scandinavian language! His sole teaching aid was a blackboard and piece of chalk, so quite a lot of miming was necessary. He started by teaching how to go shopping for food and clothes, and I watched the clothing session which was most amusing. He started off with drawing a naked man and a naked woman, and then proceeded to dress the figures. First a pair of socks for the man – much pointing and everyone repeating after their teacher "socks". Then the woman got a pair of stockings (tights were not universally worn then) followed by a suspender belt. It was surprising to see how much our Student Prince knew about women's underwear... perhaps he had a sister.

Francis Burne did have a brother who was an Officer in the Royal Navy and whose path crossed with the P&O on two occasions. The first time was in 1971 when I was P&O Purser Training Officer, a role I had for a couple of years. I realised that although our Purser Cadets were professionally qualified to manage catering operations, they could not handle men. When a 'bolshie' Steward told a Cadet or Junior Assistant Purser to 'get lost', they could not deal with the situation. So on behalf of the P&O I approached the Admiralty and a two week leadership course was arranged at *HMS Royal Arthur* in Wiltshire.

Christopher Burne, brother of Francis, was in command of this shore establishment. When *Canberra* sailed to the Falkland Islands under the command of Captain Scott-Mason in 1982, Captain Christopher Burne was the Admiralty authority on board. Francis himself didn't stay in shipping and became associated with an art gallery in London's West End.

After a spell in *Orion* I was brought ashore to work in the London office. The Company had appointed one of the senior Pursers, Seymore Hart, as Shore Purser. One of the more junior of us took it in turns to be attached to him in order to acquire an understanding of the shoreside problems, and to provide up-to-date sea-going experience as required at various policy discussions. It was an interesting time to be in the London office, whilst *Oriana* was being built at Barrow-in-Furness. Seymore Hart was keen on establishing a training programme for our many inexperienced waiters, and I found this part of his small department most interesting.

The Purser attached to the Shore Purser attended various management meetings as part of his shore time experience. I was therefore present at a meeting held in the Orient Line board room at 3.15pm on Thursday 31st December 1959, when we were told that the Managers of the Orient Steam Navigation Company were considering a merger with the Peninsular and Oriental Steam Navigation Company. After the announcement there was a stunned silence. For years P&O had held a controlling interest in the Orient Line, but we had always operated independently and as far as the senior staff knew, our ships made a profit. However, we were told that it did not make for good business practice to operate two fleets as rivals in the same trade, and with one management the whole organisation from shore offices to shipboard services could be streamlined. *Canberra* and *Oriana* were being built – two fast liners of over 40,000 tons. To run each independently would not be taking advantage of their joint potential, and maintaining two sets

Canberra

of offices all round the world to service two fleets doing the same thing was uneconomical.

All this made sense, but at the time a merger with the Devil would have been more attractive to us than with the P&O who thought themselves superior to the Royal Navy, and whose management translated the British Raj from the East to Leadenhall Street in the City of London.

A new Company P&O – Orient (Passenger Services) Ltd came into being on 2nd May 1960. For a time, for the sea-going staff, things didn't change much – the Orient ships still wore their own house flag and the Officers' uniforms remained as before. However, our separate identity didn't last for long. In October 1966 the word Orient was finally dropped and the whole fleet sailed under the P&O house flag and wore P&O livery. Although the P&O operated similar ships in the same trade as the Orient Line, their whole attitude to the task was different. The Orient Company was a small family business whose board room was dominated by the Anderson and Geddes family, and because the staff were known by the managers, there was frequent personal contact at all levels.

The P&O was a giant in international commerce, whose board room controlled subsidiary companies worldwide. We soon realised the change in attitude from the top when shortly after the announcement of the merger, those of us working in the Orient Line office near Fenchurch Street were summoned to the P&O headquarters in Leadenhall Street. We were addressed by Sir Donald Anderson, Chairman of P&O, whose theme was that we had always to remember the most important person in the group of companies which he controlled – the shareholder. He was, of course, quite right. Until now we had always thought of the passenger being the most important person and that our job was to serve passengers.

It would take some time for us to get used to being part of a larger organisation and being answerable to Superintendents and Assistant Superintendents rather than one Stores Manager in London and Directors whom we knew personally. However, we adapted. In some areas we were relieved of former responsibilities. After a couple of years we found ourselves sailing in P&O ships and P&O Pursers were appointed to Orient ships. Like seafarers generally, the sea staff integrated smoothly, especially in the Pursers' Department. The Deck Officers integration was not so easy because in the P&O Company a deck officer joined as a Cadet and there were watch-keepers with a Mate's certificate, whilst in the Orient Line the most junior Deck Officer had to have a Master's certificate, which entailed having been at sea for about eight years before he could join the Company. This of course created difficulties with the list of seniority. Thankfully, there was no such problem with the Pursers – after all, to quote a Captain who shall remain nameless, we were only 'uncertificated clerks'!

My first P&O ship was *Chusan* in 1967. There is no doubt that the Purser's accommodation in P&O ships was superior to that in Orient ships, reflecting different company policies. Orient Pursers were expected to entertain in public spaces and when a small group of passengers had to be entertained, an Orient Purser was supposed to use a small writing room or similar space. However, the accommodation in P&O ships included a bedroom, bathroom, spacious day room and private office.

The merger of the two companies affected the shore staff more than those of us at sea. As the sales and operation staff of each company was now combined, several people became redundant, and Orient employees suffered most. Throughout the world Agencies which had served the Orient Line for years were transferred to the local P&O agent.

During the second half of the last century the industry had seen many takeovers. The P&O – Orient 'marriage', like many others had, in the beginning, moments of sadness. Orient was a reluctant bride. However, from the union has been born a family of 'Princesses' – a fleet of cruise ships maintaining a great tradition.

The 'wake' that was held for the Orient Line

THE OFFICERS OF THE LATE

ORIENT LINE

solemnly invite

. . . .

to a Wake to be held in the Mortuaries
(BD5 and BD6)

to mourn the Passing of an Era

Noon   Sunday, 2nd October, 1966

Chapter 14
Oriana – **Planning** –
Building – Commissioning

O n Wednesday 18th September 1957, in response to a telegram from London, each Captain of an Orient Liner at sea gave a champagne party for his passengers. The occasion was the laying of the keel of *Oriana* at Barrow-in-Furness, when construction had begun on the largest passenger liner to be built in England. Scotland could claim the giant Cunard *Queens*, and Belfast the *Canberra*, whose keel was laid on the same day as *Oriana*'s. Discussion about a 40,000-ton ship for the Orient Line had begun in 1954 and a final decision to build made two years later.

It was some months before a name was chosen for the new ship. In the planning departments of the Orient Line she was referred to as *Orbustus* and memos were circulated in the offices under this heading until an edict was issued that this title must be discontinued. In the meantime Agents and the general public, particularly those in Australia, had been invited to suggest names. Many suggested the revival of old names such as *Omrah* and *Ophir*, once chartered as a Royal Yacht. *Otway* was suggested, but rejected on the thought that one failure of the air-conditioning would encourage the travelling public to re-christen her 'Hot Way'. The feeling was that whatever the name was to be it must begin with OR, prompting a wag to write to the Sydney office suggesting *Orstralia*! I have always given the credit for the final choice to Sir Colin Anderson, although I may be giving it to the wrong person, and whoever provided the name deserves praise.

Oriana was an excellent choice for a symbol of British achievement that would circumnavigate the world. She may have been inanimate, but to those of us who served in her she became a very living thing. Queen Elizabeth I had been referred to by poets

as 'the fair Oriana' and there is a collection of madrigals published in 1601 called *The Triumphs of Oriana*, so it was appropriate that a ship built in England during the second Elizabethan era should be named *Oriana*. Since *Orion* built in 1935, each Orient ship had a badge. For *Orion*, the stars depicting Orion's belt. For *Orcades*, the Roman name for the Orkney Islands, the badge had been an Orcadian harp. *Oronsay*, named after an island off the West Coast of Scotland, had a Targe and Broadsword; whilst *Orsova* carried a badge depicting the Iron Gate across the Danube at the town of *Orsova*. For *Oriana* a badge was designed showing a 'double E' monogram framed in a letter 'O', surmounted by an eight-arched Elizabethan pearl crown. Each ship wore her badge on the bow, high up on the bow just below the fo'c's'le. The badge was in fact the door to the Suez Canal searchlight locker!

Oriana was launched on 3rd November 1959 by HRH Princess Alexandra. Senior Officers of the Orient fleet who were ashore at the time were invited and I had a grandstand view of the ceremony from the launching platform, only a few feet away from the Princess. When the launching button was pressed, a cradle with not only one but three bottles of wine crashed on to *Oriana*'s bow – one bottle of Californian wine, one from Australia and from Europe, a Chateau Talbot claret (drunk in the first Elizabethan era and still

156

being drunk in the second Elizabeth's reign). One of the three bottles did not break, which we thought was the Californian bottle, and a tug master retrieved it after the ship entered the water. I wonder if he kept it as a souvenir or celebrated a successful launch with his crew?

At the time I did not know that I would be soon returning to Barrow-in-Furness while the ship was fitting out, and eventually sailing in her as Tourist Class Purser. It had been decided that this ship would carry two Pursers – because there would be 1,496 Tourist Class passengers, it was considered that these deserved a Purser of their own. The Senior Purser, who would look after the First Class and have overall control of our Department, was Gerald Puckle, better known worldwide as 'Puck'. Puck had joined the Orient Line as an Assistant Purser in 1936 and had made his first voyage in *Orsova* (No. 1), a coal-burning ship. He remained in the Company throughout the war, serving in *Otranto* and taking part in the Allied Landings in North Africa and Italy. He was promoted Purser in 1947 and therefore had much more experience than I did.

During the late winter and spring of 1960 we made frequent visits to the new ship and the *Vickers Armstrong* Drawing Office in Barrow, usually staying in a local hotel. By the summer more and more 'on the spot' decisions had to be made, so we moved into a cottage at Lowick Green, a village about 12 miles from the yard where *Oriana* was fitting out. Our landlord was a local farmer and the rent was three pounds a week. The landlord delivered our milk personally, usually round 11.00 at night – his delivery vehicle was a Jaguar car and often there was a dead sheep on the back seat. Our local pub was the *Farmers Arms* at Lowick to which we could walk in less than ten minutes, so we went there most evenings and got to know the locals.

One evening the talk was on fishing and the trout in the River Crake, which passed close to the hotel on its way from Coniston Water to the sea at Morecambe Bay. We asked quietly if there was any chance of a trout or two.

"Where is it you gentlemen are living?" whispered a local.

"Riddings Croft Cottage," one of us answered.

157

"If we can get a fish or two, I'll bring 'em round – early about six in the morning!"

We didn't enquire why the delivery had to be so early, but we guessed our supplier had no right to fish where he did. This suspicion was confirmed when one day Puck and I were invited to lunch with the Directors of *Vickers Armstrong* and one of our hosts remarked that he had the fishing rights on a stretch of the Crake behind the Farmers Arms at Lowick.

"Supposed to be a good stretch," he said, "but I never catch much." We thought we knew why so kept quiet about our early morning deliveries.

A small stream, or 'beck' as streams in that part of the world are called, ran right past our kitchen door. We kept our white wine in the stream, always cool, although the only disadvantage was that the labels washed off – thankfully we knew roughly what we were serving from the shape and colour of the bottle.

Each morning we set off from our Lake District cottage for the shipbuilders' yard in Barrow, watching the ship grow more like a hotel each day. For the First Class swimming pool bar there came a quantity of period engraved and sand-blown glass which had been rescued from *The Plough* at Notting Hill, London, during demolition. Inevitably, our pool bar was called the *Plough Tavern*. Eleven bars serviced the passengers, although it must be admitted that they would never all be open at the same time.

Workmen streamed aboard each day building cabins, laying lino and carpet, and fitting miles of wire for electric lights and telephones. Each cabin had a loudspeaker with individual controls giving passengers a choice of two programmes. Special lightweight telephones were installed which were. Weight was an important factor in *Oriana* – the top decks were aluminium, and even the lavatory seats were rather thin plastic (very comfortable except when a split occurred and a painful pinch was sometimes experienced). The wiring for the loudspeakers, telephones and, in some cabins, television, was complex. Unfortunately it was found that one of the builders' electricians was colour-blind and unwilling to admit this in case he was paid off. The connecting up of wires in the region of my cabin was done by this same man and on our first night at sea, when I telephoned Puck in his cabin, I got the 6.00pm news via the Radio Office, from London.

We used to lunch each day in a large dining room in *Vickers Armstrong* office block. There were Royal Navy Officers also there, as at the time two submarines were being built. One day most of the submariners were missing, and when next day we asked where they had been, we were told they had been undergoing basin diving tests. Apparently their boat had spent the day submerged at the bottom of the dock to check that it was watertight – seemed odd to us, and rather like looking for a gas leak with a match.

Our ship was the largest ever owned by the *Orient Line* and inside below decks it was difficult to determine if you were walking forward or aft. Arrowheads were set into the linoleum in the alleyways indicating which way was forward, and the colour of this large 'V' differed for each deck. However, despite this clear indication, people often got lost looking for their cabin.

Each public room was given a name. At first the Tourist Class Ballroom was called the 'Assembly Room'. It was a vast space and the name was appropriate, but it had to be changed long before the

Oriana's Princess Room

first passenger came on board, as men in *Vickers'* drawing office referred to it as the Arse and Belly room! In the Amidships Bar the tables had lights in them, and the glass tops through which the lights shone were multicoloured like images seen in a kaleidoscope. The stern galley had a sweep of windows 120 feet wide reaching from deck to deckhead, a truly impressive gallery high in the stern. Until *Oriana*, Orient Line Grill Rooms had been at boat deck level and overlooked the after end of the ship and, whilst at sea, the wake streaming away astern. Our 'Silver Grill', as it was called, was on 'A' deck and gave no view of the sea at all; nevertheless it was an attractive room where decoration included reproductions of a large Elizabethan medallion some eight inches across. The Grill Room curtains were made from a beautiful silver silk with a black stripe. The main First Class Lounge, in which was incorporated the library, was the 'Princess Room', so named after a full-length portrait of Princess Alexandra who had launched the ship. The portrait had been painted at Buckingham Palace by Judy Cassab, a Viennese-born artist living in Australia. The library part of the room was separated from the main area by a long mural called 'Landscape of the Two Seasons' by John Piper.

Each day more furniture and fittings arrived. Puck and I had seen sketches of cabins and public rooms, but it was not until carpets were laid and wall covering applied that we began to realise how different this ship was going to be from anything we had sailed in before. Some of the colour schemes were difficult to understand. The Princess Room was very sombre with a rifle green carpet and black woodwork, although there was an occasional spot of brightness provided by bright yellow, red or purple scatter cushions. However, when the room was full of people the sombre atmosphere was transformed by the women's dresses and in the evening the men's jackets complemented the decor.

The First Class Dining Room had its character changed in the evening for dinner by the use of lighting. For breakfast and lunch, the curtains were open and daylight streamed in through the portholes. For dull days there was fluorescent lighting and the whole room was bright. In the evening, for dinner, the atmosphere was transformed when bright red curtains were drawn across the portholes, thus removing the realisation of being in a ship. All the lighting was subdued, and in the centre above the Staff Commander's table the deck head was decorated with a great golden star picked out in tiny lights. The Captain's table was just forward of the Staff Commander's, the Purser's just aft, and was the first large table from the main entrance. All three tables were round, and the Captain's was designed to seat nine, while the others just eight people.

On Friday 21st October 1960, Trafalgar Day, the Queen came to *Vickers Armstrong* at Barrow-in-Furness to launch *HMS Dreadnought*, a nuclear submarine, and afterwards she visited *Oriana*. Cliff Edgecombe, Ernest Neville the Chief Engineer and Puck were presented. I stood at the point where the party entered the Tourist Class from the First Class. Beside me was 'Wally' Johnson my Chief Steward. The Queen and her entourage passed by without a glance in our direction and headed towards our Purser Cadet with whom the Duke of Edinburgh and Lord Mountbatten spoke for several minutes. When the group reached the Amidships bar where the tables were lit up, Her Majesty turned to Sir Colin Anderson and remarked, "Not good for iced drinks, Sir Colin."

"Ideal for Bovril, Ma'am," replied our Director. In fact, the lights did not generate heat. I never did get used to sitting at these tables, although they did make the room unusual and attractive.

While the Queen was on board, *Oriana* flew the Royal Standard. (I have searched ever since for a picture of the ship flying the Royal Standard and so far have not found one.) Two days after the Queen's visit we moved on board the ship. That night I lay in my bed and wondered what the future would hold for the great ship and for how long I would be associated with her.

On Friday 4th November we left the builders yard and steamed south to Falmouth for dry-docking. Technically the ship still belonged to *Vickers Armstrong* and so we flew their house flag. Cliff Edgecombe was in command by arrangement with the Orient Line.

We were at Falmouth for five days and on the sixth steamed northwards again towards the Isle of Arran, off which we were going to undergo our speed trials. First we anchored in Falmouth Bay to take on fuel and later in the day we embarked some of the P&O and Orient Line managers and their guests in very rough weather. At about 9.00pm we were rolling heavily off Land's End and then, perhaps as we began to alter course, all the lights went out and the main engines stopped. We wallowed in a short swell and

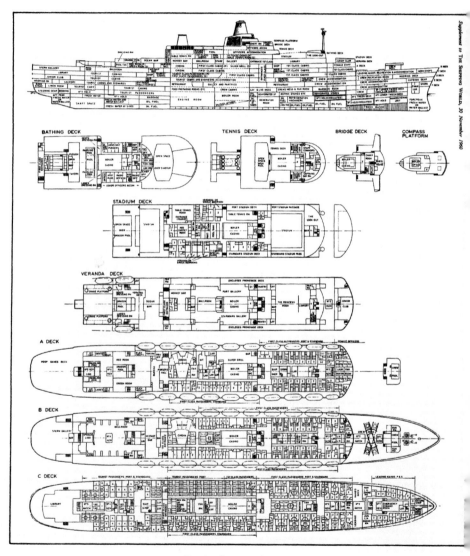

Deck plans of Oriana

pianos which were not secured broke loose, plates were smashed, and a heavy baggage conveyor crashed into the ship's side. Some of the inexperienced catering crew took fright but didn't panic – they just sat on the main companionway wearing their lifejackets.

After about 20 minutes everything was again under control. A safety device had worked better than its designers had intended –

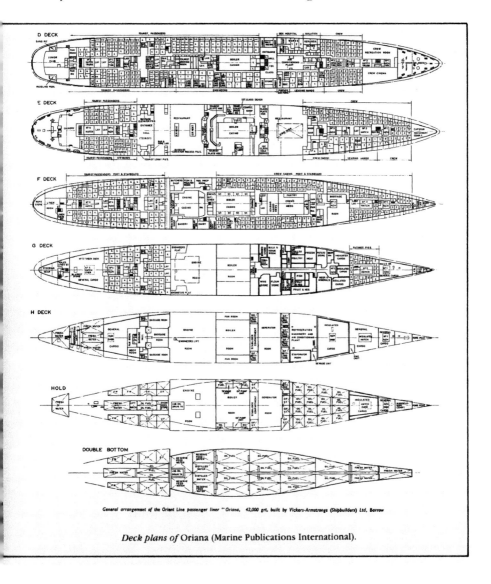

General arrangement of the Orient Line passenger liner "Oriana", 42,000 grt, built by Vickers-Armstrongs (Shipbuilders) Ltd, Barrow

Deck plans of Oriana (Marine Publications International).

provision had been made for machinery to cut out if lubrication failed and the rolling of the ship had done just this, but to an extent not expected. Anyway, we were on trials and to find out about such things is what trials are for, although the builders would have been happier if this 'trial' had not taken place on a dark winter's night close to the shore.

Off the Isle of Arran we averaged 30.6 knots over the measured mile runs. This was considered to be a great achievement, and at one stage we were reputed to have been travelling at 31 knots. I don't know what the 'top brass' did when the result was known, but I found myself playing host to the second eleven from *Vickers Armstrong* Drawing Office and Engineering Department. Over a glass of champagne, which the *Vickers* men had confidently warned me would be required, I asked, "What happens now?"

"We steam to Belfast," one of the builders said, "and drop a wreath!" *Harland & Wolff*'s Belfast yard was just completing *Canberra* whose speed trials and general performance never did equal *Oriana*'s, although her passenger accommodation was superior.

After the trials we steamed back down the Irish Sea, rounded Land's End, this time without incident, and at noon on Tuesday 15th November berthed alongside a new Passenger Terminal at berths 105/6 Southampton Docks. This was to be *Oriana*'s home port for the next 20 years until she later became based in Sydney, Australia.

Now began the social whirl which was to continue until the end of the maiden voyage. Puck had to bear the brunt of this and did not enjoy it much, although I attended most cocktail parties and really large lunches and dinners. Puck had to represent the Pursers' Department at many small functions for the very, very important visitor, such as Princess Marina, Duchess of Kent, who came with her daughter to inspect the finished product. They were charming guests, easy to entertain, with a fine sense of humour – they needed it.

Having been met on the gangway by the Captain, Staff Commander and Pursers (and I was allowed to welcome them even though I didn't join the lunch party) the Duchess and Princess entered the lift with the Staff Commander who was to take them to the Silver Grill. The rest of us remained in the foyer. However, having sent 'The Royals' on their way, we stepped back and were quietly chatting when the lift door opened again and there before us was the Staff Commander with his Princesses laughing away – it seemed they had reached 'A' deck for the Grill Room when the lift then decided to descend at once. Princess Marina thought, or pretended to think, the whole thing a great joke; poor Captain Riddlesdell, the Staff Commander, thought otherwise, especially when on the next attempt they rose to the Veranda Deck. He got over this one by suggesting that this was his intention all the time, and that he wished the Duchess to see her daughter's portrait which, fortunately for him, was hung right outside the lift doors at Veranda Deck level. They then had just one set of stairs to descend to 'A' deck which they walked. 'Ridd' had had enough of automatic lifts for one day.

During our first week in Southampton we had a special lunch each day for guests who travelled from London in an all-Pullman Car train right to the ship's side at 105/6 berth. Many weeks before, when we were still in Barrow, we had discussed these arrangements and after one meeting, whilst standing at the bar in the *Victoria Park Hotel*, I remarked to Kenneth Anderson, the Orient Line Chairman's son, that it would be nice if the special trains from Waterloo could be hauled by the Merchant Navy Class engine 'Orient Line'. Kenneth thought this a reasonable suggestion and wrote to Southern Region of British Railways who agreed to allocate this locomotive to the special trains. My suggestion was prompted by my memory of the opening of the Ocean Terminal at Southampton in 1950 when facilities designed for the use of the two great Queens, *Mary* and *Elizabeth*, had the official guests brought from London in a train hauled by 35022 'Holland-America Line'. Together with the Chairman's son, we were terrified that our trains to *Oriana* might be hauled by 35006 – 'Peninsular and Oriental SN Co!' Once, during the week, Kenneth Anderson travelled on the footplate from Waterloo. Although I could not do it at the time, I had the same privilege a couple of years later. That ride on a steam engine which I remember thundering through Winchester at 80 miles an hour is one of the outstanding thrills of my life.

Before our maiden voyage, we were committed to take the Association of British Travel Agents on a cruise to Lisbon, which was also to be the Association's Annual Conference. The five-day cruise went well, but I have always thought that our Owners took a risk accepting the most critical bunch of passengers they could possibly find for a 'shakedown' cruise. The Orient Line Management must have had faith in their ship and those of us who were to run it for them.

It was useful to have a few days in near-to-home waters before setting off for Australia and the Pacific. By now we had a full complement of crew including twelve Stewardesses who were berthed on 'E' deck close to, what was then, the Tourist Class Chief Steward's cabin. Their lavatory was the other side of the bulkhead beside his bunk. On our first night at sea he retired early, but was immediately woken up by a woman flushing the Stewardess's lavatory... then by another... and another, until he got up, put on his dressing gown and called on the Senior Stewardess, instructing, "Tell your girls to go NOW – and then to 'hold it' until the morning. Six have gone already, tell the other six to get a move on!"

"Tell your girls to go, Now "

Chapter 15
Oriana – Maiden Voyage 1960

Oriana's maiden voyage started at 2.00pm on Saturday 3rd December 1960. For several days before we left Southampton there were parties and publicity functions, including a fashion show when after parading the models, were entertained enthusiastically by the junior officers, the Assistant Pursers in particular. Four days before sailing, the passenger reception hall at 105/6 berth, Southampton Docks, was officially opened by Viscount Slim who had recently returned to Britain after being Governor-General of Australia – an appropriately distinguished person to perform the ceremony at the point from which *Oriana* and *Canberra* would make their regular sailings to Australia. This was the first of several new passenger terminals we were to tie up alongside on our maiden voyage.

Tourist Class passengers started to embark at 8.00pm on the night before departure, and more than 600 joined that evening. Embarkation went quite smoothly until an elderly gentleman felt faint and walked into the first empty cabin he came across, sat down and died. Not a good omen for a maiden voyage, but at least it happened before we had gone to sea and the local authorities were able to handle all the arrangements. All sailors are superstitious, so I suspect Captain Clifford Edgecombe felt such an unfortunate occurrence was a portent. In fact the whole voyage was a remarkable success, except for the odd hiccup now and then, which is bound to take place in a floating city of 3,000 souls.

Just before we sailed I was at the gangway with some of the Southampton port officials when a woman came down the main staircase to the foyer where we were standing, shouting, "You call this a luxury liner? That cabin isn't big enough for a midget. I'm getting off." She was followed by her Steward staggering along with two heavy suitcases. Off she went, striding past us onto the gangway. At the bottom of the gangway a group of pressmen were standing one of whom was Jack Frost, shipping correspondent of *The Daily Telegraph* and, at the time, the doyen of the shipping correspondents. He stepped forward and spoke to the still shouting woman.

"Madam," said Jack, "if you think your behaviour is going to influence anyone's opinion of this wonderful ship, you are quite wrong. You are, of course, entitled to your opinion, but I can assure you that nobody here wishes to record it or even remember it."

With that our disgruntled non-passenger stopped shouting and replied, "Then get me a porter and taxi!" Whether or not someone got her a taxi, I don't know. By then the gangway was removed and we were closing the ship's side door.

The voyage to Naples was uneventful. The weather was rough in the Bay of Biscay and Sunday's church service was cancelled, although once inside the Mediterranean things improved. On the evening before arrival at Naples we had a cocktail party for all Tourist Class passengers followed by a Gala Dance. There was quite a strong wind blowing as we berthed next morning and unfortunately we hit the wharf quite hard, damaging two cabins in the stern of the ship.

Our passage through the Suez Canal was also uneventful. The pilots remarked how well the ship handled, although it was agreed that a strong wind across the desert would present problems against a hull and superstructure towering a hundred feet above the water line. This vast expanse of top hamper turned the whole ship into a gigantic sail which, on several occasions during *Oriana*'s life, prevented her from docking or undocking.

Sunday 11th December found us in the Red Sea and dressed in our white uniforms. More work for the laundry, which was already handling around 10,000 pieces a day. Church in the Tourist Class was conducted by 'Ridd', the Staff Commander, and I read the lesson. In the evening I had a meeting with some of the 60 waiters who manned the Tourist Class restaurant, and amongst these men were the 'cowboys' of the crew from whom I was anticipating some trouble. Most had come from Liverpool and had been used to short transatlantic voyages lasting about two weeks. Our voyage was due to last 111 days, during which there would always be some passengers on board.

We discussed the layout of the restaurant and the arrangements in the servery. It was a constructive meeting and I felt that these men were surprised that their Purser and Chief Steward were willing to discuss their concerns. We did have trouble with some of the men going absent without leave in port later in the voyage, but this and other meetings showed that we cared about their working conditions. I have always felt sorry for the Dining Room Stewards who have to serve six full sittings a day and then, when the ship is full, either children's meals or afternoon tea. Often there is no let-up in port either. At least *Oriana* offered two berth cabins for all crew members – a vast improvement on the pre-war 'glory holes' and post-war ten or twelve-berth cabins.

At the southern end of the Red Sea we rounded Perim Island and the Deputy Purser, Peter Hodge, and I gave a *Pimms* party and this 'Purser's *Pimms* Round Perim Party' became a feature of *Oriana*. A few hours later we were in Aden where there was a cocktail party on board for local residents and others, amongst whom there was a big game hunter from East Africa who had several wild animals aboard a cargo ship moored close to *Oriana*. During the party a Children's Hostess and her friend, a Social Hostess, came across to me and asked permission to go off with the hunter to see his rhinoceros. I smiled and said, "Of course – remember we sail at four o'clock." Soon after we sailed I encountered the girls and asked about the hunter's rhino. I detected slight disappointment when they reported that a rhinoceros was exactly all they saw – and that was all!

Our next port of call was Colombo where the *Times of Ceylon* printed a special supplement, 'The Maiden Voyage of SS *Oriana*, 17th December 1960.' There were articles about Cliff Edgecombe, 'The Captain's Kingdom'; Riddlesdell, 'The Master of Ceremonies'; Ernie Neville our Chief Engineer, 'The Man with Drive'; Puckle, 'A

Man with a Head for Headaches'. My picture also featured together with a few paragraphs, but I did not get a descriptive annexe beyond 'The Tourist Purser'. However, I did achieve the distinction of being reported as having served in the 'Prince of Wales Dragons Guards' – now who says there are no dragons in Wales?

Our trip around the Australian coast was a social whirl. Parties for the press, travel agents, potential passengers and dignitaries kept us fully occupied, quite apart from running the largest passenger ship in the southern hemisphere, which had already become the fastest liner east of Gibraltar. During the passage from Fremantle to Melbourne we celebrated Christmas. Somehow or other we managed to entertain our 2,000 passengers with carol singing, a children's party and a Christmas dinner, at which some of my restaurant waiters became very drunk and had to be sent below.

We reached Sydney on 30th December when the Governor-General came aboard for lunch and in the evening there was a cocktail party for 400 guests. By now we had a drill for these functions and, except for the senior officers, officer hosts were not detailed to attend every party. We stayed at the new passenger terminal at Sydney Cove for a week and most days the ship was open for inspection – at a charge, which was donated to charity. At first we arranged for guides to show groups of about a dozen around at a time, but we soon changed this to having a well signposted route with 'information givers' at intervals.

We were alongside for New Year's Eve, but did not make a feature of the event in the same way that we would have done at sea. At midnight the Officer of the Watch sounded the ship's whistle in chorus with all the other ships in the harbour. I was at the New South Wales Golf Club with my friends the Longworths and our Chief Officer, having the first break ashore since Southampton. When we sailed on Thursday 5th January, as soon as we had dropped the pilot, Cliff Edgecombe turned to the Officer of the Watch and said, "I'm going below – the course is 090°." The Officer of the Watch and the Quartermaster gave him an enquiring look which prompted the Captain to remark, "Auckland."

"No, sir." replied the Second Officer. "Hobart."

"Oh Lord! Yes. We have a cruise before we go to the States. Sydney has been so hectic I quite forgot about the cruise."

The Captain had had a tough time in Sydney, although I suspect he had enjoyed a lot of it. His picture was in all the papers, he appeared on television and also spoke on the radio. He was justifiably proud of his ship and accepted every opportunity to extol its virtues. Edgecombe was a much sought after guest by Sydney socialites and he was our ambassador at many functions, so he could be forgiven for forgetting where we were going. Our cruise took us to Hobart, Wellington and Auckland, where we were all asked to appear on television. Cliff Edgecombe said to the New Zealand broadcasters, "OK – eleven o'clock on the Bridge. We have a drill for this and my senior officers know what to say."

The very embarrassed New Zealand television producer had to say, "I'm sorry, sir, we only have one camera and that is screwed to the studio floor."

"Then it's all off," replied our Captain and told us we were not needed. Nevertheless that evening there was Cliff on New Zealand television giving a solo performance, having gone up to the studio. I admired him – he always stole the limelight, but why shouldn't he? He had the responsibility for our wonderful ship and deserved the credit provided he didn't pretend he did it all by himself!

From Auckland we returned to Sydney where we stayed for just three days before setting off for New Zealand again on our way to North America and this time 090° was the correct course! We were now operating in a market for which we, unlike all previous Orient and P&O Liners, had been designed. Earlier ships had been built for the Australian trade and by chance employed on the Pacific, whereas *Oriana* had been designed with the Australia – North America run in mind. Any ship on its maiden voyage is going to be popular, but we were embarrassingly popular. During our 7.00am to 11.00pm stay in Auckland, some 600 passengers left and joined the ship and at one stage those going down the gangway were crossing with those embarking.

This was to be the pattern at Auckland for many years. New Zealand Customs officials were not the easiest we encountered, although it must be admitted that the arrival of *Oriana*, and later *Canberra*, stretched their resources to the limit. Auckland was a major storing port and on one visit in *Oriana*, we shipped 70 tons of meat. Buying the best at the most attractive price was an essential part of our stores department and the Purser's strategy throughout the world.

Those passengers in transit at Auckland had opportunities to take excursions to the thermal region at Rotorua or the glow worm caves at Waitomo. There was also an excursion to the Auckland Zoo where visitors could see a kiwi, the flightless bird which only lives in New Zealand. In 1961 there was not a specially lit house for nocturnal species at the Auckland Zoo and the poor bird (and at times there was only one) had to be woken up for shore excursionists from visiting ships. More than once this particular trip for passengers had to be cancelled in response to a telegram received on board on the day before our visit which read, "Kiwi exhausted by previous ship's call. Stop. Cancel Zoo excursion." There has since been built a splendid specially lit house at the Auckland Zoo for all nocturnal creatures (who presumably think our day is night) where night is made, for them, into day.

After Auckland, two days at sea and then to Suva where the local police and defence force band on the wharf played us in. This was an impressive group of men in scarlet or blue tunics, below which they wore a snowy white sulu or lap-lap (a skirt with large serrations). Their music was both patriotic and sentimental, especially when on our departure they played 'Isa Lei' – a haunting melody which has always meant more to me than the much commercialised 'Now is the Hour' which so often came over loudspeakers as we left port.

Music can have interesting effects on the travelling public. I well remember being at Station Pier, Melbourne, when two ships sailed at the same time. One had 'A Life on the Ocean Waves' blaring from its loudspeakers and those holding streamers both on board and ashore were laughing and cheering. The other ship was transmitting 'Now is the Hour When We Must Say Goodbye' and so the people aboard and on the wharf were crying their eyes out.

Streamers leaving Australia

At Suva *Oriana* displayed her transverse propellers most impressively – they had been built into the bow and stern of the ship and enabled the ship to literally move sideways. This was an important part of the manoeuvre to get our 40,000 tons alongside at a port which was not served by powerful tugs. We sailed from Suva at 5.00pm and then had 25th January twice, as we crossed the International Date Line. On the second 25th January we crossed the Equator and passed close to Canton Island.

Throughout the passage to Honolulu we were busy with United States Immigration Inspections. US Officers had already joined us and needed to interview every soul on board – crew and passengers – a formidable task which was completed by the day before our arrival in Hawaii. At Puck's suggestion, the evening before we arrived we entertained the United States officials in the Silver Grill, a rare treat and an evening out from the Tourist Class for me. Honolulu was a long and busy day – because this was our first American port the Coastguards and Health Inspectors kept us busy, making a thorough inspection of the ship and all our safety equipment. We had a full-scale fire drill followed by 'abandon ship' drill when all the boats on the off-shore side of the ship were lowered into the water and sent away so that the US Coastguard Officers could see how well the crew were trained, and how the boat-lowering devices worked. We passed all the tests with flying colours and received congratulations from the Senior Coastguard Officer.

I was the only crew member who got ashore in the forenoon as I went to the Port Offices with the ship's papers. I have always been surprised that in the United States of America, where the documentation is amongst the most complex in the world, the signature of a Purser carries the same weight as that of the Master of an overseas ship.

During the afternoon Wally Johnson (the Tourist Class Chief Steward) and I went for a walk ashore where we saw a man riding around a pool on the back of a shark. We returned to the ship for the inevitable maiden voyage reception for the local press and travel agents, and I noticed how Sir Colin Anderson now referred to our superstructure as being made of 'alum**inum**' – until Honolulu it had always been 'alum**inium**'.

Some Canadian officials now came on board for the passage to Vancouver, and one of these was Matt Black, a senior Immigration Officer who had served in the Canadian army and been stationed in Brighton, Sussex, at the same time as I was there. We had not met back then, but this bit of common ground made for a friendship that was to last for many years. These contacts with various government officials did more good for our ships than our Owners ever realised.

We reached Victoria early in the morning on 2nd February and embarked a large team of Canadian Customs, Health and Immigration officials who 'processed' all the passengers during the journey to our berth at the Canadian Pacific pier at Vancouver. As we steamed under the Lion's Gate Bridge we were greeted by a fleet of small boats and fire tugs giving us an impressive water display. Perhaps the most impressive of all our maiden voyage welcomes was given at Vancouver where the top concourse of the pier was lined with hundreds of schoolgirls singing 'Tie me Kangaroo Down, Sport' and other appropriate songs for a ship arriving from Australia and having amongst our passengers Rolf Harris, the (now disgraced) entertainer who was travelling to start a contract with a Vancouver night club.

Departure from Vancouver might have been a disaster because of the over-enthusiasm of the Royal Canadian Air Force. We sailed at 11.00pm and as we approached the Narrows and the Lion's Gate Bridge an RCAF plane flew low overhead, illuminating the scene with parachute flares. Most impressive, but Edgecombe knew how dangerous it would be if these flares landed on the ship still burning. Frantic wireless messages and signals stopped the display, the organisers of which could not have thought out the possibly serious consequences.

An aerial display had also been organised by a Department Store in San Francisco, but this time the arrangements were discussed prior to the event. It was proposed that as we steamed in San Francisco Bay towards our berth at Pier 35, a helicopter would drop rose petals onto the ship. Sir Colin, Edgecombe and the Chief Officer had their doubts about the wisdom of this as they thought rose petals might get washed into the scuppers and block them. Therefore they spoke to our San Francisco office from Vancouver and requested that our manager thank the store and explain why rose petals were not acceptable. The store understood the problem, but without further consultation arranged their own solution. As we passed Alcatraz and turned to approach the pier the helicopter appeared, flew low over the ship and began to disgorge hundreds of daffodils which came hurtling through the sky, stem downwards! Those on the open decks scuttled like villagers at a country fête when the thunderstorm breaks.

Apart from the rain of daffodils, our San Francisco reception followed a pattern with which we were becoming familiar: fire boats shooting jets of water into the air; hundreds of small craft crowding round us and bands on the quayside; at least one large cocktail party and often a dinner; and hundreds with tickets for our guided tour. We had to be careful to keep the occupied cabins locked and to remove everything pocketable from the show cabins and public rooms. For a few months an *Oriana* ash tray was a status symbol. These specially designed ash trays became so coveted that after the first voyage they were put on sale in the ship's shop. I overhead a tour conductor telling his group of passengers who had embarked at Vancouver that they were not to take more than one ash tray per person – beyond that he said they would be stealing!

There was also the inevitable presentation from the Port Authority, City Fathers, Chamber of Commerce and similar bodies. These usually took the form of a plaque or a framed parchment – although not always. Los Angeles gave us an attractive model of an oil rig and New Zealand a symbolic carving. The Captain usually accepted the gift on behalf of the Orient Line and in return gave a small shield bearing our double 'E' badge. Nobody was surprised when Cliff Edgecombe was asked by our San Francisco public relations department if he would accept two California Wood Ducks.

The presentation was to be at noon followed by a few drinks and lunch. The ship's carpenter was instructed to stand by to take the wood ducks and, if possible, have them on display with our other presents by the time the donors had finished their lunch. Imagine the surprise of all concerned, including the San Francisco PR party, when the rather large presentation box was opened and out waddled two live ducks! They were eventually landed at another port and presented to the local zoo but, in the meantime, rumour had it that in the Captain's bath there were three sittings – duck one, duck two and then Cliff.

After San Francisco, one night at sea and then Long Beach, Los Angeles, and another round of social events. We had travelled three quarters of the way round the world and now turned homewards to retrace our route. At New Zealand we called at Wellington instead of Auckland, but otherwise our route was the same as outward-bound. The maiden voyage of *Oriana* was truly remarkable, and as a new ship she behaved almost perfectly. There were a few anxious moments, but despite minor teething troubles we arrived back at Southampton exactly on time. Edgecombe had a trick of usually putting in his arrival signals an estimated time of arrival at fifteen minutes before or after the hour. Therefore if he was a little late or early he could apologise to the pilot or local manager with, "Sorry I was a few minutes early", or "late" as the case may have been. We did have a major delay at Melbourne on the homeward voyage when a high wind kept us pressed hard to Station Pier for 19 hours, but even so we caught up our schedule by the time we reached Suez. In addition, during our stay in Sydney, with nearly 1,000 passengers on board, all the lights went out for an hour, but for those who remembered other maiden voyages, this one was the most trouble-free they could think of.

At Naples a group of managers and superintendents from London joined the ship for the final stage of the voyage. The First Class accommodation was full so they travelled Tourist Class and because the passengers at my table had left the ship at Naples, I entertained the whole group and meals were like a radio quiz programme.

The party included the Captain-designate of *Canberra*, by then nearing completion at Belfast. Cliff Edgecombe and the P&O Captain, Jimmy Wild, were as different as chalk and cheese. With a twinkle in his eye Cliff would pull his colleague's leg with suggestions that Wild might like to start off the snowball dance or lead the conga at our final Gala Dance – these were activities which Captain Wild would never dream of doing, but which Edgecombe revelled in.

One hundred and eleven days, and more than 45,000 miles after our departure, we returned to Southampton, exhausted but proud to have been associated with the maiden voyage of a great lady.

Distant Stranger in the Night

Ah, yes, the distant stranger in the night
May leave no memory but one red light.
But you should see two sisters pass in style
No farther than a fraction of a mile.
The latest, swiftest of a splendid line,
As like as bottles of noble wine.
The houseflag flutters in a flood of light,
Salute of sirens shocking the velvet night.
Here are no strangers. Officer and man.
Are life-long members of a loyal clan.
We crowd the rails, mere passengers and yell,
Tonight, proud owners of the line as well.
Such vessels for a century and more,
Have made the sea as solid as the shore.
Such ships have made all Capricorn a friend,
And Sydney not much further than Southend.
(And may we whisper, every vessel flies
The ancient flag of Private Enterprise).
The lights, the signals die. The sisters part
But something bright long lingers in the heart:
And British breasts may be allowed to swell,
For here's a thing we still do rather well.

A.P.Herbert

(The Himilaya and Chusan passed each other in the Indian Ocean at 9.00 p.m. on Sunday, 4 February 1951)
(from P&O – Orient Reunion Dinner menu, Saturday 28 September 1996 at Christ Church, Oxford)

Chapter 16
Oriana – **Round the World**

The original team stayed together for the second voyage of *Oriana*. Time together in Barrow at the builders, the sea trials, shakedown cruise to Lisbon and maiden voyage had made us a team. This time we were to make a double crossing of the Pacific and then return home through the Panama Canal after our second visit to California – in fact, it made for a shorter voyage by twelve days than the first voyage, which had also included a cruise. For Cliff Edgecombe, 'Ridd' Riddlesdell, Puckle, Peter Hodge the Deputy Purser and me this was to be our last voyage all together. Except for 'Puck' who went to work in our London office, I sailed with each one of the original team again, but we never met all together after voyage two. By now we had the routine of running our 40,000-ton greyhound sewn up, so there were times when we could relax. For everyone at sea the ship came first, which was always accepted, even if the Chief Engineer hated the sight of the Chief Officer or the Crew Cook could not stand the Chef.

Another truism was that we 'worked hard and played hard' – in that order. I gave this advice to Purser Cadets when I later became the P&O Purser Training Officer. Every voyage is hard work and none was as hard as the maiden voyage of *Oriana* when we had little time to relax. Voyage two was better.

A lot of my laughs were provided by my next-door neighbour on 'E' deck aft, Les Hunt, Tourist Class Entertainment Officer. Les had been a Physical Training Instructor in the Army and had a delightful sense of humour – he needed it doing his job, together with an ability to stay awake all day and three quarters of the night. He did have his lapses, such as when he introduced the Hula Hula girls to the passengers as we were entering the harbour at Honolulu....

The open deck had been prepared for the girls' performance and after his introduction Les, who had been up all night, took a vacant chair at the end of the front row of the audience. Five minutes later when the heavens opened and the rain teamed down, everyone, audience and performers, rushed for cover – except for Les who was so fast asleep that even the rain did not wake him. He caught a cold and spent 48 hours in bed while our very attractive Hostess, Jill Doyle, ran the entertainment on her own.

Les lived in a London suburb and often talked about his family, his two children in particular. On one occasion, after he had been entertained by some former passengers to a barbecue in Australia, he decided to introduce this 'al fresco' cooking to London's suburbia – a type of party, in those days, unfamiliar to most English people. Les told his children to hurry back from school that day because there was going to be a surprise for them when they got home. During the morning Les and his wife went shopping and bought sausages and chops, although Mrs Hunt was still not sure about what was going to happen. After lunch together in their little semi-detached home, Les went to the end of the garden and started to build a barbecue. At about five o'clock he 'lit up' and, half-an-hour later, the Hunt family were grilling their chops and sausages.

In the suburban environment where they lived everyone was interested in their neighbours' activities, so from next door on both sides, and further down the row of houses, windows opened and neighbours leaned over fences. "Cooking in the garden!" – "Les was always a bit odd." – "Gone to sea on the big ships, he has."

While the cooking was going on, a ring and knock came on the Hunts' front door. Both Les and his wife walked the length of their garden to answer the door (seafarers tend to do this when they are ashore, forgetting that their wife has been answering the door alone all the time they have been away). The children tended the barbecue while the Hunts found their next-door neighbours standing on the doorstep.

"Evening, Les," said the man taking out his wallet, "got trouble with the gas people, have you? Can lend you a fiver for a day or so if it will help."

"My dear," said the woman to Mrs Hunt, "come and use my cooker until they put your gas on again – after all, that is what friends are for!"

The First Class Entertainment Officer was Lord Craigavon, the son of the first Viscount Craigavon who had been the first Prime Minister of Northern Ireland. James Craigavon was a delightful man, but he was a person to be avoided late at night. James (unlike Les Hunt) would not drink until his day's work was done and then, usually around midnight, he would go to a bar where he would purchase a bottle of whisky and ask the barman for the loan of a glass cloth.

He would then wrap the bottle in the cloth and set off towards his cabin with his purchase cradled in his arms like a tiny baby. Any ship's officer or friendly passenger he encountered en route was invited to join him 'for a nightcap', and he usually gathered about three or four 'victims'. Arriving at his cabin, the guests would be asked to sit down while James closed the door and positioned his own chair right in front of it, thus preventing escape before the bottle was empty. This whisky was always offered with warm water and sometimes chocolate creams – not ot the most palatable nightcap in the tropics.

James and Les complemented one another splendidly – the Peer of the Realm in the First Class and the ex-Physical Training Instructor in the Tourist Class. They went ashore together in ports abroad, James to buy an Air Mail copy of the London *Times*, Les to buy the latest edition of *Playboy*.

Entertainment Officers often have to make announcements over the ship's broadcast system or from a microphone on the bandstand, but neither James nor Les were very good at this. Les usually got names wrong, like calling a child at the children's party named Penelope, 'Penny Lope'. James was just forgetful – one of his classics was to wish all the passengers a Happy Christmas… at midnight on New Year's Eve. Cliff Edgecombe's aside, "New Year, you fool", carried into the microphone and through the speakers, making the incident even more amusing.

The wrong words coming through the speakers was a rare occurrence and therefore when it happened the event became a

"Cradled in his arms like a tiny baby"

talking point for all on board. The Radio Officers usually received the blame, and in most cases it was their fault. The night before Fremantle I decided to make a personal appeal to the Tourist Class passengers to present themselves early to the Australian officials who would board in Gage Roads the next morning. I arranged to broadcast to the Dining Room during dinner and my first words were, "Good evening, ladies and gentlemen. I apologise for interrupting your dinner but what I have to say is important...." Somehow or another in the Radio Office, where all the speaker controls are located, I got switched through to the entire ship. The Radio Officer on duty soon realised his error and rectified it, so that throughout the ship came, "Good evening, ladies and gentlemen. I apologise..." and then except in the Tourist Class Dining Room, there was silence.

It was at church services that the most embarrassing broadcasting blunders occurred. By tradition, the Sunday morning service was taken by either the Captain or the Staff Commander, but often another senior officer would be required to stand in. One Sunday Cliff Edgecombe instructed the First Officer to take the Tourist Class service, but this would be the First Officer's first experience of this job so he spent several hours rehearsing before I met him outside the Ballroom where his congregation was assembled. As he stepped up to the lectern, arranged his books before him and looked up, I saw him open his mouth to announce the first hymn, when through the loudspeakers came the voice of the Captain saying, "We will commence our service with hymn number four, New Every Morning is the Love."

The poor First Officer was dumbfounded and tried to mime. The pianist used his initiative and came in with the introduction at the same moment as his counterpart in the First Class Ballroom. I quietly, but quickly, slid off to the nearest telephone to tell the Radio Officer how they had completely deflated what little confidence the First Officer had worked up before his ordeal. By the end of the hymn things were normal and the service was a great success.

On another occasion I was reading a lesson during church when suddenly through the loudspeakers came, "That you, Iris? How are yer?"

"Iris here – you phoning from the boat? Didn't think you could do that."

"Oh yes, it's easy – Bill has gone to the church service so I thought I would ring and wish you a Happy Birthday."

"Thanks, luv – the kids are taking us over to their place for a barbecue – it's a beaut day – what's it like with you?"

"Just great, saw Ball's Pyramid yesterday and Hayman Island. Met the Captain last night, and the Purser; everyone's very friendly – do you know what the Captain said to Bill while I was dancing with the Purser – you never believe it but it seems...."

And that was that. Throughout the interruption I was trying valiantly to tell the congregation what Paul said on Mars Hill, and we never did find out what the Captain said to Bill.

Entertaining passengers was an important part of our job as Senior Officers. The weight of this duty fell on the Captain, Staff Commander and, in *Oriana*, the two Pursers. During most evenings at sea at least one of us would have a group in our cabin for pre-dinner drinks. The Captain had the largest cabin and Cliff Edgecombe, unlike some Captains, was very conscientious about his entertaining obligations. For most passengers an invitation to the Captain's cabin was considered an honour. However, on the second voyage of *Oriana*, Puckle received an unusual complaint from a lady from New York whom our shore office had asked us to look after. Due to the letter we had received, Cliff Edgecombe had asked the Hostess to include the lady in one of his cabin parties. In due course an invitation was sent requesting, "The pleasure of her company for cocktails in Captain Clifford Edgecombe's cabin."

On receipt of the invitation, Mrs New York came hotfoot to the Purser's Office and demanded to see Puckle. Puckle and I shared the same office, with Peter Hodge the Deputy Purser behind a screen in the corner. Clare Yates, a Woman Assistant Purser, showed the lady into the office and Puck invited her to sit down in front of his desk.

"What's the big idea?" asked the lady from the Bronx.

"I don't understand," answered Puck, who never did take kindly to brassy women passengers.

"This Captain of yours – wants to get me into his cabin."

"Oh yes, for drinks this evening."

"Don't give me that, boy. I know about ship's officers. Even sends me a card – what does this guy think I am – some sort of broad? I know the guys in your West Coast office – wait till I tell them about this."

"But Madam," interrupted Puck, "that's just why the Captain wants to meet you and 14 other passengers this evening."

"Who do you think you're kidding, boyo?" went on the woman. "Fourteen others, you say. You don't think I'm going to fall for that sort of stuff?"

Peter and I could no longer contain ourselves and quickly left, leaving Puckle stuttering out explanations, none of which was acceptable. Once outside we collapsed in a fit of laughter which only increased when after about five minutes a furious Puck appeared. The lady did not attend the party and probably thinks to this day that the Captain of *Oriana* in 1961 had singled her out for seduction.

Homeward-bound on voyage two we called at Acapulco before sailing on to Balboa for our Panama Canal passage which proceeded without a hitch. The extreme breadth of *Oriana* was 100 feet which meant that we fitted into the locks with only five feet to spare on either side. Some passengers travelled overland from Balboa to Cristobal while the ship sailed through the canal, but for those who remained on board we served a magnificent buffet lunch on deck.

The Panama Canal is remarkably free from flies, unlike the Suez Canal where a meal on deck would be out of the question. After Cristobal we had one day at sea and then called at Kingston, Jamaica, where we were the largest ship the pilot had ever seen – so much so that he flatly refused to take us out of the harbour at midnight, our advertised time of sailing. He made this announcement as soon as he came on board at 6.30am, but we all

Panama Canal

wondered whether he really was unwilling to move us in the dark, or if perhaps he was in league with the local hoteliers and night club owners who certainly benefitted from our sailing being delayed until daylight at 5.00am the next day.

We only had a few hours in Bermuda where there was no crew leave because only one tender served the ship which had to anchor some distance away from the wharf at Hamilton. Then we made a quick dash across the Atlantic with the clock being advanced every night so that we were losing sleep, before calling at Le Havre from 3.00pm until midnight, followed by our arrival in Southampton early the next morning. No wonder our wives said that we looked tired and accused us of having returned from 'one long party'. Perhaps they were right – a real team of professionals had knit together to produce a highly successful ship: sailors, engineers, hoteliers, communicators, entertainers and medics. *Oriana* was a 'city in the sea', and although larger ships sailed across the Atlantic, nothing the size of *Oriana* went away for three or four months, embarking and disembarking passengers as she circumnavigated the world. Cliff Edgecombe was our leader, and perhaps our greatest strength was that we received little or no interference from our managers and superintendents in London.

The next voyage we made was a single trip to Sydney and back using the Suez Canal both ways, making a round voyage of 51 days. I was Purser and my job in the Tourist Class was taken over by Alan Arkieson who had sailed with me in the past as my Deputy. The Deputy Purser was Mike Whicker, an old shipmate from *Otranto* days. In all I made eleven voyages in *Oriana* and never ceased to be proud of her (although these were not consecutive voyages, as after voyage four I was transferred to *Orion* to manage the first group of Goanese catering staff to sail in an Orient Liner).

For more than 100 years the Peninsular and Oriental Steam Navigation Company had employed Indians in their ships. On deck there were Lascars from the Malabar Coast, chiefly Hindu; in the Engine Room men from the north from what is now Pakistan, chiefly Muslim; and in the Pursers' Department Goanese from the former Portuguese colony of Goa, chiefly Roman Catholic. In 1962

Oriana in dry dock

the former Orient Line ships were employing about 2,000 Stewards and junior kitchen staff, and the National Union of Seamen admitted that they could not supply sufficient trained men to fill the vacancies. Therefore it was agreed that in the Orient ships a proportion of the catering staff would be Indian, although the Deck and Engine Room remained British.

The Goanese who joined *Orion* in Tilbury in March 1962 were all from the P&O *Strathnaver*, having just returned from Australia on her last voyage before being withdrawn from service. The new men settled in quickly and after 48 hours behaved as if they had been in the ship all their working lives. After all, they were basically seamen and to them one ship was much the same as another. We needed a few more of them to do the same amount of work as the Europeans had done, but at least they were there, and they were loyal. The Goans had two speeds – Dead Slow and Stop. Those who were not called Perera were called Rodrigues, Fernandes or Gomez – all very confusing, but we soon got to know one another.

I had a Steward of my own who looked after my cabin and served the passengers at my table in the restaurant. He came to me with that first group and stayed with me, moving from ship to ship, for nearly ten years. His name was Benedict Fernandes, known to hundreds of P&O and Orient passengers as 'Benny'. Benny gave more loyalty to me than I ever deserved – he repaired my clothes, packed and unpacked every time we changed ships, and prepared a list of replacements required which he presented to my wife at the end of each voyage. If we were arriving in port early in the morning, he would appear with a tray of tea whatever the hour; likewise he would hang around at night until I was ready for bed. On one occasion, while I was at home during a turnaround in Southampton, one of the Shore Superintendents used my cabin and my gin to entertain a friend. Benny went in and found them, and was so alarmed that he returned after they had gone and spent the night asleep on the deck in front of my cocktail cabinet, just in case they came back.

There was one difficulty with the Goanese, in that it was as hard to stop the average Steward doing something you asked for as it was to get him out of his routine to do it. One morning I felt a little 'hung over' and asked at about ten o'clock for a cup of black coffee; after that I was given a cup of black coffee every morning. The waiters also had to be restrained from serving too much food, and nobody was ever given just one egg with their bacon, however hard they tried to stop two being presented. If the Chef and Head Waiter did not watch the servery like hawks, everybody would get two steaks. It wasn't a question of stealing, it was just that each man wanted to look after 'his' passengers.

Having the first Goanese Pursers' Department in an Orient Liner was a challenge, but that particular outward voyage of *Orion* was a bit dull. We were sailing right through to Wellington and all our passengers were migrants for either Australia or New Zealand. Apart from the fact that *Orion* was a much better appointed ship, it was *Otranto* all over again, including school organised for the children. There was one bright spot when, at the end of the passengers' sports prize-giving, a man stood up and announced that on behalf of a very exclusive club of which he was a founder member, he wished to make a presentation to the Purser.

The Captain, Ronald J. Brittain, and I looked at one another and then we both looked at the Entertainments Officer who gave a surreptitious shrug of his shoulders. However, by then the passenger had taken over the meeting and was announcing, "We have been in this ship for more than three weeks and from my observations, there is one man here this afternoon who has never got it right."

"Oh Lord," I thought "what is coming next?"

"This man is the Purser and I understand so well that whatever he does, the Purser of a ship like this will always be in the Doghouse. Therefore, on behalf of the International Doghouse Club of Godalming, Surrey, England, I hereby present our Purser with this certificate and our Club tie."

The passenger then presented me with a document which certifies that I have the ability, "…to do the Wrong Thing at both the right and wrong times …". A round of applause and laughter greeted this and I breathed again.

Verse Competition

The following poem was written by Sir Alan Herbert on board the Orient Liner Oronsay.

Passengers are invited to write a reply in verse and place it in a box which is outside the Purser's Office before Noon tomorrow.
A prize will be awarded.

> Nature, answer, if you can,
> Questions vital to a man.
> Gaining years, we lose our hair:
> That, perhaps, is only fair,
> But when it declines to stop
> Where it's wanted, on the top,
> Must it blossom, more and more,
> Where it's nothing but a bore?
> Though that arid 'patch' appears
> Jungles crawl about the ears:
> Age does not a thing to check
> Horrid hairs upon the neck;
> Nature stubbornly supplies
> Eyebrows of a silly size;
> Some, with heads like Everest,
> Grow a forest on the chest.
> Why is Grandpa so thin
> On the crown, but not the chin?
> Nature, one reply we crave:
> Why do bald men have to shave?

Reply –

Chapter 17
Orion to Tahiti and Christmas on *Otranto*

O*rion* was a 'fun' ship, although by this time her days were numbered. I had made two voyages in her and then after my third she was withdrawn from service, although she did serve for a short while as a floating hotel in Hamburg during an International Festival. *Orion* was unique in the post-war Orient fleet, larger than *Otranto* and *Orontes*, but smaller than *Orcades* and her sisters.

Orion's true sister was *Orcades*, who had been sunk off Cape Town in 1942. Even though she survived for 28 years, *Orion* was modern to the end. Fortunately some of her fittings, lights and mirrors in particular, were removed before she was broken up and incorporated in an office in Sydney. In comparison with the older ships, *Orion* was easy to run and her speed and size made life in her less hectic and more comfortable than the other ships in the fleet. She also behaved well in bad weather, and thankfully it was in this ship that I experienced a gale during which the sea was snow-white on passage from Hobart to Melbourne, crossing the Bass Strait. The rigging supporting our one mast was singing, or rather screaming, yet because we were heading straight into the gale, there was hardly any movement on the ship.

Orion was the last ship to 'die' wearing Orient colours, with green boot topping, corn hull and white upperworks. She never flew the P&O house flag, although she was a part of the P&O – Orient fleet for a short while. In many ways she was the last of a line.

Orion was a happy ship, which is a result of those who sail in her. During her lifetime she had her adventures, some unfortunate and others remembered with pride. This was very much Australia's ship, built for the trade. She began her association from the start by being launched at Barrow-in-Furness by wireless from Brisbane, where the Duke of Gloucester pressed a button releasing the ship literally on the other side of the world. Soon after the start of her first voyage, off the Portuguese coast, she answered a distress call from the White Star Liner *Doric* which had been in a collision in thick fog and from which 475 passengers and 25 Stewards with 17 Stewardesses were transferred. A plaque in one of *Orion*'s lounges commemorated the event.

Throughout the Second World War *Orion* served as a troop transport and as such steamed over 380,000 miles and carried 175,000 troops, civilians and prisoners-of-war. In September 1941, whilst in convoy, the steering gear of the escorting *HMS Revenge* jammed and *Orion* collided with the battleship. The quick thinking of Ralph Underwood, the officer of the watch in *Orion*, ensured that the merchant ship took the blow on her bow, otherwise much more serious damage might have resulted.

When the United States of America entered the war, transatlantic voyages were made with more than 7,000 American troops aboard. A system was evolved whereby one third of the troops were in their hammocks sleeping, one third was inside the ship taking meals and sitting about, while another one third was exercising on deck. This was fine in theory until they encountered North Atlantic gales when the third in bed wouldn't get up and the third on deck was seeking shelter, and nobody felt like eating. Three days after leaving Halifax, Nova Scotia, a crew member remembers seeing a large Negro opening a door which led onto an open deck exclaiming, "Holy Jesus – sunshine!" For 72 hours he hadn't seen the light of day.

It took a little while for the crew to get used to ferrying American troops. Once the United States entered the war, all the troopships became 'dry' – until then there had been 'wet' canteens for troops. This restriction did not apply to the crew whose friendship therefore became much sought after. Nevertheless, the American way of life was refreshingly different – where would one hear a British padre walk into a crowded troop deck and shout, "Now, will all you men shooting craps hand your stakes to an honest man and listen to the Holy Word of God."

War service over, *Orion* returned to the Australian passenger trade in 1947. Her Captain was Commodore of the Orient fleet, Sir Arthur Baxter, whose son John served with me as an Assistant Purser for a few voyages. Sir Arthur was the last of the Orient Line Captains to be knighted, in his case for distinguished war service.

For most of my time in *Orion* my Captain was Eric Harris, a delightful Welshman with a wonderful sense of humour who gave the impression of always being vague, even though he was in fact more alert than most men. 'Ricky' Harris and I had sailed together in *Otranto* where he had been Staff Commander. We were together for a well-remembered Christmas when a Roman Catholic priest, having made arrangements for a Midnight Mass on Christmas Eve, returned to my office to ask, "Will you be letting the boys in your crew come to my Mass?"

"Oh dear, Father," I answered, knowing our *Otranto* cowboys, "I don't think they will be in the right condition to enter passenger accommodation at that time of night on Christmas Eve, but I will let it be known that you are celebrating and that they may attend; but I will insist on them being in uniform and returning to Crew Quarters as soon as you have finished."

"Leave it to me, Purser," said the priest, "I'll look after the boys – they'll be no trouble."

Ricky Harris and I decided to watch the crew arrive at the room where the Mass was to be held. Only a few turned up and they were all properly dressed. One or two did trip over the step as they entered the small lounge which had been arranged as a chapel. Having seen our 'warriors' into the service, we went to my cabin for a drink, intending to return to see the boys leave after Mass. We returned at the right time, said "Good Night" to our crew and "Merry Christmas" to everybody. The priest was clearing up and we asked, "Everything all right, Father?"

"Fine, just fine, but there's just one thing. Being Christmas and your boys being here too, I decided not to take a collection. However, halfway through the Mass, one of your Stewards got up, took a collection and walked out of the door – and I haven't seen him since!"

* * *

Thinking of Christmas, celebrating it on the *Otranto* in 1954 was particularly memorable because we spent the whole day at anchor in the Bitter lakes because a ship ahead of us had swung across and blocked the Suez Canal. We did not clear Suez until late afternoon on Boxing Day and had all the Christmas fare garbage around the galley and on the forward well deck for more than 24 hours.

The first few hours of Christmas morning were dominated by church services. In 1953 in the *Orcades* a group of female officers persuaded the Captain to have a nine-lesson carol service, and this became a tradition throughout the Orient Line. The first lesson was read by a deck boy or bell boy and the final lesson, the Gospel for the day, was read by the Captain. The printer produced a souvenir outline of the service, the actual carols being typed and then duplicated onto the outline by a Woman Assistant Purser who did a good job except that after the fifth lesson we were invited to sing *Away in a Manager.*

The Captain's service was usually held at about 10.45 on Christmas morning or even earlier so that as soon as it was over the ballroom or dance space could be cleared and tables brought up for the Chef's buffet. This buffet was a culmination of weeks of preparation and was a truly magnificent exhibition of Christmas fare.

Between them the Chef, baker and larder cook created set pieces depicting Nativity scenes, Father Christmas and reindeer; there were chocolate logs, an orchestra of angels, decorated hams, salmon and scores of other pieces. The work of these craftsmen would have been worthy of a prize in the *salon culinaire* at Hotelolympia or any other international exhibition,

Everything was there to be eaten, but not until the passengers had had a chance to take photographs, and although this was the Chef's finest hour many of them were remarkably modest. I can recall one Chef who was too shy to meet the passengers and cleared off as soon as he had arranged the display. I can also think of one who took all the credit, so much so that the baker and the larder cook cleared off. I have seen set pieces in buffet displays at many of the worlds best hotels but I have never seen one better than an Orient Line Christmas buffet.

On one occasion in the *Orontes* I decided to go to the main bar after the carol service to check with the barman about something or other. The ship's donkeyman was standing outside with a pint of beer as I went in, closing the bottom half of the stable-type door behind me. The donkeyman wished me a "Merry Christmas" and carried on drinking his beer.

A minute or two later the engine room storekeeper turned up. These two, donkeyman and storekeeper, never saw eye to eye over anything and their really quite friendly animosity was a source of amusement to those of us who had sailed with the pair for some time.

"Happy Christmas, Stores," says the donkeyman.

"What do you mean, Happy Christmas?" says the storekeeper. "It's not your birthday, it's Jesus's."

"Jesus?" says the donkeyman. "You wouldn't know who Jesus is. I've a pound that says you don't even know the Lord's Prayer."

The storekeeper was quick to respond. "I have a pound right here that says I do. Give your's to the Purser. He can hold the stakes."

As soon as I had the two notes in my hand the storekeeper started: "The Lord is my shepherd, I shall not want ..."

The donkeyman immediately interrupted. "Give him the money, Purser, I never knew 'e knew it!"

From 11.15 the crew were given their Christmas dinner in the Tourist-class dining-room. The servery was managed by officers of the Purser's Department and during the meal the Captain and senior officers wandered around the tables chatting to the men. Those serving included the female officers of the ship and while some ratings might have thought the Deputy Purser a little patronising serving slices of turkey, when it came to a pretty woman Assistant Purser offering stuffing, it was a different matter.

At noon the Captain entertained all the off-duty officers in his cabin. After this the Purser took the Captain to the scene of the buffet and a magisterial inspection took place at which all the appropriate things were said to the Chef and his staff. This progress was witnessed by the passengers and the cameras clicked throughout, until finally the Captain left to visit the bridge – after all we were an ocean liner and noon sights had to be taken.

The Purser declared to buffet open. The important thing at this stage was to make sure that the major set pieces were not broken up as they had to go on display in the Tourist-class before dinner. They were broken up and eaten on Boxing day.

There is no time for sleep during the afternoon of Christmas Day as at three o'clock perhaps the most important event of the day takes place – the children's party. Ideally Christmas should fall two or three weeks into a voyage. This gives the Children's Hostess time to rehearse her children in some sort of Christmas presentation, usually a Nativity play. Later in the afternoon Father Christmas appears often in a sleigh drawn by deck boys disguised as reindeer. One ship had an elephant provided by the deck officers – front legs the First Officer, back legs the Junior Second and seated on top with silk pyjama trousers, a turban and cocoa-treated torso, the Third Officer. Father Christmas was often an AB or Quarter-Master and more than once he appeared with perhaps a little too much of the Christmas spirit inside him; much to the consternation of the Children's Hostess who was assured by the bosun, "He'll be alright, miss, it's not proper for him to be real sober."

Father Christmas appears at a children's party

Every child got a present which, of course, they unwrapped as soon as Father Christmas had presented it. Within minutes the deck was covered with wrapping paper and toy cars, tanks and fire-engines were charging all over the place. Babies started to cry, others shrieked with joy, but all this was not the end. Next came a tea party, often on deck with decorated tables, balloons, funny hats and crackers. There were piles of food, jellies, ice cream, weird coloured drinks and finally a gigantic Christmas cake which one year the baker laced with rum so that all the children slept like logs afterwards.

The next item on the programme for a, by now, pretty exhausted Purser was a visit to the Goanese mess. Goanese joined the Orient Line after the merger with P&O and the *Orion* had the first group on board for Christmas 1962. Traditionally the Goanese entertained the Captain and his officers at a time agreed by the Captain; in my experience this was around 6pm. The Goanese mess was decorated and the principal feature was an altar upon which there was a plate for alms. I never did find out whether the money we put in the plate went to charity or paid for our drinks.

By this time we were in a mess kit having had a quick shower and changed after the children's party. Our next engagement was to act as hosts at a cocktail party for all First-class passengers; 6.30 for first sitting, a short break and then 7.30 for second sitting guests. During the short break we would adjourn to the staff commander's or Chief Engineer's room for a quiet drink. I cannot think why. Twenty minutes rest would have been more appropriate.

Orlando Sails Home.
(Chapter 6)

Cover of a children's menu

197

Then came Christmas dinner. This was a real feast in the First-class and not much different in the Tourist-class. The restaurants were decorated and some of the art work done on mirrors by the stewards was very professional. Passengers were provided with crackers, streamers and paper balls to throw from table to table – and land up in the soup!

The evening entertainment was a gala dance and in the interval the ship's choir sang carols. I cannot pretend that this performance was very melodic but it was sincere as those taking part wanted to have the passengers join with them in celebrating Christmas away from home. The choir, which sang in both the Tourist-class and First-class, processed to the centre on the dance floor, led by a nursing sister with her cape reversed to show the red lining on the outside, and carrying a candle.

The ladies in the procession, women officers, stewardesses, hairdressers and telephonist, sang the first verse of *Once in Royal David's City* and then the whole choir of about 40 came in and formed up to sing six or eight carols, the words of which were distributed to passengers so that they could join in. Our finale was *Ding-Dong Merrily on High* to which most of the Orient Line people sang "Glori – ori – ori – ori – Oriana"!

A week after Christmas comes New Year and once again something special had to be done but a similar catering effort was not expected. A gala dance was arranged and at midnight 16 bells were struck on a bell rigged in the ballroom or dance space. The first eight bells, ringing out the Old Year, were struck by the oldest crew member, usually a quartermaster. The second eight bells, ringing in the New Year, were struck by the youngest crew member, usually a deck or catering boy.

Just before the first bell ringing Old father Time shuffled across the floor wearing a long beard and carrying an hourglass and a scythe and stopped by the bell. Just after the second bell ringing a pretty young girl in a bikini burst into the ballroom with a shriek of joy and headed for Old Father Time and chased him away. The Captain wished everyone a "Happy New Year". We sang *Auld Lang Syne*. Then anyone with any sense went to bed. Few of us had any sense.

This prompts recollection of another Santa-themed event. On July 25, 1975, in mid-summer, I was Hotel Manager in the *Royal Viking Sea*. At 0800, after a night of daylight, we were almost stopped in latitude 80°44' north. The pack ice was very close. It was the sort of land-fall, or icefall, a cruise liner Captain dreams of – clear sky, no wind. We lowered a boat and collected a piece of ice which we displayed in the restaurant and upon which we laid some Aquavit water bottles to chill for passenger consumption, Aquavit which has crossed the equator the previous year.

Soon after 0900 we moved off southwards and by 1600 we were off Ny Alesund. Each passenger had been given a stamped postcard by the Royal Viking Line and on arrival we sent a boat crew ashore to the Post Office at this remote place which is inhabited only by a few research scientists. The cards were posted, the Norwegian postmaster given a bottle of Scotch whisky and the shore party returned to their boat for the trip back to the ship.

However, during their walk from the landing stage to the Post Office, which was about a mile, the boat had made a return trip to the anchorage and circled the ship with a solitary passenger on board. Santa Claus.

The Captain saw the launch approaching and identified the passenger. He quickly broadcast to all on board the *Royal Viking Sea* and the whole ship's company, passengers and crew, lined the rails and cheered as Santa waved a welcome to his Arctic home before making off again for the shore, where he rounded a headland and was seen no more.

I was part of the shore party which walked to the hut which served as a Post Office. I did not see Santa circle the ship or hear him cry out his welcome to the arctic, but I did hear that his voice sounded just like that of the ship's entertainment officer.

* * *

Returning to *Orion*, the team of senior officers in 1962-63 was so united that it would have been difficult for us not to have made a success of our voyages. Beside 'Ricky' Harris as our Captain, there was John Field (Staff Commander), Matthew Paterson (Chief Engineer) and Wally Johnson (Chief Steward). Amongst other interesting places we took our 24,000-ton yacht to Tahiti, the first time an Orient Liner had visited, and we tied up at the wharf at Papeete which was different from the present modern installation. The bollards to which our mooring lines were attached were old cannon which had been set in concrete, and one such bollard was inside the doorway of our Agent's office. That, at least, ensured the office remained open throughout our two-day stay!

The Agent was a Monsieur Poroi, who was also the Mayor and our provedore. 'Ricky' complained to him about the price of fresh water and this charming Frenchman then called on me saying, "Your Capitaine asks me to see the man who supplies the fresh water – 'e says I must tell to this man that he charges too much. 'Ow can I do this? I am the man who supplies the fresh water. Tonight everyone in Papeete has been told not to use water so that it can all come to you." Even so, we never did get all the water we needed, probably because the only supply for us came through a garden hose.

Having persuaded me that he could not charge less for his precious water, M. Poroi then explained other arrangements that he had made for our stay. *Quinn's Bar*, which was right at the foot of our gangway, was to remain open throughout our stay. The police would arrest all drunks and keep them in jail until just before we sailed, when they would be returned uncharged at no cost to the Orient Line.

I began to appreciate how practical these people were. Then we discussed the arrangements for an official lunch to be held on board later in the day, where M Poroi would make a speech and he hoped that our Captain would do the same. He had prepared the seating plan which showed that I was to sit next to the wife of the Minister for Tourism.

"Can she speak English?" I asked.

"No, I don't think so," he replied. "You can use your hands – underneath the table – she will understand, and then maybe she will take you to her home this afternoon. Her husband is in Paris!" She didn't, but that evening we were entertained at a native feast where the dancers moved their hips faster than I have ever seen before or since. They were not gyrating like the Hula dancers in Hawaii, but were vibrating like a pneumatic drill.

The cruise was a great success and on our return to Sydney early one Sunday morning we woke up the whole town by steaming down the harbour and under the bridge, making a quite unnecessary noise with our whistle. Round our stern we had a massive grass skirt made from rope! After the passengers disembarked the ship was dead, and so 90% of the Ship's Company went to bed for 24 hours.

At Christmas we were cruising again, this time to New Zealand, and a call at Port Chalmers for Dunedin was another first for most of us. During the morning of our arrival we were taken to the Otago Harbour Board where we were seated round an impressive board room table and had to listen to some boring speeches about the commercial activity of the port and Otago in general. 'Ricky' Harris was presented with a picture of the harbour, which he received on behalf of the ship, and then we thought that at last the meeting was going to break up. No such luck – another New Zealand Scot stood up and told us how much wool passed through Port Chalmers each year. I was seated between Matt Paterson and John Field, when Matt whispered to me, "Do we no get a drink here? They're all Scots; it's about time we had a tot!"

"Don't worry, Matt," I muttered. "This can't go on much longer."

Just then there was a grinding of machinery when a booming bell began to strike midday from a clock above the building. The Chairman thumped the table (even though his colleague was still rattling on about wool export figures) and announced, "It's noon!" He walked over to a wall cupboard, produced glasses, whisky and water, and we settled down to a cosy chat about everything except shipping, port facilities and exports.

After Dunedin we called at Lyttelton, the port for Christchurch. During our stay here I flew to Mount Cook in a DC3 piloted by Geoff Williams, a fascinating New Zealand aviator. I was the official escort for a passenger excursion and my place in the aircraft was 'up front' in the pilot's cockpit, where I was allotted the navigator's position, meaning that I sat on a tiny seat looking sideways at nothing. However, once we were airborne I was transferred to the co-pilot's seat while he went back to the passenger cabin to 'chat up' our excursionists. As we approached Mount Cook, we called up the local landing control, which was the barman at the Tourist Hotel, who had a radio set amongst the bottles and glasses behind the bar. Approaching aircraft called up the hotel and the barman, cocktail shaker in one hand, microphone in the other, looked out of his picture window and advised, "Runway clear," or otherwise.

We received our clearance and began to descend. As we approached, Geoff Williams opened the throttles and we climbed high again. At the same time he called the barman, saying, "What do you mean – runway clear? Get someone to chase the sheep off!" This was a safe, well-run airline. Later whilst cruising to Central America, I flew to Copan to visit a Mayan temple in a DC3 when they didn't even bother to close the door!

There was usually an opportunity for at least one Ship's Officer to accompany each excursion which had been arranged for passengers visiting the shore. A place on longer trips, sometimes with a night ashore, was much sought after. The shorter half-day tours were not always so interesting, and junior officers were usually sent on these to write a report and gain experience. The report was a useful indication of how efficient the tour operators were, and also showed the ability of the officer concerned at observing and reporting. During a call at Lisbon, Stan Rawdon (then an Assistant Purser) was sent on a Night Club tour. The following morning he was asked for his written report. A very washed out looking Stan asked, "Report on what?"

"The shore excursion you went on last night," he was told.

"What shore excursion?"

"Lisbon Night Life. Here – read the brochure."

Stan took the brochure which gave a description of where he had been and remarked, "So, that's where I was. I don't remember much about it."

Another Assistant Purser told him. "You had better think hard; the Purser is asking for an account of the tour."

Stan sat down at a typewriter and made a word-for-word copy of the leaflet. "The coaches leave the ship's side at 9.00pm, returning on board at 2.00am." The whole description with double spacing filled his sheet of paper. The Purser, who never read shore excursion pamphlets, congratulated Stan on his report. Stan doesn't remember a thing about the evening to this day!

Senior officers were usually invited ashore by the Manager of the local agency. The Lisbon Agent told an amusing story about a wartime British Consul in Lisbon who received an instruction from London to find a clean brothel for British seamen. It seems that the authorities in the United Kingdom were alarmed at the number of sailors returning home with venereal disease whose last port had been Lisbon. The Consul was instructed to select a suitable brothel and arrange for regular inspection of the girls. He was then to tell each Ship Master, when he boarded the ship, where his crew should go to avoid infection. The Consul himself had no experience in these matters so he sent his Portuguese clerk to select somewhere suitable and then to give him the address for passing on to the seamen.

Several weeks later the Consul received a letter of appreciation from London. His selection, the letter said, must have been satisfactory as the number of seamen arriving at British ports from Lisbon with VD was diminishing. The Consul congratulated his clerk and decided that he must take a look at the outside of the house – perhaps he should recommend the 'Madame' for an MBE award, something not unheard of for 'ladies' who protected and entertained troops and seamen during the war. Walking his dog one evening, the Consul decided to stroll down the road where the brothel was situated. He was not amused to see a Royal Coat of Arms beside the door with the inscription, 'By appointment to His Britannic Majesty's Consul'.

At Funchal, Madeira, another Portuguese port, our Agent was the head of an English family who seemed to carry as much, if not more, weight than the island's Governor. One morning, sitting in the Captain's cabin shortly after our arrival, this agent said, "I forgot to tell my wife you are here today, but you must come home for lunch."

Funchal, Madeira

This was an invitation we gladly accepted, knowing the excellence of his hospitality from previous visits. As we drove up to the front door of the Agent's residence (I hesitate to call it a house, it was more like a mansion) his wife, looking like a duchess awaiting the Royal Carriage, greeted us from the steps with, "Captain, Purser, so nice to see you. If I had known you were coming, we would have had peacock!"

All agents were not like our host at Funchal. On the other side of the world, in the Marquesas at Nuka Hiva, the Agent, although a European, did not bother to wear shoes to call on the Captain when our ship arrived at 7.00 one May morning. He did, however, appreciate our cold rum, milk and honey. When I conducted the Frenchman to Captain John Wacher, John announced that he intended to call at the Residency and sign the Visitors' Book at 11.00. This request clearly surprised the Agent who told me that this would mean that he would have to go home and change.

I wasn't surprised, as all he was wearing was his crumpled khaki shorts with a shirt. We arranged to meet on shore at 10.45am. John Wacher insisted that I accompany him to the Residency and that we wear our full white uniforms with high collar and long trousers. For such a visit white shorts and uniform shirt would be inappropriate, and he was quite right. I was interested to see what the Agent would wear, but when he met us with his car (an open jeep-type vehicle), he looked the same as when he had left us a couple of hours before.

I whispered, "I thought you said you would have to go home and change?"

"I did," he replied. "I've got my shoes and a hat."

The shoes were an old pair of sandals and the hat was a faded Panama. We set off for the Residency with the Agent driving and the Captain sitting beside him. I had to squat sideways in the back on a box over a rear wheel. On the way we passed several of our passengers who were ashore for a stroll. Arriving at the Residency, we were introduced to a charming French secretary and taken to meet the Resident who did not speak English, and seemed surprised that the Captain of a cruise ship (they didn't get many) would wish to make an official call. From the enquiries he was making through our Agent as interpreter, I gathered he thought that John Wacher wished to make some sort of complaint. However, we left after five minutes of handshakes and smiles.

All he was wearing was . Crumpled khaki shorts and a shirt.

Returning to our transport John announced that he would travel in the back of the jeep. This surprised me, but I knew that Captains can be unpredictable. As soon as we were on the road where our passengers were walking John stood up, and grasping a support which must have been for a canvas roof, he waved and smiled at his passengers as we made a 'Royal' Progress back to the island's landing stage. There we embarked in our launch for return to the ship… and the Agent removed his shoes.

Before the merger of the Orient Line and P&O each Company had its own Agency at Colombo. Those wishing to travel to Australia or Europe had to go to the appropriate Agent to make a booking.

There was a senior P&O ship's officer who owned a parrot. When the officer knew that he was to go on leave when his ship reached the United Kingdom he would leave his parrot in the care of an agent abroad. The parrot talked a lot. One of his favourite phrases was, "Go to hell!" When ashore in the P&O's Colombo agency the parrot is reputed to have called out to visitors as they entered the office, "Go to hell!" The prospective passengers then went straight to the Orient Line agent to book their passage.

Chapter 18
Difficult Passengers

The Captain has only the ocean to fear;
The engines are fun for the Chief Engineer;
But the Purser has people to manage, poor dear.
And heaven help the Purser!!!

A.P. Herbert's appreciation of the Purser is welcome. Most of a Purser's expertise is gained by experience and he never stops learning. The principal requirement is to be able to handle people – not just passengers, but Captains, Bell Boys, Directors, Shipping Clerks, Port Officials and Dockers. A Purser's business is, 'People Business', the ultimate goal being to satisfy passengers, who are people. To achieve this a Purser must manipulate a crew and shore staff – all people. There are Directors, Superintendents and Captains who have strong views on how the ultimate goal is to be achieved, and they too are people. In many ways the Purser is 'piggy-in-the-middle', trying to satisfy the employer, the customers and the staff. I had, and still have, a theory that the most important group to keep happy and give personal attention is the staff. If the staff are content, they will give cheerful, willing service, and thus the customer is satisfied, and so then the employer remains happy.

It is most important to be a good listener and not rise to taunts. When Charles Pinkney was a Staff Commander, a passenger began to harangue him in the middle of a Gala Dance. The man went on for several minutes about the service, the music, the officers, and then he started in on the food, his cabin, the short time the ship stayed in port – in fact, he complained about everything and everyone, the Staff Commander in particular. After a while he stopped, waiting for an answer. "Pinks" remained silent so the man began again with, "Don't you have anything to say about your lousy shipping company?"

After a moment or two he got his reply. "Sir, I am paid an adequate salary to receive your insults which I have noted." A man with less stature and rank than Pinkney could not have answered in such a crushing yet dignified manner.

The behaviour of passengers is quite unpredictable. In a series of cruises, each calling at the same ports at the same times with identical entertainment programmes, the reactions of each group of passengers could be different. On one cruise the fancy dress dance would be a roaring success, whilst on the next when the arrangements were exactly the same, the evening was deemed a flop.

Some people were demanding, expecting continuous personal service; others approached the staff meekly, requesting the simplest of things. Of course, our passengers came from various backgrounds and the fare they had paid did not necessarily reflect their background. A charming old man embarked in *Orcades* where he had bought the sole use of a two-berth suite with private bathroom. Soon after the ship sailed, the Steward called on the old boy and asked, "What time would you like your bath, sir?"

"Friday, if it's all the same to you," he answered.

There were occasions when a passenger had to be spoken to about his or her behaviour. Sometimes a Captain would instruct that a passenger's 'tap' was to be stopped – in other words, the barmen were ordered not to serve this person alcoholic drink. In *Orontes* when I was an Assistant Purser, there was a man of military appearance who managed to get drunk by lunchtime each day. He was harmless, but he annoyed other passengers by attaching himself to groups and regaling them with accounts of his experiences in India. The final straw was when he turned up at the Fancy Dress dance very drunk and dressed as the Captain. Our Captain was Ivan Goldsworthy, a formidable man whose Master's Certificate entitled him to command in sail where he had previously served before joining the Orient Line. (A steamship Master needs an additional certificate before he can command a sailing ship.) I was the Sports

Assistant Purser doing my best to organise the Fancy Dress Parade, which was difficult enough without a drunk going around dressed as the Captain. As soon as he saw our military man and his condition, Ivan called me over and said, "French, get rid of that man and bring him to me tomorrow at noon – sober!"

"Yes, sir!" I blurted out and went to find Thorp, the Purser, with the hope that he would somehow persuade the drunk to go away. Thorp was marvellous, as always – he took the man to another bar, gave him a drink, and told him he was making a fool of himself and that he must go to bed. The man stood up, saluted, and went off like a lamb. The next morning it was my job to take Mr Campbell to the Captain at noon. I was surprised that the man did not call himself Colonel or Major Campbell. On reflection, I realised that the man never mentioned a regiment or rank – most of his banter was, "The natives, you know," and "When the monsoon broke we would…" and how he used to have his 'chota peg' at sunset. To be on the safe side, I arranged to meet him half-an-hour before we were due in the Captain's cabin. Although I feared he might not turn up, he did and so we had time to kill. He had guessed what was going to be said to him and asked quietly if, "We might have a small gin and tonic before we set off to the Bridge". I saw no reason why he should not have a final 'snort'. After all, the Captain had not yet told the man his 'tap' was stopped. While we were drinking, I asked, "Exactly where were you in India, Mr Campbell?"

"North West Frontier, Peshawar, Rawalpindi, Nowshera."

"Good Lord!" I said. "Those are the very places I was at. Did you ever go to Risalpur?"

"Risalpur!" he cried. "Know the place like the back of my hand. Served there with the Third Carabiniers, Prince of Wales Dragoon Guards."

"That's interesting," I continued. "I was a Carabinier. I commanded Three Troop 'B' Squadron when the regiment was at Risalpur."

"My God!" he exclaimed. "Mr French – of course!" He then stood to attention and reported, "Corporal Campbell, 'C' Squadron, Leader's Driver, sir."

I took Campbell to the Captain. As expected, the Captain stopped him being served at the bars, but I managed to buy the Corporal a gin now and then in the seclusion of my cabin. I hope he made a success of life in Australia and eventually forgot the last days of the Raj.

'Ordering' a passenger ashore is the prerogative of the Master. 'Suggesting' to a passenger that they should leave the ship is the job of the Purser or sometimes, for different reasons, the Surgeon. Soon after the start of a long circle Pacific cruise which was to take us from California to Hawaii, Japan, Australia and back again, I realised that we had a problem passenger. The Head Waiter informed me that a lady I shall call Mrs Ella May Dunn was causing him trouble, in that wherever he seated her, the other people at the table asked for her to be transferred elsewhere. Fortunately Ella May Dunn also asked the Head Waiter to move her after each meal.

I had already noticed the lady in the public rooms when she would, uninvited, join a group of drinkers and after a short while take over the conversation, telling those present all about her husbands, Chicago, her clothes, her jewellery and whatever else she could think of. Several people made mild complaints about Ella May and most tried to avoid her, and before we had got as far as Honolulu, it was clear that we had a problem on our hands. The last straw was when she accused an elderly Canadian man, travelling on his own, of stealing her rings. She made this accusation in a loud voice in one of the lounges. The Steward in charge of the room came to tell me and I asked him to try and persuade her to come to my office, which he succeeded in doing. I asked her if she wished to make an official complaint about a fellow passenger.

"Sure," she said. "This guy tried to rape me."

"But I thought you were accusing him of stealing your jewellery."

"Yeah, that too," she answered. "What are you going to do about it?"

I continued. "I think the first thing we must do is make a thorough search of your cabin. Can you tell me exactly what is missing?"

"Five rings, and three of them are engagement rings, each worth a thousand dollars."

"Thank you, Mrs Dunn. I will ask your Steward to look for these. In the meantime, do you mind not mentioning this to anyone?" I asked – a bit late because she had told half the ship already. After she had gone, I rang her cabin Steward who appeared in less than five minutes with five rings. He reported, "Found them behind the dressing table, sir; surprised she hasn't mislaid anything else; leaves her stuff all over the place, never puts anything away."

"Thanks," I said. "Tell me, does she entertain? Has she got any men friends?"

"None that I know of, sir. The night watchman says that a Canadian gentleman on 'B' deck escorted her to her door last night, but he didn't go in. We've all heard what she is saying about being raped. Wishful thinking if you ask me. I've never seen any sign of a visitor having been in her cabin. She keeps a bottle in the wardrobe, but there's never more than one glass used."

Armed with this information, I went to see the Captain, who already knew about her constantly changing tables in the Dining Room. We decided that I should try and persuade her to leave the ship at Honolulu, so I arranged that one of my Woman Assistant Pursers should bring Mrs Dunn to my cabin at noon. I also told the Assistant Purser that she was to stay with us and not leave me alone with the lady. I had no wish to be accused of rape. It is a good thing that I did ask the girl to stay, as it was almost the other way round. My Assistant brought the passenger in, I poured each of us a gin and tonic, and began what I expected to be a difficult interview. "Mrs Dunn." I said.

"Call me Ella May. Ella May from Chicago, have you ever been to Chicago? Now there's a fun place. You should come sometime. We've got...."

"Ella May!" I almost shouted. "Your rings, here they are. They were in your cabin."

This didn't stop her starting up again with, "Oh yeah – the guy brought them back, did he? I guess he got cold feet."

"The gentleman you refer to as 'that guy' did not get 'cold feet', madam. He never had your jewellery nor did he enter your cabin. It seems to me that you are unlikely to enjoy your cruise if you intend

211

to suspect everyone who shows you some consideration. You do not seem to be able to absorb the atmosphere of shipboard life. We are all literally 'in the same boat' and we must get on with one another, the passengers as much as those of us who run the ship. You, Mrs Dunn – sorry, Ella May – have managed to upset a lot of your fellow passengers. We have been at sea a week now and you still haven't found a permanent table in the Dining Room. You have accused a fellow passenger of stealing from you and have made other accusations about this passenger. Ella May, I cannot see you enjoying the next eleven weeks for which you have paid a lot of money. I suggest you leave us at Honolulu tomorrow and have a holiday in the Islands."

I paused, waiting for a reaction. My Assistant was sitting staring at the bubbles in her tonic. For a good 15 seconds silence reigned. Then – like a bull elephant (Ella May was no lightweight) my troublesome passenger leaped up and charged towards me. She threw her arms around me, gave me a big wet kiss and nearly broke my ribs.

"Boy, oh boy!" she cried. "You're the first real man I've met since Wilbur died. That's what I need, a man to tell me what to do. Don't make me get off, I'll be good. Just keep telling me what to do.

My troublesome passenger leapt up and charged towards me

I'll be good – real good." She looked at the girl Assistant Purser and said, "Ain't he just great? Boy, oh boy, a real man. Is he yours, honey?"

The poor Assistant girl didn't know what to do with herself. She had never witnessed a Pursorial interview like this before. However, she felt she had to do something, so she grabbed Ella May's empty glass saying, "Another gin and tonic, Mrs Dunn?"

"Gin and tonic?" cried Ella May "Champagne – let's get some champagne. You are all such lovely people. You are my friends – not those crummy bums up there in the bar."

I managed to quieten Ella May down and we made a pact. She could stay with us as far as Yokohama, but if there were any more complaints about her behaviour, she would leave the ship there. I arranged that she would sit at my table for a week and I would advise her by raising my finger surreptitiously if she was saying the wrong thing. Things went remarkably well, at least on board the ship.

At one port Ella May went on a shore excursion which included dinner with a Malayan Prince at his palace. The Prince presided and asked round the table where his guests came from; each replied quietly until it came to Ella May who stood up, put one foot on her chair and started to sing at the top of her voice, "Chicago! Chicago!" I hope Ella May found a fourth husband or at least someone to tell her when to calm down.

By the mid-sixties we were cruising more and more as regular travellers took to the air. Our great ships were becoming passenger's tramps. Wherever the trade was, there we went – Olympic Games in Tokyo, we were there; Empire and Commonwealth Games in Canada or Australia, we were there. The cruising programme became more ambitious and for us more interesting.

I paid my first visit to South America in *Arcadia*, where we called first at Salvador, arriving a little late due to adverse currents during the previous night. When I met the shore excursion organiser at the gangway, she asked excitedly, "So, the pilot was late again. Yes?"

"No," I said. "We were late."

"Okay, Okay. Maybe you were late, but if you had come on time he would not have been there. He is always late. He lives below me

Arcadia

and when I see the ships come I throw a brick at his roof – then, and only then, does he get up and go down to the harbour." Very friendly I thought, and wondered what state his roof was in after a busy cruising season!

Two days later at Rio de Janeiro, after we had concluded our immediate arrival business, the young enthusiastic British Agent, Max Johnson, informed me that his firm was also Agent for *British United Airways*. Apparently there were two crews resting in Rio, and he had invited twelve Air Hostesses to dinner on board.

"You can't do that," I said. "I have a full ship and everyone of these geriatrics will be on board for dinner." His face fell and I felt I must do something for the poor chap.

"However," I continued, "we can have a buffet supper here in my cabin and I will ask some of our officers to come and help entertain your grounded hostesses."

His look of despair changed to elation as he said, "Will you really? That's jolly decent." He was so 'frightfully' British it was a treat to meet a hard-working Englishman in this Brazilian setting of surf-washed Copacabana and natural harbour, watched over by the peaks of Sugarloaf Mountain and Corcovado, the humpback mountain.

"Yes, but don't bring them until nine o'clock; we've got enough to do getting our own people organised before we start on your girlfriends."

The evening was a roaring success. The senior Air Hostess was Marion Sandersford and she presented her 'girls', who I immediately presented to an equivalent number of ship's officers. I took Marion to meet the Captain and he personally showed her the Bridge and then entertained her in his cabin. It was more than an hour later when I got back to my cabin to find the party in full swing. By 2.00 the next morning things had quietened down a bit, and I found myself left with Marion, Max Johnson and a *British United Airways* wireless operator. I took this group to the gangway and invited Marion back on board for lunch with our Agent, Max. I suggesting she brought any of her girls who wished to come.

The next morning my Senior Assistant Purser, Dick Rutter, came to my cabin and said, "On behalf of all the officers invited to the party, I wish to thank you for a splendid evening."

I thanked him for his kind remarks and said, "I have news for you; they are coming back for lunch."

He replied. "Respectfully, sir, except for yours, they are all still here!"

Oh well, the only married man in the team had to pass up the best-looking guest. However, he did follow up his luncheon invitation, and I went with Max Johnson to the hotel by Copacabana beach where the air crews were staying. While we were waiting in the bar for Marion, a typical South American 'lover boy' type of man strolled into the bar and stood a few feet away from us whilst ordering a drink. Max whispered to me, "If that man offers to sell you a piece of jewellery, accept the offer."

Having got his drink the man moved down the bar towards us and greeted Max who introduced him to me as Pedro de Silva. After a while, when Max was engaged in conversation with someone else, Pedro de Silva said quietly to me, "Are you married?"

"Yes," I replied.

"Would you like a piece of jewellery to take home to your wife?" he continued.

"Well, yes," I said. "What do you have in mind?"

"How much money do you want to spend?"

I put my hand in my pocket and produced a number of cruzeiro notes, saying, "That's all I've got – is it enough?" He took my money without counting it, knocked back his drink and walked out without another word.

"Hey," I said to Max, "your friend Pedro has just relieved me of about 20 quids' worth of cruzeiros and walked off."

"Don't worry," said Max. "I told you to accept any offer he made. He'll be back."

Just then Marion came into the bar and for a few minutes I forgot about Pedro the Jeweller. We were just about to set off for the ship when Pedro reappeared and pulled from his pocket a soft leather pouch, from which he took an aquamarine stone on a light gold chain. Marion went into raptures about it, saying, "It's beautiful, it's gorgeous; can I put it on? How much is it?"

"It is not for you, my dear," said Pedro. "It is for the wife of the Purser." To me he then said, "If you give me five more pounds in sterling notes, it is for you." None of us had any sterling on us so I had to invite Pedro back to the ship to collect the money. Arriving in my cabin, I poured everyone a drink and went into my bedroom to get five pounds for de Silva. When I gave it to him, I naturally expected him to give me the stone, drink up and go. However, he didn't – he took the money and made no attempt to give me the goods.

"The stone, please?" I asked.

"Later," he said. "May I have a look round your ship?"

"Yes, of course," I answered, "but what about my aquamarine?"

"You will get it – don't worry."

Marion stopped what was developing into a nasty situation by taking Pedro de Silva's arm and saying, "Come on, I will show you their lovely ship. I went everywhere last night."

This clearance of my cabin for a while suited me as I had a few things to do, but I was becoming worried about friend Pedro, despite Max's assurance that he was an honest trader in precious stones. Pedro was still with us at a quarter-to-four when an Assistant Purser came in and told me that we had our Clearance from Port Authorities and were ready to sail. I now had to go up to the Bridge and tell the Captain that departure formalities were complete – but I still hadn't got my stone.

"Pedro," I said, "it's time to go. My present please."

"I will give it to you when we say goodbye."

"It's goodbye now, I'm off to the Captain. Dick Rutter here will take you and Marion to the gangway while Max and I go to the Bridge. I'll see you both on the gangway in a few minutes."

"Right," said Pedro. "I will see you at the gangway."

At the very last minute, literally at one minute to four o'clock, when we landed the gangway, Pedro de Silva handed over the leather pouch containing my aquamarine stone.

"Why couldn't I have had it when I paid for it?" I asked.

"Because, my friend, the way you were going with that Air Hostess, you would have given it to her. Now she has gone down your gangway and I know your wife will get the present you bought for her."

Soon after my return home, we had to get various things valued for insurance purposes, so I suggested we had the jewel from Rio valued as well. The valuation was five times the price Pedro had charged me.

Seagull

AP Herbert got hit on the head by a seagull, that did a dropping on the deck of Otranto:

Oh seagull we're grieving
To see you relieving
Yourself on the merchant marine
You have all the oceans for your little motions
Otranto is not a latrine
But if it must be a liner
Then what could be finer
Than choosing a nice P&O?

Chapter 19
Oronsay to Alaska

There are milestones in all our lives. Passing exams, first job, marriage, first child and things like that. Monday 8th September 1969 was a great day in my life. Ever since my marriage in 1954, I had been hankering after either a shore job or a change in the Company regulations to enable wives to travel in the same ship as their husband.

My second wish was granted to Senior Officers within weeks of my leaving the P&O in 1974. How ironic! I thought my first wish, to have a shore job, had been granted when in September 1969 I was invited to become the first P&O Purser Training Officer. However, it was not for the rest of my career as I had hoped. Nevertheless, for two-and-a-half years I was the Company's Purser Training Officer. This meant training personnel from bell boys up to the Purser himself when necessary. The event which created the appointment was a Management decision to require their Purser Officers to have a professional qualification. The qualification to be achieved was membership of what was then called the Hotel and Catering Institute (now the Hotel Catering and Institutional Management Association).

My first task was to arrange correspondence courses for all the existing junior Purser officers, and to ensure that new Purser cadets had achieved a qualification before entering our service. Newly appointed Purser cadets were under my care for six months before they were appointed to their first ship. Although they had their professional qualification, they knew nothing of Marine Catering or shipboard practices. As a result my programme, which included two weeks with the Royal Navy to learn about leadership and staff control, also took them on a cruise. There were eight or ten young men in each group, and during a two-week cruise I had them working in pairs all over the ship including the Engine Room and the Bridge. I have always believed that understanding other people's jobs is important in any large organisation.

These cadets were nice young people and it was interesting to see them develop from shy boys to confident young officers during their time with me. They weren't all shy – I well remember one young man who when asked to address his course and tell us, amongst other things, how he wanted to be called said, "My name's Paul, but I want to be called 'Sir' – but I doubt if I ever will be."

I also ran courses for Leading Hands when we tried to give them an understanding of how the Head Office and Company Management worked. I would have like to have run courses for some of the shore staff to tell them how the ships worked. There were far too many 'bosses' who had no idea of how the end product – the ships – operated at sea and abroad, which often led to misunderstanding and resentment that could have been avoided.

Each ship had some Women Assistant Pursers and so I ran an introduction course for them before they were appointed to their ship. Some of these girls were Dutch, a policy the Company adopted when trying to woo passengers from Northern Europe. They all spoke perfect English, but occasionally I put my foot in it by using idioms. When explaining that a complaining passenger should be allowed to keep on talking without interruption until he had got 'the dirty water off his chest', I had the girls in hysterics and for a moment couldn't think why.

There was a dozen or more boy ratings in each ship (before they came to join us the boys had been to a sea school, usually the National Sea School at Gravesend). I had always been critical of our reception arrangements for them when they joined their first ship. Instead I arranged for them to join as a group at the same time on the same day, and for them to report at the London office of the Company, rather than on board. I then sent them to Southampton in the care of my training staff and they spent their first night in a seamen's hostel. During the evening and the next morning they were given an introductory talk about the P&O Company and I arranged for the Mission to Seamen padre to talk to them. One of my instructors checked their gear to see that they had sufficient clothes for what might be a six-month voyage. Each boy was given a stamped postcard with a picture of the ship he was about to join and told to write home and say he had arrived safely in Southampton – although we checked that it was addressed to his home and not a girlfriend. As Training Officer, I tried hard to improve the welfare of crews, and the boy ratings in particular.

Despite my happiness at being ashore and going home every night, I soon realised that I was losing touch with shipboard practices. This was a time of change and I soon found out that I was telling people how to do things that I had not done myself. After two years I therefore asked to be allowed to return to sea for at least six months. There was another reason for my wanting to get back to sea – I discovered in 1972 that the Management was taking less interest in what I was doing. Courses I proposed and submitted for approval were put on one side, while personnel were no longer made available for training. A squeeze had begun and I saw 'the writing on the wall'. There were days when I could not find anything to do and used to wander around London or Southampton, keeping up with my contacts, in the hope that I would soon use them again. During my career I had struck up a rapport with a great number of people who helped me with my courses.

A leading cosmetics manufacturer gave lessons in the West End of London to my Women Assistant Pursers and Hostesses on how to wear make-up in different situations, including ashore in the tropics. *Constance Spry* gave instruction to Hostesses on flower arranging. I had some adverse comments from my girls in connection with *Hardy Amies*, from whom they had to buy their uniforms, and the final straw was when one of our Dutch Assistant Pursers, who was having a fitting for a uniform for which she would have to pay herself, was asked to leave by the back door as a customer had just entered the salon.

I often lunched with my contacts at the Admiralty who arranged the leadership courses at *HMS Royal Arthur*. The Canadian Military

Attaché was helpful letting me borrow some excellent films on drug abuse to show to new recruits at all levels. Sometimes I went to Ealing Technical College where I earned my lunch by talking on Marine Catering and Opportunities at Sea for Catering Students. I also had a couple of tame Chinese cooks in the East End of London who gave our senior cooks tips on Chinese cooking before a ship set off for the Far East.

Near Oxford Street there was a place where *Gaumont British* taught Assistant Pursers how to work a cinema projector. In Southampton I called on the local Fire Brigade who had put together a frightening one-day course on fire fighting, at which many of the female trainees distinguished themselves, especially the attractive Assistant Purser who was congratulated on walking through a wall of fire with her hose without any hesitation. Afterwards she admitted she couldn't see where she was going. "I'm not surprised," said the instructor, "you have the helmet on back-to-front."

I wasn't surprised when I was told that I was to return to sea in *Oronsay* sailing on 15th April 1972. Looking at the itinerary, I realised that I really had been thrown back in again at the deep end – the voyage was to last nearly six months and would include four two-week cruises to Alaska from San Francisco. First we were to sail to Australia via the Cape of Good Hope, then from Sydney inside the Barrier Reef to Rabaul, Hong Kong and Japan; across the Pacific to Honolulu and on to Vancouver and San Francisco, from where we began a series of cruises to Ketchikan, Juneau and Sitka, calling southbound at Victoria on Vancouver Island.

We sailed from Southampton at 1pm on Saturday, April 15, and early next morning were picking up a pilot off Hook of Holland on our way for a five-hour call at Rotterdam. For some time P&O-Orient passenger ships had been calling at a north European port, usually Rotterdam, to pick up passengers from the lucrative, principally German, market. German-speaking Assistant Pursers were recruited and considerable efforts were made to make the European passengers feel welcome in our British ships.

We were alongside at Rotterdam from 8am until 1pm and then spent a pleasant afternoon steaming to the open sea and setting

Alaska

course for Lisbon, where we arrived on Tuesday evening. During the night before the arrival a Goanese cook died but mercifully this was to only death to occur during the long voyage.

We arrived alongside at 6pm, an hour ahead of schedule, and this enabled passengers to get out to Estoril for dinner and an evening at the casino. Many chose to dine on board and then join an evening tour of Lisbon's night clubs and by 9pm the ship was quiet with most passengers and crew, including the Chief Engineer and myself, ashore. This was to be our last run ashore in Europe for nearly six months.

The following day, before we sailed at 1pm, there was a sightseeing tour of the town for passengers and before dawn a group of Goanese cooks and stewards set off for a visit to the shrine at Fatima where the Virgin Mary was said to have appeared in 1917.

Two clear days at sea and then came Dakar, capital of Senegal, where we stayed from 2pm until midnight. Apart from a coach trip around the town few passengers went ashore and nearly all were back on board for dinner followed by entertainment from a group of African native dancers. These dancers with their straw skirts, and very little else, were entertaining but the spectacle was best observed from up-wind of the performers.

Now at last we had a decent long passage to Cape Town, a whole week at sea in which to settle down and get some routines operating which would be the pattern for the voyage. Our first Sunday at sea was two days before Anzac Day and for the Australians and New Zealanders at church appropriate hymns and prayers were chosen. After the service I entertained some VIPs and later in the week the Captain entertained in his cabin before dinner. We had already had cocktail parties for all passengers on board during the run between Lisbon and Dakar.

On Monday, which was very hot and sticky, crew members who did not have valid certificates were vaccinated against cholers. On Tuesday we crossed the equator and Neptune with his court visited the First-class and Tourist-class swimming pools. A cast of 30 officers and leading hands supported by the ship's orchestra provided a spectacle for the entertainment of our passengers.

About six or eight specially selected and rehearsed "victims" were chosen in each class and that night at dinner every passenger received a "Crossing the Line" certificate.

On Wednesday, Cape Town and Durban shore excursions were on sale at the Purser's Office and the documentation of passengers finally landing in South Africa began. Stores orders were telegraphed to Cape Town.

Thursday, April 27, brought some sad news from London. The *Orcades* and *Chusan* were to be withdrawn from service early in 1973 and a hint was given that the *Oronsay's* future was under discussion. Competition from the "jumbo jets" was beginning to bite and the news was hardly a morale booster for the crew of the *Oronsay* just a week out on a long voyage.

On Friday the weather was still hot and sticky and an American woman passenger wanted to send a telegram to London because she considered our air-conditioning was not good enough. I gave a cocktail party for all the parents with children on board.

The next day the weather was a bit rough and we were moving about a bit but at 8am on Sunday, April 30, we reached Cape Town. Two weeks down, 23 to go, and crew lists, there were more than 600 of us, were sent to Australia. We sailed at midnight for Durban where we arrived at five o'clock on Tuesday evening and stayed until lunchtime the next day.

Now there began the long haul across the bottom of the world to Fremantle, with eight and a half days without a sight of land during which we had to alleviate the boredom of our 1,000 passenger guests.

Thursday, May 4, was Ladies Night, not one of my favourite evenings. The ladies are supposed to wait on the men, pull out their husband's chair at dinner, choose the wine and later in the evening ask the men to dance. How I wished one could retire to an all-male smokeroom as in old ships for the most embarrassing part of the evening was *not* being asked to dance.

Every evening we provided some sort of diversion to entertain our passengers in both First and Tourist-class. Each class had an entertainments officer and a hostess but for major events such as

Island theme night

the Fancy Dress Ball, Country Fair and Tropical Island Night we had to give support. After a full day of work in the Purser's Office, Assistant Pursers often dressed up for such things as a Music Hall Night, chaired by the staff Captain resplendent in tail coat and his normally clean-shaven face bewhiskered.

Arrival at Fremantle at 10am on Friday, may 12, had a psychological effect on the passengers; we had reached Australia. Although the eastern states were still a few days away, from now until Melbourne on Tuesday and Sydney on Thursday there was a feeling of anti-climax as goodbyes were said at innumerable farewell parties.

The stay in Sydney was from eight o'clock on Thursday, May 18, until noon on Saturday. There were passengers on board throughout, although not many, and the crew had a well-earned break before we set off for the second leg of our tramp around the world.

We sailed at noon on Saturday, May 20, the next day being Whit Sunday. We sailed inside the Great Barrier Reef and passed through the Whit Sunday Passage on Whit Monday, running exactly 199 years behind Capt James Cook in the *Endeavour*.

Wednesday found us in Rabaul in torrential rain and the passengers' shore excursion transport consisting of open lorries.

During the five-day passage to Hong Kong I had a birthday and the baker and his staff presented me with a splendid cake with chocolate icing, but not being very keen on fruit cake I sent it down to the restaurant for serving at the children's tea. When I mentioned to the baker what I had done, and hoped that he appreciated my gesture as I thought the cake too big and beautiful for me not to

Ship's bakers at work

share it, he told me the mixture had been laced with neat rum and kirsch. No wonder several parents remarked how well their children had slept that night.

In our two and a half days at Hong Kong a lot of work as done in and outside the ship so that she left looking like a lady with a set of new clothes after a visit to the beauty parlour.

After a lunchtime sailing we headed for Japan, arriving at Kobe at 8am on Sunday, June 4. On our arrival, Japanese officialdom delayed clearance of the gangways for passengers booked on a variety of shore excursions, and then it rained all day. We sailed at 10pm and I listened to several hundred Australians expressing compete disenchantment with "The Land of the Rising Sun". However, Monday afternoon saw us at Yokohama where the gangways were cleared at once and shore excursions for shopping and dinner left on time. First impressions were forgotten and for the whole of the next day and until noon on Wednesday, Tokyo was enjoyed by tourists and crew members alike, all of whom were able to get a few hours ashore.

Some 3,370 nautical miles and six and a half days later we were off the breakwater at Honolulu waiting to pick up a lunch load of hula-hula girls who danced for the passengers and distributed leis as we proceeded to our berth beside the Aloha tower. As soon as we had taken in a gangway the dancers hurried ashore as most of them worked in Woolworths and had to be at the store when it opened.

The next stop was Canada but we had five days at sea before the first of several calls we would make at Vancouver. On that occasion we spent just nine hours in port and then we were off to California.

The day at sea before San Francisco was one long farewell party given by passengers who had been with us from Australia, and enhanced by my Deputy Purser who decided that this was an appropriate day on which to celebrate his birthday. This day, Tuesday, June 20, was an important one for all of us in the *Oronsay* as we were approaching what was to be our home port for a series of cruises to Alaska.

* * *

Arcadia had cruised to Alaska the previous year and the programme had been so successful that our office in San Francisco had requested a repeat series of cruises in 1972. When they heard that the ship allocated to them was *Oronsay*, the Californian offices complained bitterly. They wanted *Arcadia* again, they had no faith in *Oronsay* with her European deck crew, and I don't think they wanted me as Purser. For some reason or other they thought I did not like American passengers, which was quite untrue – although I had said some unkind things to American shore staff during my visits in *Oriana*.

Our Captain was John Crichton, a P&O man in command of a large passenger ship for the first time. We were old friends and had sailed together when he was Chief Officer and Staff Captain. We both had the same outlook on life, believing that the ship came before everything else, and we both deplored inter-departmental strife on board. The fact that North America did not want our ship was a glorious challenge to which the entire ship's company rose, as even the normally scruffy deck department took up the challenge and their turnout at ports where the ship's launches had to be used was very smart indeed. Their behaviour with passengers was remarked upon, and perhaps the best backhanded compliment came from a lady who put her hand on some grease on the gangway and to whom the Quartermaster rushed with a clean cloth. "God dammit!" she said. "These British are inefficient – but they're so polite about it."

When we visited Alaska, cruising to those waters was still a novelty. Today the ports we visited must have become prosperous from the number of ships calling almost daily during the summer months. It is interesting to remember that more than 200 years ago Captain Cook was charting the headlands and inlets we passed. There is Point Seduction where Indian lovelies tried to persuade Cook's crew to step ashore, and relics of gold mines long since exhausted remain at Ketchikan. Trappers' trading posts now trade with tourists wearing coats of simulated fur made from nylon, selling 'local' souvenirs probably made in Japan. At Juneau, the capital of Alaska, the *Red Dog Saloon* looks little different from the gold strike days, except that the bartenders are trim, young ladies with delicate hands. A hundred years ago a bartender was chosen by the size of his hand so that when he took a 'pinch' of gold dust from a miner's 'poke' he got good value. Today's Dry Martinis and sophisticated cocktails would have been rejected by 'Six Finger Jack', 'Gold Stick Johnny' and others of their time.

During one of our four calls at Ketchikan, the Chief Officer and I made our mark at the *Fireside Lounge*. We knew the place quite well, having been entertained there by the local Chamber of Commerce during our first call. After a short stroll around the town, we called in for a drink when the barman asked, "What's it to be, gentlemen?"

The Chief Officer replied, "Two pink gins, please."

"What the hell's that?" said the barman, while a couple of locals added, "That's a new one, Mac," and to the Chief Officer, "Tell him how to mix it – is it some kind of woman's drink?"

"Oh no," we answered. "Pink gin is very much a man's drink, drunk extensively in the Royal Navy," and to the barman asked, "Have you got any Angostura Bitters?"

"Sure," said Mac behind the bar.

We soon showed him how to put the drops of bitter in the glass and swirl them round the inside before putting in the gin and handing us the water. Needless to say, the locals had to try one, and then two… and then another. We managed to miss lunch that day and sailed in a haze of pink gin at four o'clock for Juneau. Two weeks later we were in Ketchikan again and as the Chief Officer and I walked into the bar, our friend Mac greeted us with, "Hi, fellers, have some pink gins on me; the whole town's on them!" No wonder the British have left their mark all over the world. Alaska 1778 *HMS Resolution* with Captain Cook; 1972 *SS Oronsay* with Captain Crichton and his Chief Officer and Purser!

When we made our first visit to Ketchikan and were entertained at the *Fireside Lounge*, we all attended in uniform, and some local 'souvenired' my cap. At the time I was furious, but had to accept the situation when I realised how embarrassed our hosts were. I was assured that the town was so small that the culprit would be found before our next call and although my cap was not found, on our last

…The British left their mark all over the world

call I was presented with a real fur hat as worn throughout the winter by the residents.

The highlight of each cruise was our day in Glacier Bay. For each visit we carried a United States Ranger who gave a commentary on points of interest and we stopped for several hours close to the foot of the Muir Glacier, amongst tiny icebergs called growlers. Usually the sun shone and we saw seals basking on the slowly drifting growlers. Whales are not uncommon in Alaskan waters and occasionally we caught sight of a bear in the woods which spread right down to the water's edge.

During one of our calls at Juneau, I left the ship and flew up to *The Glacier Bay Lodge* which offers tourist accommodation. Officially I was visiting on behalf of the Company and therefore I took with me a Woman Assistant Purser, Sheila Tattershall, who could report on the facilities from a woman's point of view. I did not see much of Sheila during our brief overnight stay. We arrived in the early evening and as the Manager, Frank Kerans, showed us to our cabin-like rooms about 50 yards from the main hotel reception, dining and bar complex, he pointed out the deep scratch marks on the outside doors.

"Bears," he said, "get down here at night and try to get in. Don't have too much trouble with the guest rooms, but they create hell in the garbage area!" I could see Sheila going pale as he spoke. Immediately after dinner she went to her room and we didn't see her until next morning.

At breakfast I asked, "Have any bear trouble?"

"No, I bolted the door to stop the bears and put a chair under the door knob for the likes of you!" Some shipmate – she need not have worried!

During these two week cruises we had a series of set menus. This practice had been introduced by the P&O to control costs and to ensure that no ship could outshine the rest of the fleet with its menus. The idea was that whichever P&O ship passengers travelled in, they could expect the same standard of cuisine in each one. At first the Chefs didn't like it, but they got used to the idea; like all of us they let the assurance of employment outweigh their principles.[23]

The set menu routine meant that every time we were in, for example, Sitka, we had the same lunch and the agent began to wonder if we had steak and kidney pudding for lunch every day of the cruise. We always left Juneau at 12.30pm and that evening we had a Caledonian Night, one night when we persuaded the Head Office to let us use an old Orient Line menu from pre-war days. Our ship was named after an island off the coast of Scotland and we felt entitled to have this dinner once a cruise.

The menu is shown opposite.

At the point where the menu reads, "HAIL TAE THE CHIEF", over the loudspeakers there came some bagpipe music and from the galley the Head Waiter appeared bearing a salver on which there was a bottle of scotch and three glasses; he was followed by the Chef with the Haggis. The pair of them paraded around the tables finishing up at either the Captain, Staff Commander or me. Then through the loudspeakers came my voice disguised as a Scot with part of Robert Burns 'Ode to the Haggis'. As soon as this was over, the Head Waiter poured three neat whiskies and we toasted the Haggis. Of course our American and Canadian passengers loved this pantomime. There were occasions on other voyages when we had a piper on board and he led the procession and joined in the toast, but for four cruises to Alaska we could not find a piper; nevertheless our tape-recorded music and address went down very well.

Our last Alaskan port was Sitka which did not have much to see but it was interesting as the place where, on 18th October 1867, the United States of America took over Alaska from Imperial Russia, having purchased the territory for $7,200,000. Several Russian buildings remain to this day. Unfortunately, the Russian Orthodox Cathedral of St Michael was burned to the ground in 1966, but Sitka people of all faiths and no faith at all risked their lives at the time to save icons, relics and paintings.

Turning south after leaving Sitka, we spent a day at sea and then called in at Victoria on Vancouver Island where we were greeted by, amongst others, Norma Fitzsimmonds, a local florist who presented each female passenger with a rose. Norma was a great character who entertained us at her home and a lakeside cabin. Our Surgeon and I

CALEDONIAN DINNER

A wee drappie and a bit o' snack.
Some o' the things wee'l hae.

Prawn Cocktail **Chilled Tomato Juice**

Twa kinds o' soup:

Cockie Leekie **Scotch Broth**

Fush:

Caller Saumon Frae the Spey

Ae coorse:

Asparagus wi' Sauce
Stick to Whusky, lads.
Many a nicht we've merry been,
An' many more we hope tae be.
Haud yer wheest a wee; here. it's comin'.
"HAIL TAE THE CHIEF"

HAGGIS

Fair fa' yer honest sonsy face,
Great Chieftan o' the puddin' race,
Aboon them a' yer tak' yer place,
Painch, thripe or thairm.
Foorth coorse:
Mon, sic a dinner; weet yer whussels.

A Muckle Sirloin o' Beef **Roastit**
A Haum **Bakit**
Champit, Bakit, Biled Tatties
Mashed Neeps **Kail**
Here's tae ye.

Anither coorse:

Down on the Farm, Bubbly Jock, Roastit
Wi' Thairm an' Stuffin'

Last coorse:

The pruif o' the puddin's the preein' o't.
Tremlin Tam **Russet Tairt**
Coupe St Andra
Whangs o' Shortbread
Apples Oranges Pineapple Nuts
An' ony ither thing ye can lay yer hauns on.
Slaint gu mhah
DEOCH-AN-DORUIS.
Jist anither drappie to keep a' doon.
Seas atween us braid hae roared syn Auld Lang Syne.

233

were her most regular guests and an hour or so away from the ship at the Fitzsimmonds' home was really relaxing – which it needed to be after the drive there with Norma behind the wheel!

When we had completed our series of four cruises, the San Francisco office staff were so delighted with the results and the reputation *Oronsay* had gained that they gave John Crichton and me a small silver ingot upon which is engraved a picture of the ship. Each member of the crew was given a picture of our ship in the ice at Glacier Bay with a card which read:

> A special thanks to all of you from all of the staff in
> North America for making the *Oronsay* Alaska
> cruise season of 1972, the most successful ever.

We felt like sending one of our pictures with the citation to *Arcadia*, but I don't suppose they would have appreciated it.

I never did discover why the senior staff of the P&O lines in North America thought that I was antagonistic towards our American passengers. It may have been that when they tried to persuade me to slant my service in *Oriana* towards their market by serving quantities of 'junk' food, hamburgers in particular, I stuck out for traditional British fare such as roast beef with Yorkshire pudding and in particular afternoon tea with pastries and, maybe, cucumber sandwiches. I still feel that in the long run I was right – they were travelling British and so with me they got British. The success of *Oronsay* cruises proved my point.

The great thing about passengers from North America, both Canadian and United States citizens, is that if you explain what gave rise to any complaint they might make, they accept your answer. Never try to make excuses, just tell the facts.

"Sir, I am very sorry your Steward was drunk; I understand it was his birthday."

"Okay, okay, I get the picture. Hope he doesn't have too many birthdays this trip," would probably be the answer. British passengers might not accept this and probably demand a refund, writing to the London Office. However, if it was an Australian or

New Zealander, then he probably got the Steward drunk in the first place!

There is no doubt that Americans have their own views on procedures we consider to be immutable. An area where this often reveals itself is food and drink. In *Oriana* we had a most attractive bar in the First Class section of the ship called the *Monkey Bar*. The head barman was Carlos from Southern Spain who had several sales gimmicks purchased in the States, such as drip mats, swizzle sticks and, from a Mediterranean port, a brandy balloon mounted on a model gun carriage beneath which was a small spirit lamp to warm the balloon. As it took some time to rig up this contraption it spent most of its life decorating the back of the bar.

One evening during the quiet time after the second sitting had gone down to dinner, a first sitting passenger from Texas appeared in Carlos' Bar. Few first sitting passengers took their coffee in the *Monkey Bar*, they as were usually fighting for the best seats at the evening entertainment. The large Texan with an impressive cigar sat down at a table at the side of the room, glanced at the drinks list and said to the waiter, "Bring me one of those Bisquit-Dubouché. What is it, some kind of Brandy?"

"Yes, sir," answered the waiter. "A very fine Cognac – an excellent choice, sir."

"Great – make it a large one."

The waiter crossed to the bar where Carlos was cleaning up after a busy pre-dinner session, and ordered, "One large Bisquit-Dubouché."

"The Bisquit-Dubouché?" says Carlos. "For who is the large Bisquit-Dubouché?"

"Chap over in the corner with the big cigar."

"I will serve it myself," says Carlos. "Tell him Carlos himself will serve the large Bisquit-Dubouché." The waiter shrugged his shoulders, walked over to the customer and explained that the barman would serve the brandy himself.

"Great, great," responded the Texan chewing on the end of his cigar.

Carlos prepared his gun carriage by lighting the lamp beneath the large glass. He then sallied forth from his bar bearing the carriage, lamp and glass on a large silver tray, and was followed by the Steward with a bottle of Bisquit-Dubouché held at shoulder-height on a salver. The passenger watched their approach muttering, "Great, great."

At the table Carlos rotated the glass over the lamp saying to himself, "The large Bisquit-Dubouché." At last he was ready and, turning to the Steward, he took the bottle from the salver. With a flourish he poured once, 'glug, glug, glug' – a tot and then, saying yet again, "A large Bisquit-Dubouché," he tipped the bottle once more, 'glug, glug, glug'. With a theatrical gesture after passing it beneath his nose, he placed the glass in front of the Texan who was still muttering "Great, Great", before announcing, "On the rocks – plenty of ice, boys."

Chapter 20
A Wedding at Sea

Acting as a host to our passengers was one of the principle functions of an Orient Line Officer. Every Executive, Purser, Medical and many Engineer Officers had their own table in either the First Class or Tourist Dining Rooms. Who sat at your table was the luck of the draw for junior officers, although friendship with the Head Waiter could be an advantage. Senior Officers often had to take commended passengers, some of whom could be a bit heavy going, although most were easy to get on with. As an Assistant Purser I had an advantage over my equivalents in other departments in that I worked closely with the Head Waiter, and as Sports Assistant Purser I often found myself looking after the children of distinguished parents sitting at the Captain's table. If I did not have them with me in the Dining Room, I was often told to find them a job on the Sports Committee.

It was in this way that I met the daughters of the great Australian wine families, Seppelt and Penfold.[24] They were usually in their late teens or early twenties and always great fun. Most of the girls had been to a school called Frensham, the Australian Roedean, and therefore knew one another and conversation was easy, as we were all around the same age. However, not all of the girls lucky enough to be travelling to Europe were fortunate enough to have been educated at an expensive private school. There was an amusing friend of mine, Zelle Wilkinson, travelling as the companion of the widow of a New South Wales property owner. One evening a rather snooty socialite asked, "Did you go to Frensham, Zelle?"

"Oh no," she answered. "I was educated at *Prince's* and *Romano's*" (Sydney night clubs).

The daughter of one of Australia's principle meat exporters sat at the Staff Commander's table. Soon after leaving Adelaide the ship ran into bad weather and started moving about a bit, and under these conditions the Stewards often dampened the table cloth to prevent plates sliding about. The young lady remarked that the table cloth was wet.

"Oh yes," commented the Staff Commander. "We always wet the table in rough weather. Stops things falling off, you know."

"What a wonderful idea," says the girl. "I think I will wet my bed tonight."

Australians have an accent and idioms of their own, which we soon got used to, and often used ourselves. "Too right", came as naturally to me as "I agree". I must admit I didn't instinctively run to such phrases as, "Don't come the raw prawn", which means "You can't fool me", or use, "A one-pot screamer" to describe someone who can't hold their drink. Joe Chapman was Second Officer in *Orion* when we were cruising to New Zealand from Australia. He was referred to by the crew as 'Telescope Jack' because whenever he was on gangway duty at an anchorage he carried his telescope – he was very 'pukka' and British. We were in Auckland for two days and at breakfast on the first day Joe asked his table companions what they were going to do that day.

"Going to Takatour," was the reply from one of the men.

"Really," said Joe, assuming Takatour was some place with a Maori name that he hadn't heard of. He continued, "And what plans have you for tomorrow?"

The man's wife answered this time. "Going to tak' another tour."

Language difficulty nearly ended in disaster for a Mexican boxer and his trainer who travelled in *Orontes*. These two did not sit at an Officer's table and perhaps they would not have encountered the difficulty they did if there had been an Officer present. It was not until the trainer came to me with an interpreter that I became aware of any problem. It seems he was concerned that his champion was not getting enough to eat, so with the aid of the man who could speak Spanish I went through a set of menus, asking which dishes the boxer needed to keep his strength up. There were plenty of steaks on our menus and I couldn't really understand the problem, until it became apparent that the boxer and his trainer did not realise they could order the whole menu – they had been going into meals and pointing to just one item on the menu, and after they had been served they got up and left. Sometimes all they had was soup. I told the waiter I thought he was a bit dim, but all he said was, "He's supposed to be a flyweight – I thought he was on a diet."

When I was Assistant Purser I had an 'all-in' wrestler at my table called George Penchoff, and although we became firm friends he was a constant embarrassment to me. Half the trouble was the other passengers at the table, Colonel and Mrs Horton. The Head Waiter knew that I liked Service Personnel, as soldiers, sailors and airmen were always good value, so it was a kind thought on his part to put a Colonel and his wife with me. What neither of us knew in advance was that Colonel Horton was a Colonel in the Salvation Army and that his wife held equal rank in the same army. I was never quite sure what George, the wrestler, would say or do next.

Orontes was not air-conditioned and my table was on the ship's side close to a porthole which was always open in hot weather. One evening at dinner there was quail on the menu, and I explained to George that it was quite in order to pull off each leg and eat it from his fingers. This was right up George's street, so he ordered six quail and devoured them in Henry VIII style, throwing bones over his shoulder through the porthole and straight into the Red Sea. Mrs Horton's face was a picture.

A couple of days later we called at Aden and then sailed at about 2.00pm. That night at dinner I asked the Hortons and George what they had done in Aden. Colonel Horton didn't seem to have done much except escort his wife who had bought a silk scarf, whereas George had met a beggar boy who had said to him, "No mammy, no pappy, no brother, no sister," and then held out his hand. I asked "So what did you do, George?" He answered "I gave 'im sixpence – poor bastard." Mrs Horton was not amused.

I have always admired the Salvation Army. In 1965 in *Orcades* we carried a large contingent of Salvationists to the United Kingdom

Sally Army girls

and steamed up the Thames estuary wearing the Blood and Fire flag of the Army. Ron Brittain, the Captain, and I appeared on the front page of the *War Cry* – a distinction not achieved by greater P&O personalities than us.

One of my gimmicks was to give a 'Coke' tail Party for the children, around the date upon which the Captain gave his Cocktail Party for all adult passengers. Even this innocent event got me into trouble when I was in *Orcades* with my old friend Ricky Harris in command. I arranged for parents to collect their child or children from the party at about 6.00pm, and I also arranged for the barkeeper (who was serving innocuous 'Man-hat-on' and 'White Laddies') to have some sherry and gin and tonic available to offer the parents when they came to collect their offspring. Around seven o'clock I was tidying up my desk before going to change for dinner when a fierce-looking woman walked into my office asking, "Are you the Purser?"

"Yes, madam."

"My child has been exposed to alcohol, and I understand you are responsible," she complained.

I was taken aback by this remark and could only say, "What do you mean – exposed to alcohol? I have just given a 'Coke tail' Party for the children. They were not served any alcoholic drinks."

"But you and the Captain were drinking gin."

"Not until the very end when the parents came to collect the children," I replied.

"Maybe," said my inquisitive visitor, "but my children were in the same room and were therefore exposed to alcohol. I intend to write to your head office and report the incident."

I don't know if she ever did write to London, but I do know that within minutes I was subjected to almost the same interrogation. As I walked from my office on 'D' deck back to my cabin one deck lower, I met an old friend of mine who had travelled with me before. He asked me, "Say Froggie, they tell me there was hooch at that kids' party you just gave?"

"Oh Lord," I answered. "Not you too."

"Well," he said, "my daughter had to drink coke which is bad for her teeth, when she could have had a decent Scotch!"

one of my gimmicks wasto give a 'COKETAIL' party for the children   20

Although plenty of members of minor religious groups travelled with us and often held meetings and services, the Captain led the whole ship each Sunday at sea for a non-denominational service, very much on the lines of Anglican matins. Travelling clergy sometimes contributed to the Sunday worship and could be called upon for funerals, migrant chaplains baptised, and one Bishop held a confirmation service. On 22nd October Bishop Cecil Muschamp of Kalgoorlie conducted a wedding aboard *Oriana*. Jens Sorensen was a champion racing cyclist from Holland who was engaged to Dorrit Bauer, also Dutch. Their original plan had been to get married in Western Australia, so Dorrit was booked to travel in *Oriana* and Jens was going to take part in an important race and then fly on to Perth.

Last-minute alterations to Jens' plans enabled the couple to travel together in *Oriana* and hearing that there was a Bishop on board, they asked if he would marry them. They had already asked the Captain, Cliff Edgecombe, but he had explained that the Captain of a British ship did not have authority to perform a marriage ceremony. Bishop Muschamp expressed a willingness to marry the couple if he could be satisfied that the ceremony would be properly registered and that all the formalities (such as reading of banns) had been carried out. Several telegrams to Europe and Australia convinced the Bishop that a wedding had been arranged in Perth, Western Australia, and that there the local church held a certificate confirming that the banns had been read in Holland. In addition, both sets of parents were contacted and gave their blessing. By now we were beyond Suez, so it was decided that the ceremony should take place the afternoon of the day after Aden, from where we were due to sail at midnight.

While we were in Aden I dined with Jack Playfair, our Agent, and his wife Nina who were living in the Agency house high on Steamer Point. Sir Austin and Lady Anderson were also in the party as Sir Austin, who had been chairman of the Orient Line, was travelling with us to Australia. With the aid of a torch, after dinner Lady Anderson, Nina and I picked flowers from the garden to make a bouquet for the bride. The garden of P&O House was one of the few places where flowers grew in Aden.

The marriage took place at four o'clock in the Red Carpet Room. The Captain gave the bride away and afterwards we had a jolly reception with a cake which had been made on board. The couple, who were travelling in the Tourist Class, were given a First Class cabin for the rest of their journey as a wedding present from the Company. Having given the bride away, Cliff Edgecombe spent the whole evening dancing with the bridesmaid. After the ceremony I took a press release I had prepared for Cliff to approve before I sent it to London, which he read and said, "Leave me a copy. It's fine, don't bother to send it now but leave it until tomorrow and then send it cheap rate – there's no urgency."

First thing the next morning I took my press release to the radio office addressed to the P&O Press Officer in London. The Chief Radio Officer took my message himself and started counting up to the number of words to be transmitted but immediately stopped, looked up and said to me, "The Captain sent this message last night, full rate, direct to the Daily Express." Cliff deserved to be in command of *Oriana* – he never missed an opportunity.

Not very many film stars, statesmen or other well-known personalities travelled on board our ships. Captains and Pursers on the North Atlantic liners were always encountering the rich and famous, but I doubt if they ever got to know them as well as we got to know the few who sailed with us – after all, we had them for weeks, they only had them for days.

Sir Robert Menzies, former Prime Minister of Australia and a Senior Commonwealth politician, became ill during a visit to Europe in 1968. He recovered and returned to Australia towards the end of the year in *Iberia* where I was Purser. The Captain and I escorted Sir Robert and Dame Pattie from the gangway to their suite, close to my own cabin, and as soon as the Captain left us to return to the Bridge, Sir Robert said to me, "I want a jug and a table spoon, Purser. I need them to make Dry Martini."

"Of course, sir," I answered, "but we can give you a proper mixing glass and filter."

"No, sir," he insisted. "All I want is a jug and a spoon."

Iberia

Most evenings, and always before a port, I called on the Menzies to discuss their arrangements for the following day. Every time I called I was given an excellent Dry Martini, mixed in the large white jug I had provided. At Cape Town they left the ship to visit Pretoria and rejoin at Durban. When they returned I met them at the gangway and walked to their suite with them, and on the way I asked Sir Robert, "Have you sorted out with Mr Vorster the problems of South Africa?"[25]

"No way," he answered. "I only went there to get to the bottom of the D'Olivera business." D'Olivera was a South African cricketer about whom there had been some controversy and cricket was a great love of Sir Robert. While the Menzies were away in Pretoria, St Andrew's Day occurred. Many passengers had left for the Cape Town to Durban overland tour, so I decided that we would have our usual St Andrew's Night dinner after we left Durban. Knowing that Sir Robert had a reputation for addressing the Haggis, I persuaded him to do this in the First Class Dining Room.

This was the first of three things I asked the former Prime Minister to do and which Dame Pattie insisted had helped to complete his recovery from the recent illness. I do not think she was just being polite, because if it had been otherwise she would have asked me not to project him in public. There were several migrants in the Tourist Class and the Tourist Class Entertainment Officer was keen to have an 'any questions' session with Sir Robert on the panel. He agreed to do this, together with an Australian judge and others, including a journalist. I acted as chairman and the whole event was a great success.

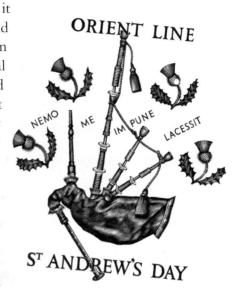

ORIENT LINE

NEMO ME IMPUNE LACESSIT

ST ANDREW'S DAY

The third public involvement in a shipboard activity was within hours of the couples' disembarkation at Melbourne. As we were due to arrive at Station Pier in the early evening on a Sunday, the Captain instructed me to conduct the usual Sunday church service because he would be on the Bridge at the time. I invited Sir Robert to read the lesson, and he was excellent. He stood before the congregation and said, "I'm going to read you the story of David and Goliath." Then, after a few verses, he said, "The next bit is quite irrelevant," and left out a few verses before continuing with the story.

Just after we left Durban the Chief Officer and I had the bright idea of signalling London and asking for a Cinque Ports Flag to be sent to the ship, so that we could fly this in Australian waters to indicate that we had the Lord Warden aboard. Sir Robert Menzies held this office and was delighted when we steamed into Fremantle with this personal standard at the masthead which had been brought on board by the pilot. We created confusion at HMAS Leeuwin, the nearby naval base, where it was felt that the Lord Warden of the Cinque Ports must be entitled to a gun salute. However, they were not sure of how many guns and I think they settled for 19. The disembarkation of Sir Robert and Dame Pattie was amusing, in that as we all stood stiffly to attention on the gangway of *Iberia* at Melbourne, Captain, Staff Captain, Chief Officer and Purser. Dame Pattie then went down the line and kissed each one of us, while to me she whispered, "You have done so much for him, thank you."

On 27th June 1966 Cary Grant and his wife Dyan, together with their baby daughter, joined *Oriana* for the voyage from Los Angeles to Southampton. Our first meeting was when during embarkation I called on them in their stadium deck stateroom. The room was full of friends of theirs and I felt a bit foolish when I had to ask, "Which one of you gentlemen is Cary Grant?"

We became friends and had many quiet meals together in the Silver Grill. During the voyage he spoke to the Tourist Class passengers and was superb. He did not have any notes – in fact, he didn't have anything prepared – but he just sat on a platform in front of more than 300 people and said, "Here I am – what do you want me to tell you?"

Cary Grant and the crew

Southampton docks

At once questions began to flow and with each answer he included an amusing anecdote. The hour went by, it seemed to me, in less than five minutes. I had been warned that Cary Grant might be temperamental, but he proved easy to keep happy in *Oriana*. The only upset we had was caused by a *Daily Express* reporter who joined at Le Havre, a few hours before Southampton. A press conference had been arranged for the morning of our arrival at Southampton and he was not amused by a reporter turning up the night before, trying to get in ahead of other newspapers.

Googie Withers and her husband John McCallum were well known to Orient Line and P&O Pursers. We often took parcels from Australia to England for them. June Bronhill was very fond of *Orion* and I remember well a party which went on in my cabin until dawn after a group of us had been to see June appear in *The Sound of Music* in Melbourne. It seemed to me that we had the entire cast on board that night – perhaps we did.

Max Wall, the English comedian, travelled in *Orion*, although he didn't go down well with most of us. One cold, wet and rough afternoon in the Mediterranean he demanded that I went to his cabin immediately. When I arrived he gave me hell because his wife was seasick and although she "fancied a bit of gorgonzola cheese", the Steward had already been gone 20 minutes and the cheese had yet to arrive. Mrs Wall is the only person I have known to ask for gorgonzola when feeling seasick.

The film actress Hayley Mills did not actually sail with us in *Oriana*, but she was on board for several hours during a call at Singapore – in fact, for an hour she was asleep on my bed! Miss Mills was filming in Singapore and the producer wished to take a sequence aboard a passenger ship. About noon I asked the unit if they would like to take lunch on board, and although they declined lunch, they accepted an offer of beer and sandwiches in my cabin. As soon as they arrived, Hayley Mills announced that she was exhausted and asked if she could borrow a bed for an hour. My bedroom was next door, so while the rest of us drank and ate, the star was fast asleep.

Tennessee Williams, the playwright, and David Bowie, the pop star, were on board at the same time. I hardly ever saw Williams, but Bowie joined in all the shipboard activities and was a charming travelling companion.

General Hershey of the United States Army told some interesting tales about the way in which people had tried to avoid service in the Armed Forces. At a lunch in port on board *Oronsay* Mrs Nimitz told us how the Admiral was handling retirement, "after having commanded a million men." "At first," she said, "he thought I was those million men. I told him to go and look through the telescope he stole from the Japanese, and I would tell him when lunch is ready."

The wife of Ed Mitchell, sixth man on the moon, kept our table in fits of laughter describing her time as a *Disneyland* Hostess. It seems that guests in the hotel who demand to see the manager are confronted with a larger-than-life-size Mickey Mouse squeaking, "You got problems?" Ed himself was a most interesting table companion and was kind enough to speak to the crew about his trip in Apollo 14.

Sharada Raje Holkar, the daughter of the Maharajah of Indore, sat at my table from Vancouver to Bombay. Thirty-nine dinners together and never once did the Princess wear the same sari twice. We became great friends and still correspond, more than 20 years later.

Chapter 21
Women at Sea

When the *Oriana* was commissioned in 1960 there were 38 women on her Articles. At the time the *Oriana* was an Orient liner with an all-European crew but with the introduction of P&O Goanese into the Purser's Department the number of women in the crew was reduced. The introduction of Goanese laundrymen meant the paying-off of laundresses, who were the great characters of the female staff.

My first encounter with the "steam queens" was in the *Orontes* which I joined in 1948 as a Junior Assistant Purser. There were several occasions on which I had to visit the laundry to see the chief laundryman or perhaps the linekeepe, who seemed to spend most of his time sitting on piles of dirty linen on the after mooring deck outside the laundry, quietly smoking his pipe and chatting to the laundryman.

All round was a hive of activity amplified by the threshing of the propellers and the roar of the wake just a few feet below. The activity was accompanied by the hiss of the steam presses, the gentle throb of the calendar and the voices and laughter of the laundresses. These were not young women and most had been at sea during the war. During the Red Sea passage they worked their presses wearing just a towel around their waist and a bra. Professionally they were experts but they did play tricks from time to time.

"Any more cheek from you, young man, and we'll put so much starch in your trousers that you won't be able to put them on" – and they did.

A junior deck officer was to be married on our return to Tilbury... and found his last laundry of the voyage returned with little blue bows sewn all over his pyjamas.

The "steam queens" found a contraceptive in the pyjama pocket of one officer. His laundry was returned with the flies of his pyjamas and his underpants sewn up.

When the *Strathnaver* was withdrawn from service in 1962 her Goanese crew were transferred to the *Orion,* where I was Purser. Our laundresses had all been found jobs with other shipping companies but one declined an offer from Union-Castle. "Sail in that company!" she exclaimed. "My old man's an AB there and you won't get me sailing in the same ship as him – it's bad enough when we're on leave at the same time."

When the laundresses left the Orient ships some delightful people moved out of our lives and all of us, from Captain to boy rating, lost some good friends, loyal servants and colourful characters.

Stewardesses presented a different image. The laundresses were "behind the scenes" workers while the stewardesses were very much in the public eye and their appearance was important as they came into close contact with passengers. A few were young and attractive but most were motherly types who inspired confidence in children and women travelling alone.

Few passengers in Orient and P&O called on the services of a cabin stewardess but at least one cabin stewardess in each class was essential to run meals to sick women and be of assistance to mothers of young children. Ladies lavatories were serviced by a stewardess, another was attached to the playroom staff and in the *Oriana* where, for the first time, fully equipped laundrettes were installed, there was a stewardess in attendance for most of the time to assist passengers with the machines or even carry out the whole process.

Towards the end of my time at sea I sailed as hotel manager in a Royal Viking Line ship where all the cabins were looked after by stewardesses, and very attractive and efficient girls they were, mostly Scandinavian. During the forenoon while cleaning and bed-making they wore a serviceable working rig but in the evening they appeared in Norwegian-style uniform dress and their very pleasant appearance enhanced any pre-dinner function in a passenger suite

Uniform for the girls

or elsewhere about the ship. Some of the public room staff were women although the restaurant waiters were men.

Standing on the bridge of the *Royal Viking Sea* one afternoon talking with the Captain I thought how different the appearance of the fo'c'sle was with half the crew sun bathing in bikinis and all looking clean, young and healthy – in comparison with my early days in the *Otranto* and *Orontes* where frequently the officer-of-the-watch had to send a quartermaster forward to instruct a dirty oiler, greaser or utility steward to make himself decent,

Telephonists appeared on the scene when all First-class cabins were provided with a telephone. The equipment they handled became more sophisticated as telecommunications advanced and eventually the switchboard operator became unnecessary in many passenger ships.

With the older type of switchboard it was possible (in fact it was initially necessary) for the operator to hear the conversation of the parties she conneted. This meant the telephonist was privy to many conversations but in fairness I must say that few bothered to listen in on passengers talking from one cabin to another. The ship's officers conversed on a separate dial system and could not be overheard. There was however, one feature in the *Oriana* which caused amusement and sometimes embarrassment.

There was a baby alarm system which was linked into the passenger cabin telephone network. Parents could obtain a microphone box which they plugged into their telephone and which alerted the switchboard operator if the child was crying in the cabin. The parents then told the switchboard where they would be during the evening and were contacted there if necessary.

The system was fine and a great advance on having to rely on a disinterested night watchman who kept wailing kids quiet by giving them a piece of sugar soaked in gin; but there was a snag. If the parents forgot about the alarm when they came back to the cabin after an evening of dancing and drinking on deck their conversation, and other noises, were transmitted to the telephone exchange!

The ship's shop included, until a concessionaire was appointed, the passenger hairdressing salons. The shop's manager's staff included a manicurist who was, in fact, a fully qualified ladies hairdresser but being a member of the shop team she was expected to turn her hand to any task, from stocktaking and serving in the shop to cutting the Purser's hair. Many regular women passengers inquired, when booking their passage, who the manicurist was in that particular ship. Her hairdresser is an important person in the life of a society woman and many booked daily appointments throughout the voyage.

In 1972 P&O appointed a concessionaire to provide a hairdressing service but retained the ship's shop as part of their passenger services department. All the concessionaire's staff were women and it took ship's officers a voyage or two to adjust to having their hair cut by a woman; some never did adjust and went to a barber ashore. Personally I had no objection; the girls were attractive with pleasant personalities and it was more than their job was worth to make a mess of the Purser.

Post-war bureaucracy required a Purser's Office to prepare comprehensive lists of passengers for immigration departments and detailed crew lists, and the improvement of air mail increased the correspondence to be dealt with by Captains and Pursers. Liner companies therefore appointed stenographers and the Orient Line gave these women officer status. This was partly because of the confidential nature of their work but a far-seeing management also realised the advantage of having attractive, intelligent women as receptionists at the Purser's Office, hosting a table in the saloon and mixing with passenger in the public rooms.

Uniforms for Women Assistant Pursers in the Orient Line were at first the same as WRNS officers with the rank insignia the same as Male Assistant Pursers. After several years a specially designed day-time uniform, unique to the company, was designed. The skirt and blouse were similar to those worn by airline stewardess or hotel receptionist but for evening wear the company commissioned an exclusive couturier to design an evening dress.

In my time there were several such dresses, not all of which pleased the girls who had to wear them. One dress had a pocket flap bearing the initials of the Orient Steam Navigation Co. At a cocktail party I overheard one of our Women Assistant Pursers telling a persistent male passenger that the letters stood for "Only Sailors Need Come".

When the *Orion* was re-commissioned in 1947, after trooping, two Women Assistant Pursers were appointed and this number steadily increased until on the *Oriana's* maiden voyage there were eight. Two held the rank of Senior Assistant Purser and carried considerable responsibility for the passing on by radio of vacant passengers accommodation, and the accurate preparation of ship's papers for entry into foreign ports. There was every justification for giving these women officer status as inaccuracy in their work could have held up a ship's clearance. Indiscretion at the office counter or over confidential documents could also have caused considerable embarrassment to the ship, the company or, indeed, to Britain.

The senior Woman Assistant Purser in each ship had responsibility for the welfare of the female ratings and leading hands, a role which the type of woman employed by the Orient Line carried out most efficiently. Male Assistant Pursers also had responsibility for the welfare of ratings. The whole department was split into Divisions and Junior Purser Officers acted as Divisional Officers in the same way as RN officers.

Many of the "old school" Captains enjoyed the idea of having a female secretary at their disposal. Before sailing on one voyage I was given a small dictating machine by the stationery manager from the company's head office. He suggested it might be useful as most of the WAPs were experienced audio-typists. Soon after rounding Ushant I received a telephone call from the Captain.

"Pay? Send me up a stenographer, the new one who joined this voyage. I haven't met her yet."

I answered "Sir, I have something better than her."

"Oh really? " he said. "Well I'm waiting."

This Captain was an old friend of mine. I sent the dictating machine by bell boy and a note in a sealed envelope which read, "Take this to the grill-room for lunch."

Within minutes there was an explosion down the telephone.

"Send me that girl! This thing is broken and if it isn't it soon will be."

Children's Hostesses were key officers of the Purser's Department, especially during the years when ships outward bound to Australia carried migrant families. During the late 1940's and the throughout the '50's I served for most of my time in the *Otranto*, *Orontes* and *Orion* and developed a theory that if the children were happy and out of the way for most of the day, then Mum was happy. If Mum was happy, Dad was happy. Thus everyone was happy but without a good Children's Hostess this could not be achieved.

The ships carried two Children's Hostesses and two stewardesses who worked with them but with more than 400 children on several voyages we had to give all the help we could to the Senior Children's Hostess to enable her to the keep the young people amused.

The Children's Hostesses were usually talented young women who could turn their hand to various tasks, like painting, making fancy dress costumes and Christmas decorations and, not infrequently, piano playing. One Children's Hostess who agreed to play for a Church service in the Tourist-class of the *Oronsay*, for the Chief Officer who was conducting the service, said that she could not look at the words and the music as the same time.

It was therefore arranged that the Chief Officer would turn and look at her when the last verse of each hymn had been reached. All went well for the first hymn but half-way through the second a door slammed in the direction of the piano; the Chief Officer turned quickly to see what had caused the noise… and the hostess stopped playing.

Before flying became the way for the average long-distance traveller, liners provided the link between the continents. There was little competition between the shipping companies, except perhaps on the North Atlantic; regular sailings in comfortable ships were provided and this was all a passenger asked for. Maintenance of the itinerary and timetable was the traveller's main concern – Union-Castle to South Africa, Royal mail to south America, P&O to India and the Far East, Orient or P&O to Australia.

When flying alternatives became available, however, shipping companies began to offer services which had not, before, been considered necessary. Entertainment became a feature of shipboard life and hosts and hostesses were employed to make the passenger feel welcome.

The first hostesses were mature women who would mingle with the passengers and, with discretion, chat to those who appeared lonely, advise on the choice of a library book, a shore excursion or what to wear for the Captain's cocktail party. These officers did not wear uniform but were an important part of the team. Later, the hosts became entertainment officers and then cruise directors controlling orchestras, cabaret acts and themselves directing musical extravaganza on the high seas. The hostesses still have a role but passenger's requirements have changed and in many cruise ships the hostess has been absorbed into the entertainment staff.

Nursing sisters in the Orient Line were the darlings of the crew. During those post-war years, when joining the Merchant Navy excused a man from service with the armed forces, there were some pretty tough characters in ships with large, all-European, crews. Malingers were common at the surgery and fights in the crew quarters were frequent but the presence of a nurse when treatment was being given had a remarkably sobering effect on the toughest men.

A sharp "Go and wash your feet before the doctor sees you" met with instant obedience from a man who might have injured his foot trying to kick the daylights out of a shipmate.

Towards the end of my time at sea, which was before the advent of cruise directors and professional entertainers, P&O introduced into each passenger ship a discotheque operator; a nocturnal young lady, seldom seen in daylight hours, who went on duty around 11pm and played music for dancing until the small hours.

The "Disco Dollies" were amusing girls and hard workers. I remember a jolly blonde who was at a meeting I held to co-ordinate arrangements for a fashion show at which passengers were going to show off their Hong Kong purchases. I remarked, "If we're going

BOAC offered more flying alternatives

to do this properly we should finish up with a bride and bridegroom. I suppose we could have the groom in uniform, but what about the bride?"

"Oh," says the Disco Dolly. "I have a wedding dress. I never travel without one!"

The appointments held by women at sea, and in particular those I have mentioned with, the exception of Disco Dolly, are well established. Stewardesses are traditional and it would be interesting to find the first woman, other than a Captain's wife, recorded on a British ship's Articles.

Blue Funnel had a woman Engineer when I was at sea. Lady Doctors are not uncommon on cruise ships. The twenty-first century has seen the rise of the role of women at sea. There are 100,000 ton cruise ships with crews of 1,000 and 3,000 passengers commanded by women – the 'Mistress under God' now exists.

⊢

Postscript

There are no longer passenger ships plying regular routes, providing a Commonwealth lifeline. A new breed of purpose-built cruise ships now sail around in circles to remind their passengers of the days when travelling by sea was the only way to get beyond our shores. Those who choose the holiday afloat unwittingly compliment those of us who manned the Mail Ships, Migrant Carriers and true Liners of not so long ago. Our efforts to entertain during an enforced journey are rewarded by nostalgia which has warranted the construction of new passenger ships. On board routines have changed.

Satellites tell the navigator where the ship is. The Purser receives almost daily telephone calls from shore offices where 'experts' tell him how to run his hotel. The Stewards' Foo-foo band, with tea chest and broomstick double bass, is replaced by a sophisticated orchestra supporting a team of professional entertainers. Nevertheless, I know the hard core of men and women who believe 'the ship comes first' still exists.

The liners I have written about have had their day. New ships have been commissioned and have been built.

May God Bless Them and All who Sail in Them.

IF

If you can keep your head when half the boat train
Lose steamer trunks and blame the loss on you;
If you can be mistaken for the Boatswain,
And not get rattled at that error too …

If you can dance with those not young and pretty,
Stick at your job for twenty hours on end,
And help to organise the Sports Committee,
Yet still count every passenger your friend …

If you can drink till dawn and not get blotto,
Avoid the Boat Deck when the moon is bright,
And never quite forget that little motto
Which runs – "The passenger is always right" …

If you can keep your temper and your books straight,
Give sound advice to those who fear the "Bight ",
Deal tactfully with Captain or with Cook's mate,
And answer silly questions day and night …

If you can meet the ship's vamp and resist her,
Learn to look on at sports, yet play the game,
Fall for one girl though you dislike her sister,
And treat those two inseperables the same …

If you can act just like an elder brother
To hopeful maids who want to learn a lot,
And steer to leeward of some scheming mother
Who's marked you plainly as a sitting shot …

If you can wear a look of deepest sorrow,
When last goodbyes are said at Sydney's shore,
Then work like blazes, knowing that the morrow
You must give welcome to two hundred more …

If you can flirt with dowagers through dinner,
Then to doubting ladies be a little terser,
Yours is the ship, and every soul that's in her,
And, what is more, YOU'LL BE A PURSER! ...

The adaptor of Rudyard Kipling's 'IF' is unknown, probably a pre-war Assistant Purser.

⊢

Ships

ORMONDE (1917 – 1952)

Gross tonnage 14,981; Length 580ft 5in; Breadth 66ft 7in; Draught 27ft 4in

Ormonde was laid down at John Brown's Clydebank yard in 1913 and then took an unconscionable time being born. When war was declared the following year, work on merchant ships was stopped to enable the yard to concentrate on warships. However, in 1917, there was a need for troopships and *Ormonde* was completed. At first her accommodation provided no more than the basic requirements of troops in transit.

The ship became part of the Orient Line passenger fleet in November 1919. She was an immediate success and became the crack ship of the Australian mail liners. Between the wars *Ormonde* maintained her popularity and became a favourite with cruising passengers.

Throughout the Second World War the ship was again engaged in trooping and the carriage of prisoners of war. *Ormonde* was employed evacuating troops from France and Norway in 1940, and the landing of troops in North Africa in 1942. Despite several near misses by the enemy the ship survived the war.

From 1947 for five years *Ormonde* carried new settlers from the United Kingdom to Australia and occasionally to New Zealand. She carried the New Zealand contingent to Korea, thus achieving the distinction of trooping in three wars.

OTRANTO (1926 – 1957)

Gross tonnage 20,026; Length 657ft l0in; Breadth 75ft 2in; Draught 29ft 9in

During the 1920s the Orient Line built five 20,000-ton ships. *Otranto*, built by Vickers at Barrow-in-Furness, was the third of these ships.

Until the outbreak of war in 1939 *Otranto* ran on the mail service to Australia and made several cruises. In 1937 she was present at the Coronation Naval Review at Spithead.

Otranto's war service began in Sydney when she carried part of the first contingent of Australian troops to Egypt. Later she was involved in 'Operation Torch' in North Africa, the Sicily landings, and was present at Salerno.

Having survived the war with a distinguished record and little damage, *Otranto* returned to commercial service in 1949 as a Tourist 'one class' ship. Many assisted passage migrants travelled to Australia in *Otranto*. Homeward-bound young Australians travelled to Europe, many on working holidays.

Her final voyages to and from Australia were made round the Cape of Good Hope, calling at Cape Town and Durban, as the Suez Canal was closed. She was sold, for breaking up, to the British Iron and Steel Corporation at Faslane in 1957.

ORONTES (1929 – 1962)

Gross tonnage 20,186; Length 663ft 10in; Breadth 75ft; Draught 30ft 2in

Orontes was the last of the Orient Line's 1920s building programme. Launched at Vickers, Barrow-in-Furness, in February 1929. She made her début in September off Ryde Pier for the Schneider Trophy races.

For the next ten years *Orontes* maintained the mail service to Australia and made cruises to the West Indies, Norway and the Mediterranean.

After September 1939 *Orontes* made two commercial voyages to Australia before being requisitioned for war service. Between May 1940 and the end of the war she steamed 371,409 miles carrying troops, civilians and prisoners of war. She was present at the landings in North Africa, Sicily and the Italian mainland. Frequently under fire, *Orontes* survived the war.

After an extensive re-fit by John I. Thornycroft's at Southampton, *Orontes* returned to the Australian trade, as a First and Tourist Class ship in 1948. Five years later she became a Tourist 'one class' ship. Throughout a long life *Orontes* was a popular ship until finally sailing to a breaker's yard in Spain in early 1962.

ORION (1935 – 1963)

Gross tonnage 23,371; Length 665ft; Breadth 84ft 6in; Draught 30ft

Built by Vickers at Barrow-in-Furness, *Orion*'s single funnel and a foremast only, with an entirely new approach to shipboard interior decoration, ushered in a new concept of a passenger ship.

Launched by the Duke of Gloucester, then Governor-General of Australia, from Brisbane, by radio, she entered service in August 1935 with a Mediterranean cruise before sailing for Australia.

Orion was Commodore Ship of the first large convoy carrying Australian troops to the Near East. In December 1941, after completing repairs to damage caused by collision in convoy with *HMS Revenge*, she sailed from Singapore with wounded troops and civilian evacuees for Australia. *Orion* carrying 5,300 troops was present at the North Africa landings. During 1943 the ship was employed ferrying US Forces to England with over 7,000 troops on board each voyage.

This was the first Orient ship to return to commercial service as a First and Tourist Class liner after the war. In 1951 *Orion* resumed cruising from the United Kingdom. In 1954 she crossed the Pacific on the recently introduced Orient Line Australia – North America service.

During the ship's last years she sailed as a 'one class' Tourist ship. *Orion* never lost her popularity and justified her original forward-looking features to the day in 1965 when she was delivered to the breakers at Antwerp.

ORCADES (1948 – 1973)

Gross tonnage 28,472; Length 708ft; Breadth 90ft 5in; Draught 31ft

Having lost half the fleet by enemy action during the war, the Orient Line embarked on a building programme and ordered from Vickers their first post-war ship in March 1945, while hostilities were still in progress.

Orcades was designed to reduce the passage time to Australia by about a week. With a service speed of 22 knots this was achieved.

Externally, the ship was something entirely new. The Bridge, a tripod mast and a fat funnel grouped together amidships, gave a businesslike warship appearance.

Besides maintaining a fast schedule to Australia, *Orcades* was employed cruising from both the United Kingdom and Australia. In June 1953 this was the principal Admiralty Guest Ship at the Coronation Review of the Fleet in the Solent.

After the merger of the Orient Line and P&O, *Orcades* was painted white and wore the P&O house flag. Nevertheless her distinctive outline always marked her as an Orient Liner. Her end came in February 1973 when she was delivered to Mitsui and Company at Kaohsiung for breaking up.

ORONSAY (1951 – 1975)
Gross tonnage 28,136; Length 708ft 7in; Breadth 93ft 5in; Draught 31ft

Oronsay was the second of the three post-war ships to be built at Barrow-inFurness to replace wartime losses. She had a difficult birth in that whilst fitting out she caught fire and nearly capsized. In the end she was the last of the sisters to die. Although there was some rivetting, much of the ship was welded and prefabricated.

Once in service, *Oronsay* maintained with *Orcades* and P&O's *Himalaya*, a fast service to Australia. On 1st January 1954 she sailed from Sydney to Auckland, Suva, Honolulu, Vancouver and San Francisco, inaugurating an Orient Line transPacific service, which was to become a round-the-world service using the Panama Canal. Eventually *Oronsay* became as familiar in North America and the Far East as she had been in Europe and Australia. In 1972 *Oronsay* made a series of cruises from California to Alaska; by now she had a white hull and wore the P&O house flag.

Although far from being worn out, the ship was withdrawn from service, and sold to a Taiwan shipbreaker in 1975. The Jumbo Jet had killed the market for which she had been built.

ORSOVA (1954 – 1974)
Gross tonnage 29,091; Length 722ft 6in; Breadth 90ft 6in; Draught 31ft

The Orient Line had always been trend-setters in passenger ship design and construction. With the last of the three post-war sisters they introduced a 29,000 ton all-welded, mastless, passenger liner.

Entering service in March 1954, *Orsova* immediately broke the speed record to Australia. A year later she was on the Pacific, becoming part of the service started by *Oronsay* the previous year. Another speed record was broken, this time between San Francisco and Honolulu. In 1960 *Orsova* embarked at Los Angeles over 500

passengers for Europe. The Jumbo Jet may have been on the drawing board but the threat to sea travel was not yet apparent.

By 1964 the Orient Line's corn-coloured hull had been painted over with P&O white. *Orsova*, together with her sisters, continued to maintain a service to Australia and across the Pacific. Additional ports of call were introduced to make the voyages more interesting. Regular business travellers were already travelling by air. The not inconsiderable cargo space was no longer in demand. Fast container ships could deliver as quickly as the former mail ships.

Orsova was broken up at Kaohsiung in 1974.

ORIANA (1960 – 2005)

Gross tonnage 41,923; Length 804ft; Breadth 97ft; Draught 32ft

The last Orient Liner was built at Barrow-in-Furness and was the largest passenger ship built in England. She entered service in 1960 and on her maiden voyage broke every speed record east of Gibraltar. The ship was designed to serve the Australian trade and, the by now well established, trans-Pacific route. Adelaide had to be omitted as a port of call, but with her shallow draught and transverse propellers at both bow and stern, Suva presented no problem as a Pacific port of call.

For ten years *Oriana* was the undisputed "Queen of the Indian Ocean and the Pacific". As the impact of the Boeing 747 was felt on passenger liners worldwide, Orient and P&O ships, built for line

voyages, searched for new markets. The great liners became 'passenger tramps' conveying people to international events like Olympic and Commonwealth Games wherever they were being held. Cruising occupied most of *Oriana*'s time although this had never been intended as her full-time role.

Inevitably, operating a 40,000-ton greyhound with 172,500 cubic feet of cargo space solely on pleasure cruising became uneconomical.

In mid-1986 *Oriana* was towed from Sydney to Japan, although she could have steamed under her own power if necessary. For nine years the ship served as a static resort at Oita, near Beppu. In 1995 the ship was sold to a Chinese department store and moved to Qinhuangdao where she remained for three years before being sold again and moved to Shanghai becoming a tourist attraction and conference centre. A final move in 2002 took *Oriana* to the Chinese port of Dalian. On 16th June 2004 a storm severely damaged the ship and in 2005 she was sold to ship breakers.

Oriana (1995 –

Gross tonnage 69,840; Length 260m; Breadth 32m; Draught 9.7m. On 6th April 1995 Queen Elizabeth II named a new, German-built, Oriana at Southampton. This is the first of the large 'cruise ships' with lounges, bars, restaurants and a library designed for the British cruise market.

HM launching the new Oriana in 1995

Ships' Ranks

A SHIP'S SURGEON is said to be a man
who knows a great deal about very little,
and who goes on knowing more and more about less and less.,
until he finally knows practically everything about nothing.

A PURSER, on the other hand, is a man who
knows very little about a great deal,
and keep son knowing less and less about more and more,
until he knows practically nothing about everything.

A CAPTAIN starts out knowing practically everything about
everything,
but ends up knowing nothing about anything,
due mainly to his association with Surgeons and Pursers.

End Notes

1   Long distance aircraft had to rely on landing fields, which also increased the strain to the undercarriage of early passenger planes. Hence, landing on water was much kinder to the fuselage. The flying boats also took a long time, as they did not fly at night, and required frequent refueling stops.

2   Formed from two famous cavalry regiments that amalgamated in 1922, the 3rd Prince of Wales' Dragoon Guards and the 6th Dragoon Guards (Carabiniers).

3   *Thornycroft* were ship builders named after their founder, John Isaac Thornycroft, founded in 1866 and located primarily in Southampton, later to merge with *Vosper and Company*.

4   At one stage, there was probably a ship taking hundreds of migrants from England to Australia every fortnight.

5   The importance of the Suez Canal, completed in 1869, for international shipping and trade cannot be underestimated. It allows ships to travel between Europe and South Asia without having to travel around Africa, reducing the distance by over 4,000 miles.

6   A coolie was a term used during the nineteenth and early twentieth century to refer to locally-sourced unskilled labourers.

7   In the post-War period there were two classes, First and Tourist, although pre-War there had been three.

8   During the early stages of World War I, *HMAS Sydney* was involved in supporting the Australian Naval and Military Expeditionary Force, and escorting the first ANZAC convoy. On 9 November 1914, the cruiser defeated the German cruiser *SMS Emden* at the Battle of Cocos.

9   At this time the Head Office was located in Bishopsgate, in the City of London. They also had offices at Cockspur Street, near Trafalgar Square.

10   Sir Donald George 'Don' Bradman, AC (27 August 1908 – 25 February 2001), often referred to as 'The Don', was an Australian cricketer widely acknowledged as the greatest test batsman of all time. His career t batting average of 99.94 is often cited as the greatest achievement by any sportsman in any major sport.

11   William Richard Morris, who took his title Lord Nuffield from his home village of Nuffield, Oxfordshire, was a noted motor manufacturer and philanthropist.

12   The Spithead Review was a traditional ceremony at which the monarch reviews the assembled fleet, and originated in the days when Kings served in the Royal Navy and were in command. Due to the need for a large, sheltered anchorage, it is traditionally held in the Solent off Spithead.

13   A British soldier who had received the Victoria Cross and later served as the seventh Governor-General of New Zealand from 1946 to 1952.

14   Clement Attlee was Prime Minister immediately after the war from 1945 to 1951, and Leader of the Labour Party from 1935 to 1955.

15   The Archbishop of Canterbury from 1945 until 1961 was Geoffrey Fisher.

16   *The Bing Boys Are Here* was a series of musical reviews popular in the West End, especially before the First World War.

17   This practice went on for several years as the ships carried thousands of migrant passengers in that early post-War period.

18   Cousin to The Queen, Princess Alexandra, The Honourable Lady Ogilvy, is the youngest granddaughter of King George V and Queen Mary – prior to her marriage to Sir Angus Ogilvy (now deceased) she was known as Princess Alexandra of Kent.

19   The Suez Crisis, also named the Tripartite Aggression, was an invasion of Egypt in late 1956 by Israel, followed by Britain and France. The aims were to regain Western control of the

Suez Canal and to remove Egyptian President Gamal Abdel Nasser from power who had nationalised the Canal as a response to increasing political strife. After the fighting had started, the United States, the Soviet Union, and the United Nations eventually forced the three invaders to withdraw.

20 For the uninitiated, the forecastle is the upper deck of a sailing ship forward of the mast, often abbreviated as 'fo'c's'le'.

21 Playwright, screenwriter and novelist who was also active in the Labour Party – known for films such as *The Blue Lamp*.

22 In 1957 Indonesia faced a series of political rebellions, and as a result martial law was declared. Due to the conflicts many people sought to leave Indonesia and find homes elsewhere, particularly in Holland where they could claim citizenship.

23 Eventually I had to make a personal decision in a similar respect and stuck to my principles, although I should never have done it!

24 Seppeltsfield is one of Australia's oldest wineries, founded in 1851 by Joseph Ernst Seppelt. Penfolds was also a famous wine brand, now owned by the Foster's Group.

25 BJ Vorster was the Prime Minster and then Fourth State President of South Africa from 1966 to 1979.

BV - #0017 - 231020 - C0 - 229/152/13 - PB - 9781909075450 - Gloss Lamination